THE STRAIN OF OTHER BLOOD

THE STRAIN OF OTHER BLOOD

The Life of the Reverend Mother Ruth from Harlem

Patricia Allen

WILLIAM B. EERDMANS PUBLISHING COMPANY

GRAND RAPIDS, MICHIGAN

Wm. B. Eerdmans Publishing Co.
2006 44th Street SE, Grand Rapids, MI 49508
www.eerdmans.com

Published 2026
Printed in the United States of America

32 31 30 29 28 27 26   1 2 3 4 5 6 7

ISBN 978-0-8028-8354-4

Library of Congress Cataloging-in-Publication Data

Names: Allen, Patricia, 1965– author.
Title: The strain of other blood : the life story of the reverend mother
    from Harlem / Patricia Allen.
Description: Grand Rapids, Michigan : William B. Eerdmans Pub-
    lishing Company, [2026] | Summary: "A historical biography of
    Reverend Mother Ruth, a Black Episcopal nun who overcame
    personal, cultural, and institutional obstacles as she followed
    God's calling to work for social justice"—Provided by publisher.
Identifiers: LCCN 2024039218 | ISBN 9780802883544 | ISBN
    9781467469159 (epub)
Subjects: LCSH: Ruth, Mother, C.H.S., 1897– | Nuns—New York—
    New York City—Biography. | Harlem (New York, N.Y.) | Commu-
    nity of the Holy Spirit (New York, N.Y.)
Classification: LCC BX5974.R87 A55 2025 | DDC 271/.9002 [B]
    —dc23/eng20250606
LC record available at https://lccn.loc.gov/2024039218

CONTENTS

1. Four Words—"Strain of Other Blood" ... 1

2. Ruth Awakening ... 9

3. Blood Relations ... 14

4. 1897-1918, the Death of Ruth Elaine Younger ... 20

5. Little Nun on the Prairie ... 36

6. A Monastic Manifesto ... 47

7. Repatriation I—Detroit ... 57

8. A Veiled Threat—Expelling Sister Ruth ... 71

9. She Said, She Said—Sister Ruth on Trial ... 83

10. The Bishop's Move ... 91

11. Repatriation II—White Saviors, White Saboteurs ... 96

12. Becoming the Reverend Mother Ruth, CHS ... 117

13. A Dream Deferred or Mission Aborted ... 132

14. The Kids of St. Hilda's & St. Hugh's ... 148

15. Mother Ruth and Madeleine L'Engle—
Keeping Up Appearances ... 153

16. The Nice Black Families ... 163

Contents

17. Runaway Nun   178

18. Middle Sister—Along Comes Mary   186

19. Resistance—Challenging a Ruthless Regime   194

20. The Incognegro and Black Episcopalians   206

21. The Beginning of the End   213

22. Elegy   226

Acknowledgments   235

Photos   237

1

FOUR WORDS—"STRAIN OF OTHER BLOOD"

Protestant nuns really do exist!

This biography necessitated establishing that fact. As I embarked on this research, rarely did anyone find it unusual that there are diverse people of color in monastic or cloistered religious vocations. Yet some were shocked and even incredulous at this notion of nuns in the Episcopal Church. It repeatedly elicited quizzical gazes and requests to repeat or clarify what I meant when I discussed my work on this Episcopal nun, the Rev. Mother Ruth.

And more often than not, that shock and disbelief came from my fellow Episcopalians who were not aware that these monastic brothers and sisters—who, like their Roman Catholic counterparts, took vows of obedience, chastity, and poverty—were our very own.

Despite my use of the terms "an Episcopal nun" or "an Anglican nun" to describe the Rev. Mother Ruth, in two instances the follow-up response was "Mother Ruth became a Catholic." Those words were not even uttered to me as a question, but more like a foregone conclusion drawn because this scenario of Episcopal nuns was as far-fetched as Kosher pork farmers.

One of the sisters interviewed for this biography recalled a debate with a dubious docent while on a tour of the Washington National Cathedral in the 1990s. Also known as the Cathedral Church of Saint Peter and Saint Paul, it is the mother church and seat of the Episcopal Church for the presiding bishop and primate along with the bishop for the Diocese of Washington.

"We don't have nuns," the guide told the tourists. Yet there stood Sister Heléna Marie of the Episcopal order the Community of the

Holy Spirit, founded by Mother Ruth, in full old-era black habit with a veil. "I am one," she declared. Despite the sister's embodiment of evidence to the contrary, the guide continued to challenge her on this point.

Just as the docent found the existence of Episcopal nuns unbelievable, the life story of the Rev. Mother Ruth from Harlem at times was downright inconceivable. I feel it is not being presumptuous to file this biography under the heading of Mark Twain's century-old chestnut, "truth is stranger than fiction." Hollywood's most iconic fictional and fictionalized nuns portrayed by Whoopie Goldberg, Julie Andrews, Audrey Hepburn, and Sally Fields combined don't hold a church candle to this real-life story.

* * *

In the final, five-mile stretch of a twelve-hour drive from Cincinnati to upstate New York, the three-lane highway that I traveled on in my battered, older model Prius abruptly dissolved into a rural, single-lane road. From New York's State Route 22, my GPS navigated me onto Milltown Road. I meandered along, and then, after two quick, sharp turns, I began a gentle ascent up Federal Hill Road in the town of Brewster in Putnam County.

Along the drive, modest ranch houses, quaint Colonial-era farmhouses, and rustic bungalows on the lower elevation gave way to much grander estates, set far back beyond the paved Federal Hill Road. Expansive homesteads dotted with icy ponds and circular driveways with Land Rovers and Teslas sat enclosed and protected behind wrought-iron gates. Finely manicured opaque hedges and clusters of statuesque maples sectioned off property ownership and maintained privacy.

The high hedges were reminiscent of those I'd seen surrounding homesteads in the English countryside just five months earlier. My Oxfordshire, England, odyssey, during which I lived in an intentional community with an organic vegetable farm alongside White Europeans, was part of a middle-aged "gap half-year" of self-discovery, new connections, travel to neighboring European countries, visits to Anglican convents, and spiritual awakening. Emerging out of that half-year, I now pinned my hopes on my home country and Brewster, New York, to begin a new and more stable chapter in my life.

As my car crested the hill, a small white sign hanging from an old, rusted metal arm ushered me into the entrance of Melrose Convent, Community of the Holy Spirit. Here I anticipated farming with an ultimate goal of helping to launch a new ministry that would serve women—specifically women of color—coming out of incarceration.

During my Zoom interview for the Community of the Holy Spirit (CHS) farm apprenticeship program, Sister Heléna Marie, a telegenic White woman, told me her community had hoped this new ministry would preserve the legacy of their religious order's founder, the Rev. Mother Ruth, "a woman of color." Once again, I would find myself in an environment of all White people. In contrast with the past, this time, there was reason for cautious optimism because of the promise of an expanding and more diverse community. That was the historical mission of CHS, so I was told. After a long career of peddling institutional propaganda to the masses as a public relations professional, this type of career change represented a promise of redemption. Still, I had to wonder how the neighbors in this haughty enclave might receive the influx of former inmates, especially Black and Brown ones. And even me, for that matter, without a criminal record.

"Arrived," my Prius's voice navigation announced. The auditory conviction of the little Toyota's global positioning satellite rivaled the combination of my own sense of faith and my African heritage. Upon entering the compound inhabited by a "Community of the Holy Spirit" (CHS), as a believer who followed the Spirit's leading, I knew this wasn't the end of a journey but the beginning of a new, uncertain one. In this new setting, my diasporic faith, steeped in traditional African spirituality, helped assure me of protection by the Ancestors, as they had during all my recent travels.

I parked in one of three spaces in the center of the circular driveway. I stepped out of the car and walked over to a fence adjacent to the side of the main house. It was Easter Monday, and a gauzy April snow lightly covered the fallow garden beds in an unseasonable lacy blanket. Stretched out before me were two acres of open field, an orchard and garden beds. Very soon I would sow seeds as the resident farm companion. Besides attending chapel with the nuns, I was not yet certain how much contact I would have with the sisters as a farm companion. I only knew I would not be cloistered with them in their convent. The convent was an annex of the shuttered school the sisters used to operate. It was situated on the other side of the circular driveway. On the other side of the circle, the impressive Second Empire Victorian that stood before me was my new home.

The three-story, pre-Revolutionary War manor would one day become the home for those women coming out of incarceration, and potentially, I would serve as the resident house manager. It was big enough to house a lot of people. Ultimately, I hoped and prayed that the lofty aspirations and ambitions the farm sister presented during our Zoom would manifest in this place. I had read that the property was once owned by Broadway musical lyricist Dorothy Fields, most known for *Annie Get Your Gun.* Eager to learn more about my new home and filled with a curiosity that harkened back to my news reporting days, I turned to the *New York Times*'s Time Machine digital archives, where I found a May 17, 1946, article that reported on the sale of the property. It described the residence: "a manor house containing 17 rooms, five baths, a five-car garage, with six rooms and a bath, greenhouse, and a chicken house. There are two brooks and a lake, swimming pool, and double tennis court on the property."[1]

The CHS website indicated that it was in the late 1950s that the estate became the second convent—a country home and retreat center—for the CHS nuns whose "Mother House" was based in Harlem. And like the people that join monastic religious life, the house was christened with a new name—St. Cuthbert. Now upon laying my eyes on this expansive estate coupled with the 1946 *Times* description of the property, it begged a bigger question for me: How did "a woman of color" acquire all of this, which included more than one hundred acres?

---

1. "Real Estate: Dorothy Fields Acquires Radin's Country Estate," *New York Times,* May 17, 1946, 32. https://timesmachine.nytimes.com/timesmachine/1946/05/17/91615174.html?pageNumber=32.

The aged manor's ramshackle exterior aside, architecturally, the house still looked impressive and full of potential. I strolled to the front of the house and opened the farm gate. I climbed the steps to the sweeping, covered wraparound porch. Marred by a clutter of farm equipment and a massive oil tank near the ledge, there were several aging rocking chairs on the porch landing that lent the house an air of country charm. I pictured myself rocking back and forth with a glass of wine and a book, glancing up from the pages to take in the wooded splendor. I had to wonder how many African American girls from Dayton, Ohio, could lay claim to moving from one historic landmark manor house in England—which had been home to celebrities (including the author of James Bond novels, Ian Fleming, and, briefly, the musicians Marianne Faithfull and Mick Jagger)—to this one, formerly owned by a Broadway doyenne. Where I stood, I wondered if perhaps Duke Ellington, Ethel Merman, or other stars who performed Dorothy Fields's songs visited the house and sat on this very porch enjoying cocktails. I prayed that other women of color freed from the harsh life of imprisonment might also enjoy this view.

During the early days of my arrival, Sister Heléna Marie astutely recognized my need to live and work in a racially diverse setting. Sister Heléna Marie, adorned in a hipster-variety, multicolored knit hat during the Zoom interview, projected more ebullience than any nun I had ever met from either my Roman Catholic schooling or the traditionally habited Episcopal order in Cincinnati where I was a lay associate. Several times she alluded to Mother Ruth's being "of color" and CHS's commitment to creating a multiracial community. The farm sister's occasional invocation of the Rev. Mother Ruth's racial background was something I was accustomed to as a Black woman who worshiped in a predominately White denomination. Even though I was already a member, it harkened to that old chestnut "some of our best friends are . . ." by a church in a constant effort to prove diversity and inclusiveness.

To further prove CHS's Episcopal brand of street cred, Sister Heléna Marie gave me a breakdown of forthcoming farmworkers who signed onto the projects. The others included a Black Canadian who was a former Broadway performer turned yoga teacher/

social activist/life coach; two recent graduates from Union Theological Seminary from Ghana; and a Dominican woman, the director of a county-sponsored re-entry program for the newly released from prison. Our coterie of talent to launch this new ministry, Sister Heléna Marie concluded—specifically our "diversity"—would make Mother Ruth proud. After all of my post-election 2016 travels that took me to the UK and now here in New York, it sounded wonderful to me.

That Mother Ruth was a "person of color" (who in the late 1940s and through the 1950s founded schools and religious institutions and was considered a leader in the Episcopal Church) was, on the surface, gratifying, but it seemed she should have been more widely known. Then again, unknown Black women who have done monumental things and received little credit was a cliché. After the naming of Barbara Harris as the first woman bishop (an assisting bishop) in 1988—a seismic, moon-landing moment in Episcopal Church history—it would be more than twenty-five years before another Black woman, Bishop Jennifer Baskerville-Burrows, was elected to lead a diocese. Buoyed by Bishop Jennifer's election and the previous year's consecration of the soon-to-be renowned royal wedding preacher, Bishop Michael Curry, I thought the church had entered its "Black is Beautiful" moment and that an opportunity for a lay career in the church might be possible. Two rejections later, I thought the farm apprenticeship and the re-entry ministry with the CHS sisters might be my third-time charm. Twenty years of languishing in middle management in office buildings were in my rear-view mirror, or so I thought.

By the end of my first week, I received a copy of a book—purported to be an autobiography of founder Mother Ruth and a history of the Community of the Holy Spirit and its schools—along with other orientation materials, the schedule for Daily Office prayers in the chapel, documents that explained monastic religious life, and information about biodynamic farming. In the first weeks, only the farming materials held any interest to me. On one particular Sunday, during downtime from my new farm apprenticeship duties of tending to vegetable seedlings and learning the Gregorian chants in chapel with the sisters, I settled into one of the rockers on the porch and hunkered down with Mother Ruth's purported autobiography and history of CHS, *In Wisdom Thou Hast Made Them*. She was born more than one hundred years ago, in 1897, and as I read, although it was not explicitly stated, I suspected that Ruth Elaine Younger lived in Harlem. In the opening paragraph Harlem's historic St. Philip's Episcopal Church, the first "free Africans church of New York," was identified as her place of confirmation.

I was a mere four pages into the book when I abruptly braked the back-and-forth pitch of the rocker. I read a phrase that would require a complete recalibration in my mind: ". . . rejected because of a strain of 'other blood,' an unacceptable accommodation at the time to southern members." It was those four words in the middle—"*strain of 'other blood'* "—that struck me as alternately absurd and amusing. The words "other blood," curiously quoted on the page, made me think of the outdated, outmoded dioramas of New York City's Museum of Natural History—especially given that the book was written in the mid-1980s. Was this how she conceived of being biracial; a person of color? All human blood essentially was the same. A "strain of other blood" was definitely not on my acceptable list of racial and ethnic identifiers, and the term "other" signified to me an effort to extricate herself from her true origins.

My efforts to finish reading the book amounted to skimming in search of more details about this religious matriarch. The more I read, the less I learned and the more annoyed I grew over the gaping holes in the biographical story. Ruth was both her secular birth name and her religious one—she had a progression of three aliases: born Ruth Elaine Younger, then Sister Ruth, SSJD (Sisterhood of St. John the Divine), and finally, the Rev. Mother Ruth, CHS. As both the author and the supposed subject matter of the book, Ruth gave a 30,000-foot macro autobiographical view, with just a few measly paragraphs out of 135 pages dedicated to her personal background, her biological family, and life before becoming a nun. The main thrust of the book was the details related to the acquisition of the properties for the convents and schools and a supporting cast of others—mainly bishops and clergy—who helped make it happen.

It was those four words, "strain of other blood," that revealed the single most-defining biographical and personality trait I first associated with Mother Ruth. There was no doubt in my mind that Ruth's Blackness was a strain on her life, especially in a mainline church of the early twentieth century. In the twenty-first century, I myself had experienced various forms of rejection from the Episcopal Church that I perceived as racially motivated. But I wanted to know why Ruth's Blackness was a strain to such an extent that she omitted the basic words of "race" or "racial" from her writing of *In Wisdom Thou Hast Made Them*. The "*strain of other blood*" turned into a trail I was impelled to follow beyond the book's hardcover.

2

RUTH AWAKENING

Closing in on the second week of my farm residency, I had been avoiding doing laundry because I dreaded going down into the dusty, cobweb-draped cellar where the washer and dryer were located. On my first day at the farm, Sister Heléna Marie escorted me down into the cellar and pointed out a small cubbyhole in a wall. "We were told that it was a shooting window used during the Revolutionary War to shoot at the British. Then, I met a Native American woman who told me it was probably used to shoot at her people." After hearing all of that, the cellar came to symbolize a dungeon with a sinister history.

Unsurprisingly though, an untenable situation arrived. My underwear supply was running short, and I could no longer avoid doing my laundry. Alone, I finally descended the uneven, creaky basement stairs. I discovered a large portrait of a woman who I knew was the Rev. Mother Ruth. She was propped up against the wall on the cellar floor. The Reverend Mother's placid, thin-lipped Mona Lisa smile and bespeckled dark eyes gazed through ancient grime and cobwebs caked on the glass frame. I didn't want to touch it, yet I felt it was my duty to rescue Mother Ruth from that horrible condition. I ran back upstairs to retrieve a wet rag from the kitchen. Upon my quick return to the basement, I squatted down on the floor to clean as much of the debris off of the frame and glass as I could. I brought the portrait out of the darkened basement and into the sunlit kitchen upstairs with me and polished it some more, this time with Fantastic cleaning spray. I scrubbed until the pall of smut on the glass was cleared to a shine.

The only other place I had seen a clear picture of her face was on *In Wisdom*'s dust jacket. Both portraits, the book jacket and this one, were black and white. As I studied Mother Ruth's expressionless face closer, with its duo chromatic options, I could not discern with certainty her racial identity as either Black, White, or biracial. I took the portrait into the living room, found a picture hook, and hung it on the wall opposite the fireplace. Later, I googled the name of the portrait studio, Bachrach, and learned it was an acclaimed presidential photography studio.

As an associate of another Episcopal order and as a visitor to two other Anglican convents in England, I knew "the Reverend Mother Foundress" was often regarded with saint-like reverence. In every case, her portrait was prominently displayed—like any family matriarch or ancestor—and often in multiple places throughout the convent. At the Community of the Transfiguration in Cincinnati, of which I'm an associate, the Rev. Mother Foundress Eva's body is even buried beneath the high altar in the convent's opulent chapel. It dawned on me that after three weeks at the Melrose Convent, I had not seen the Reverend Mother's portrait hanging anywhere in the three buildings of the property. So, finding the Rev. Mother Ruth's portrait in the most degraded condition in the macabre, old cellar made me wonder if she had been purposely cast aside.

The Bachrach portrait and strain of other blood transformed Ruth into a white whale I was obsessed with. My long-dormant journalistic instincts were awakened, activated, and kicked into high gear. I felt called to do more digging. I started questioning the CHS sisters more about Mother Ruth. "Controversial" was how the farm sister described her. I would come to learn that the Rev. Mother Ruth wasn't universally cherished and beloved. Equally compelling, some of the nuns who lived in the community with Mother Ruth during her lifetime knew very little about her past religious life in Canada and even less about her secular years, including her family background and racial heritage.

"I didn't know that Mother Ruth was Black until she died and Bishop (Frank) Griswold told us." That was the startling revelation from Sister Heléna Marie when I asked about the "strain of other blood" phrase in the book. Sister Heléna Marie had joined the Community of the Holy Spirit in 1978, eight years before the Rev. Mother Ruth's death. I noticed that in this conversation, Sister Heléna Marie referred to Mother Ruth as Black, where she had initially said she was a "woman of color" and "biracial" during my interviews for the farm companion program and subsequent conversations.

Next, I wanted to find out more from one of the other farm sisters, Sister Emmanuel—the "Livestock Sister"—I so named her because of her expertise in farm animals. In my experience with Episcopal and Anglican religious community, sisters often took on the name of the roles they played, for instance, the Novice Mistress or Hospitality Sister. Like Sister Heléna Marie, Sister Emmanuel also entered the order in the late 1970s, before Mother Ruth's death.

"I knew she was Black," Sister Emmanuel answered, "but it was supposed to be a secret." I noted that she did not use the word "biracial" to describe Mother Ruth. Sister Emmanuel also told me that if I wanted to learn more about Mother Ruth, I should reach out to a former CHS sister, Mary Winifred, who was now running an animal rescue center in a small town on Maryland's Eastern Shore.

For the time being, I mentally filed away the name of Mary Winifred. The two conversations with the CHS sisters for the moment steered me away from amassing more flimsy and contradictory anecdotal information from the women who obviously knew little about their Reverend Mother. I decided to use the Internet tool America now relied on to discover their "true identity" and ethnic origins—Ancestry.com. While I didn't have a DNA sample to submit, Ancestry.com still felt the most logical place for me to find out how Ruth Elaine Younger identified—Black, Negro, Colored, or "Mulatto," a term used by the US Census in a bygone era.

Ruth Elaine Younger, of New York City, immediately popped up. Her name led me to a 1905 US Census: Address: 24 134th Street. As I suspected, she was indeed from Harlem. Head of the household, William—under race for him, "B" (B = Black), and age fifty-eight—and the Younger mother, Ruth, "B," age thirty-two. Seven-year-old Ruth was a "B."

Then an unexpected occurrence surfaced between 1891 and 1910, contradicting other scanned Census records before and after 1910:

the entire family was now listed as "W" or White in the scanned Census entry.

Time was ticking. I was using a free Ancestry.com account that lasted only thirty days. I continued to download all the Younger family data, only pausing to review and cross-reference data entries like those that intrigued me or that had information that conflicted with other documents. Meanwhile, I also obtained the email address for the former Sister Mary Winifred, CHS, and reached out to her. I explained who I was—or had been career-wise—a former newspaper reporter, public relations professional, and writer. As I wrote that I was researching Ruth Younger's life story, it felt important to also let Sister Mary know that I was both African American and Episcopalian. In turn, she provided information about her life. Her legal name was Emily Shepherd, and she had entered the convent in 1969 and departed CHS in 1994. She had been the Reverend Mother's personal assistant. She was now living under the moniker "Sister Mary." She portrayed herself as still a religious monastic, yet admittedly not canonically or officially recognized by the Episcopal Church as a nun.

Sister Mary said that before leaving the convent, she had wanted to write a full and accurate biography of Mother Ruth's life. However, she claimed that her sisters in the CHS community harbored such hostility toward Mother Ruth, she felt her proposal to pursue the biography would be doomed. Even after her separation from CHS, Sister Mary thought she might still thoroughly research and write the CHS's founder's biography. Over subsequent decades, working with one of the sisters still with the community, she compiled information about Mother Ruth's life before she became a nun, with the intention of writing her biography. One of Sister Mary's stumbling blocks, she admitted, was Ruth's "complicated life," especially her racial heritage and family background.

"Mother Ruth rarely spoke of her family, although she would mention Loretta and Arthur," two siblings, Sister Mary wrote. Then she closed out a week of back-and-forth email to me this way. "Mother Ruth's life story needs to be told. I can't write about her—it's for you to do. I believe you are the one I've been waiting for." She also cautioned me: "Be careful of looking for easy or obvious answers/ motivations for Mother Ruth."

Days later, a large FedEx envelope arrived. It was filled with old brochures about the CHS religious order and the St. Hilda's & St. Hugh's School; a tarnished award medal in a decaying jeweler's box; and the disintegrating pages of a 1957 *Look* magazine article with a photo spread featuring the Rev. Mother Ruth and her schoolchildren. I was considerably impressed by the excerpted pages from *Look* magazine, which I knew from my journalism history to be a famed national general interest photography magazine that was launched as a competitor to the renowned *Life* magazine. Yet, the one item that instantly commanded my attention was a typewritten letter on yellowing paper. The letter, Sister Mary explained in a note, "was written by Arthur Younger, Ruth's youngest brother."

After reading the letter several times over, I felt like an archaeologist uncovering a never-before-seen fossil that provided evidence of an undiscovered life being and an uncharted world. The letter illuminated the darkened recesses of Ruth's life before she became cloistered. Arthur's words were key to a passageway that Ruth herself, I concluded, tried to cut off.

3

BLOOD RELATIONS

The letter that Sister Mary sent to me in that FedEx package was written by Arthur sometime in the late 1980s after his sister's death. Born in 1911, Arthur was Ruth's youngest brother, born fourteen years after his sister. By the time Ruth left for convent life in 1918, Arthur was seven years old.

From the time I sat on the rocking chairs of the Brewster manor house astounded by the *"strain of other blood"* followed by the arrival of Sister Mary's FedEx, four years had passed. That's how long it took to find a member of the Younger family who responded to my emails and gave me what I most desired, a blood relative. Two years earlier, in 2020, before the pandemic lockdown, I left the CHS farm after the sisters failed to launch the new ministry for women of color coming out of incarceration. My consolation for yet another failed vocational venture had become working on what I hoped to be the definitive and comprehensive life story of the Rev. Mother Ruth. There was no shortage of former nuns and Episcopal school and church folks who had met and known the Reverend Mother. But those who both knew and were related by blood to Ruth Elaine Younger eluded me from 2018 until 2022. It was then that I was finally able to speak with Peter Younger, the seventy-eight-year-old son of Arthur and nephew of Ruth Elaine Younger.

I was ecstatic when Pete agreed to talk to me. To me, Pete felt like a long-lost relative who held missing pieces to a family puzzle I had started four years ago. My first attempts at reaching out to Ruth's older biological family, whom I was able to identify and locate through my Ancestry.com trolling, were unsuccessful. My new tactic involved using social media, specifically Instagram. Instead of reaching out to the older members of the family, who were alive when Mother Ruth was still living, I retrained my focus on the younger generation of the Youngers who might answer emails or DMs (direct messages) and also have influence with their elders. I first chose to contact a grandnephew in Massachusetts, who didn't respond. But Ruth's grandniece, Jaclyn Younger, a dancer with the New Mexico Ballet Company, did. I was able to identify her after locating her grandfather Arthur H. Younger's 2001 online obituary. Instagram, LinkedIn, and her profile on the ballet company's website enabled me to locate an email address for her.

Jaclyn, born after Mother Ruth's death, put me in contact with her father, Arthur G. Younger, in New Mexico. Born in 1961, Arthur G., who goes by Art, was the second and last child of Arthur H. with his second wife, Irene. A retired police detective, Art had never met his aunt Ruth. Consequently, an hour of phone conversation only yielded a few useful morsels that would flesh out Ruth's family life. Some of what he shared put me in the uncomfortable position of having to refute the scant information he offered with all the information I had collected over four years verified with government records and his father's letter. He finally admitted that his father didn't talk about her.

"It seemed like he didn't have a lot of communications with Ruth," Art said. "I didn't find any letters from her. The only thing that I have about Ruth is a brochure about the school."

There were even gaps in some of Art's knowledge of the Younger history. "I knew my father had a brother named Willie," he said, seemingly oblivious to the fact that his father had seven siblings. Finally, Art said he would put me in contact with his half brother Pete, who had actually met Ruth.

The years of online sleuthing and trolling Ruth's biological family on Ancestry.com finally paid off, so I thought. Feeling that I had hit the mother lode, I was excited to learn that Arthur's oldest son was close by, only a short car drive across the Mario Cuomo Bridge from where I lived in Nyack. And the best part, he was willing to talk face-to-face.

I met Pete at the horse stable at Yonkers Raceway. Like his brother Art, Pete had been a police officer. After retirement from the New York City Police Department, Pete began a second career in 2000 as a racehorse owner and trainer. Before our meeting, I googled Pete and learned through online media for harness racing that he had been the director of the Standardbred Owners Association of New York and was the association's trustee.

Pete and I converged at the entrance to the Yonkers racetrack. He rolled up to the intersection in his late model SUV and waved me to follow. I fell in behind his car in my smaller hooptie. We turned off the paved lanes that led to public parking onto a rocky and uneven back road to the horse stables. After parking our cars, Pete and I walked into his area of the stable. A light blue square banner with Pete Younger Stable and an insignia of a harness racing horse in white stitching marked his area. Pete pulled over a dusty chair next to a large storage container, wiped it down with a rag and then offered it to me.

Flies buzzed overhead and dust and the smell of manure permeated the air. Pete kept apologizing for the setting for our interview. I reminded him that it was I who requested to meet him at the stable. After all, my work with goats and chickens on the CHS farm was how I became acquainted with his aunt Ruth, I explained. I enjoyed being around farm animals, including all the olfactory sensations that came with it. I felt as if I was in my element among the horses and hay. I asked for an introduction to Pete's horse before I sat down. Banski was his name, and he was a bit standoffish, jerking his head away when I attempted to rub his nose. I was certain it was a gesture to let me know he was a working horse and not some petting zoo attraction.

Pete perched himself on a stool and I sat down across from him. I placed a notepad and my iPhone, to record our interview, on the storage chest. Banski looked on from his stall.

"As I told you on the phone, I did meet Ruth, once," Pete said, leaning back in his chair, a horse whinnying in the background. "I was really young, maybe four, five, or six. My aunt came to stay with us in our apartment. My father explained that my aunt Ruth was a religious sister. What I remember most is how my father reacted to her. My parents were having an argument over something. And I remember my aunt Ruth yelling out my father's name, 'Arthur!' My father immediately froze. She just called his name as if she was scolding him, and he immediately stopped arguing with my mother. He backed down. I never saw anyone who had that effect on my father."

In terms of how Ruth treated Pete, he said, "I remember my aunt being really nice to me, while she was visiting us. I wasn't scared of her or anything like that. She did say one thing to me that I have never forgotten. She said, 'you're going to be all right.' I never forgot that."

These memories of his aunt were all Pete said he had to offer. "I remember my father and Aunt Miriam talking about my aunt Ruth, but they were whispering so I couldn't hear them," he said. I started to ask questions about his father's life and upbringing with the hopes that at least I could paint a picture in Ruth's biography of what her secular family life might have looked like.

"I really don't know much about my father's childhood or what his family life was like growing up," Pete said. That admission left me completely deflated. "All my father would say to me was he had it rough."

Still, as my journalism education taught me, I persisted with my questioning. "Do you know what neighborhood he lived in, where he went to school? Your father had four other siblings besides Ruth and Miriam, did you ever meet any of them?" Each time he answered no. However, he remembered one detail.

"Oh, I can tell you I'm named after one of my father's brothers, Peter, who died before my father was born."

Then, Pete excused himself because he remembered something he left in his car. He returned with a large manila envelope and deposited its contents on the storage container that served as our desk as we spoke. "These are my grandparents," he said, pointing to two portraits. "Ruth and William Younger." I had seen their portraits before. Art, in New Mexico, had emailed scans of the images to me. It appeared I was now looking at the original, finely preserved or at least well restored. I knew Pete's grandparents died three decades before he was born, his grandfather in 1914 and his grandmother in 1925.

Pete flipped over another photograph. "This is me with my mother and father." The faded black and white photo showed a family getaway to the Jersey Shore. Pete later said that when he was still a young child, his father and mother divorced.

Pete indicated that his father had always taken care of him throughout his life; however, there was a bit of estrangement between Pete and his father. Arthur had remarried and moved to New Mexico. It was outside of Albuquerque, New Mexico, where his half brother Art grew up, where decades later, a small family reunion took place. Pete shared photos of that family reunion, the two brothers with their father in the 1990s, a decade before their father's passing in 2001.

"This is pretty much it," he said, shuffling through the photographs.

I knew that wasn't it. There was a lot more. It had become abundantly clear that I knew more about Art's and Pete's father's life—especially his childhood—than they were ever privy to. It was contained in the yellowing pages I possessed, written by their father more than thirty-five years ago. While Arthur only told his sons that "he had it rough," to Sister Mary, in the three-page letter written after the Rev. Mother Ruth's death, Pete's father depicted in more detail a childhood filled with tragedy and trauma.

"Mr. Younger, I have something to share with you," I said to Pete after I finished snapping photographs with my iPhone of his parents' and grandparents' portraits arranged on the makeshift desk in the stable. "I have a lot more information about your father's childhood. That information is in his own words. I have letters that your father wrote to a former CHS nun about your aunt Ruth, after she died in 1986. He wrote about his relationship with your aunt Ruth and some memories of his childhood. I can confirm to you, he did indeed have it rough."

* * *

"My mouth was hanging open when I read the letters," Pete said a week later when we spoke on the phone. "Actually, it's still hanging open. I'm still trying to process it all.

"The shocking thing to me was that my father really didn't like his sister. Maybe he loved her, but what it seemed to me was he didn't like her," Pete said. "It seemed like my father was blaming Ruth for their mother's death because she left to become a sister. I don't think my father was being fair. She had a calling and a life to live."

After reading the letters, both of Ruth's nephews commented on what they characterized as the unreasonable amount of blame their father placed on her for some of the family's misfortunes.

But after four years of reading archival documents of several hundred letters and talking to dozens of people—from both Ruth's religious family and her secular blood relations—there was a shared consensus—animosity toward Ruth Elaine Younger/Sister Ruth, SSJD/the Rev. Mother Ruth, CHS, abounded.

4

1897–1918, THE DEATH OF RUTH ELAINE YOUNGER

In his undated letter to Sister Mary, Ruth's youngest brother Arthur
wrote, "My sister has never been talked about with members of the
family. I have decided that at this stage in my life I am not going to
start explaining." She was persona non grata and Arthur's reasoning
was clear: "I don't believe she ever considered herself a member of
the Younger family."

Arthur wrote, "I do remember some of the very negative things
that happened, mainly because of my mother. My mother was depressed about my father's death and the death of my oldest brother
Peter. Theodore and Miriam had left home to marry and live their
own lives. That left Ruth as the oldest child to help my mother with
the younger children. It appears that Ruth did not want this responsibility." In his letter, he makes references to his mother's struggle with
depression. "She couldn't support the children (Gertrude, Loretta,
William, and Arthur) without some help."

Arthur's bitterness toward Ruth most likely took shape in 1914,
the year their father died, when, as a four-year-old, he was sent to live
in an orphanage with his older brother William. Ruth was still living
at home in Harlem when the two youngest Younger boys were sent to
Howard Orphanage and Industrial School in Smithtown, New York,
a village on Long Island—a world away from their Harlem home.

The Howard Colored Orphan Asylum was founded in Brook-
lyn in 1866 by two African Americans, a Presbyterian minister,
Henry M. Wilson, widow Sarah A. Tillman, and a White general,
Oliver Otis Howard. An 1894 *New York Times* article praised it as
"Comfortable and Spacious Quarters and Excellent Care and Teach-

ing."[1] In 1915 when the Younger boys arrived, "Howard provided a dozen 'industrial' teachers of cooking, shoe repair, shop and like, and taught farming to boys by having them work on a farm. However, according to a government report, much of the Howard farm equipment was in bad condition, and the shop equipment was inadequate. Howard simply lacked the money to become a first-rate industrial school."[2]

By 1917, when the Younger brothers left the facility, it was in financial crisis. A March 29 *New York Times* article's attention-grabbing headline declared, "NEGROES INVADING NORTH; Teams Organized to Raise $100,000 for Howard Industrial School."[3] In a May 3, 1917, article in the *New York Age*, "Mrs. Ruth Younger," the boys' mother, was one of "the captains of the colored teams" in Harlem for the fund-raising campaign.[4]

Arthur admitted in his letter, "I really don't recall much about that time that stands out in my mind." He says, "I don't remember when Ruth started going to work, but I do know she worked in the parish office of St. Philip's Church." The historic Episcopal church, on 134th Street (the same street as one of the Younger's apartments), was founded in 1809 as the "Free African Church of St. Philip's." It was the parish where all the Younger children were baptized and confirmed. The world-famous Dr. W. E. B. DuBois was a St. Philip's parishioner and had also served on the orphanage's board. He very likely crossed paths with both the child and elder Ruth Youngers.

A widely accepted view of monastic life is that a person is "born again" into a new life as a religious. Ruth's life span is depicted in

---

1. "Little Colored Orphans," *New York Times*, July 22, 1894, retrieved from: https://timesmachine.nytimes.com/timesmachine/1894/07/22/109720845 .pdf?pdf_redirect=true&ip=0.

2. Carleton Mabee, "Charity in Travail: Two Orphan Asylums for Blacks," *New York History* 55, no. 1 (1974): 55–77. JSTOR, http://www.jstor.org /stable/23169563. Accessed March 13, 2023.

3. *New York Times*, March 29, 1917, page 12, retrieved from: https:// timesmachine.nytimes.com/timesmachine/1917/03/29/121602168.html ?pageNumber=12.

4. "Howard Orphanage to Continue Campaign," *New York Age*, May 3, 1917, accessed May 14, 2023.

Christian monastic years in this way: 1897—1922—1986. The three years represent biological birth, rebirth as a "religious" through final vows of "life profession," and death of the physical body. It is a standard format on tombstones and other grave markers for many nuns and monks.

In Ruth's case, there appeared to be two birth dates—1897, the year of her biological birth, and 1922, when she took her vows and became Sister Ruth Younger at the Convent of St. John the Divine in Toronto. There were also two death dates—1918, when she first decided to enter the monastic life, and 1986, the year of her bodily expiration. In neither case did death come swiftly. The life of the woman born Ruth Elaine Younger entered into death throes that lasted sixty-five years.

"My life began in October 1897 in New York City during the days of horse cars and buggies and elevated trains."

This was a sentence penned by the Rev. Mother Ruth in an unpublished draft for her autobiography, *In Wisdom Thou Hast Made Them.* The pages were in a second package of items mailed to me by Sister Mary. Two and a half of the typewritten pages, out of eleven in total, were dedicated to Ruth's childhood. From that draft, only one paragraph made it into the final published history given to me when I first entered the CHS as a farm aide.

"Why the text never made it into the final manuscript for the book was unknown," said Sister Mary, who quickly understood that questions about her Reverend Mother's secular life were off limits unless she broached the topic herself. And what Mother Ruth often offered was trivial.

"The (memories) she shared were so random," Sister Mary said. "I remember she once told me, 'my brother Arthur hated green beans.' She also told me she used to warn her sister not to touch her things and that her father nicknamed her Rudy. She told me that when her father proposed marriage to her mother, he told her, 'You will always be Younger.'" Those were the only anecdotes of Ruth's secular life Sister Mary ever recalled hearing.

The brittle, frayed pages from 1984 are the only documented account directly from Ruth about her childhood. Frustratingly, the short narrative was flimsy, and some of the information dramatically contradicted the history as told in her brother's letter and archival government records. I regarded the erasing of Ruth Elaine Younger's life between 1897 and 1918 as intentional.

There was one other source of information about the childhood and teenage years of Ruth Elaine Younger, the society column of the legendary African American weekly newspaper, the *New York Age*. During its heyday in the late nineteenth and early twentieth centuries, the paper billed itself as "The National Negro Weekly." Similarly to Sister Mary's account, they only produced random snippets of Ruth's secular life. Using the newspaper.com database, I unearthed a half dozen news briefs in which Ruth Elaine Younger's name appeared. It was mostly in listings as an attendee for a social gathering or as a member of arts and culture clubs, one of which she founded. While initially the findings thrilled me, they did little to satisfy my yearning to know more about Ruth's home life and family. At the most, the short news items added a new dimension to Ruth's youth as evidence that her life was about more than religious piety. A May 27, 1915, article listed Ruth Younger as a member of the Beaux Arts Club, "a dramatic and literary club."

Another news brief corroborated a reference Mother Ruth made to her childhood illness in the published version of *In Wisdom Thou Hast Made Them*: "A long period of serious illness meant months in St. Luke's Hospital and subsequently recuperative time in Virginia."[5] An August 15, 1907, mention in the *New York Age* noted the nine-year-old's travels out of state: "Miss Ruth Younger of 6 W. Ninety-ninth Street, has returned home from a visit to her aunt in Danville, Va."[6] Virginia, as noted in Arthur's letters and government records, was the birthplace of their mother. Historically, Danville was a major center of the nation's tobacco industry and had a large settlement of formerly enslaved African Americans who shared political leadership with White residents until Virginia legislators and a White mob forced the Black residents out of office in 1883.[7]

---

5. The Reverend Mother Ruth, CHS, *In Wisdom Thou Hast Made Them* (New York: Adams, Bannister, Cox, 1986), 3.

6. *New York Age*, August 15, 1907.

7. Molly Castle Work and Rachelle Keaton, "In the 1880s, Election Fraud

The long period of serious illness as a child reported by the Rev. Mother Ruth in her book was an aspect of her secular life she did willingly share. According to a former student of Mother Ruth's school, Mother Ruth herself had told the student that she suffered with discoid Lupus, which only affected her skin and which she gave as the reason for wearing makeup. Ruth's childhood illness disclosure eclipsed other family trauma. Missing from Ruth's account of the Youngers' family life was the dire, tragic tone of poverty, the untimely death of their father and two siblings, and a mother's struggle with mental health, all captured in Arthur's letter. In fact, in the published book and the unpublished drafts, all of that information was omitted and, in a couple of cases, contradicted Arthur's letter. One such contradiction had to do with their father's occupation.

"There was some account of my father's life at sea before marriage and later he went into building and engineering," Mother Ruth wrote in the unpublished pages. However, according to Arthur's letter and Census reports, William's work is described as "very menial jobs," with Census entries citing his occupation as a janitor and in other entries a fireman—the work of stoking furnaces and maintaining building heat. Ruth made no mention of her mother's work as a seamstress, which was also documented in some Census entries and Arthur's letter.

In the published pages of *In Wisdom Thou Hast Made Them*, just a single sentence is devoted to the parents of Ruth Younger: "She also had good and devout parents who attended the Presbyterian Church. Bible reading and praying together was the norm of her family life."[8] It is in unpublished pages that a more expansive view is provided: "We children were sent to the local school early and always to Sunday School, for my mother was a devout young woman who also read the Bible to us faithfully and had family prayers. Father had no objection to this but took no active part in it.

---

and a Massacre Stopped Black Progress," Word in Black, https://wordinblack.com/2021/10/in-the-1880s-election-fraud-and-a-massacre-stopped-black-progress/. See also Gregory Schneider, "Reckoning in a Small Town: Civil War Meets Civil Rights in the Last Capital of the Confederacy," *Washington Post*, September 19, 2020.

8. The Reverend Mother Ruth, CHS, *In Wisdom Thou Hast Made Them*, 3.

"We first three children were normal in every way though interest on the part of my brother (Theodore) in tenor singing and in figure skating were above average and were highly praised. I was, from the beginning, very much interested in books and in school subjects, especially English, history, mathematics, and science."

Mother Ruth did shed some light on her parents and even alluded to some family struggles, writing in the unpublished draft: "My father, who was twice my mother's age, found the making of a home and family life quite difficult but my mother's innate religion and sense of responsibility and the love they had for each other made their lives together quite possible.

"The family observed the great and public holidays very fully as well as their birthdays and other holidays in family style alone. We were very self-contained and therefore did not develop a wide circle of friends at this early stage though I had two cherished friends, May Chinn, who became a doctor, and Carmen St. Clair, who did excellent handwork."

May Chinn grew up to become an acclaimed physician who broke both racial and gender barriers as the first African American woman to graduate from Bellevue Hospital Medical College in 1926 and the first African American woman to intern at Harlem Hospital. Both May Chinn's and Carmen St. Clair's names appeared with Ruth's in the *New York Age* news briefs, as members of the same arts and social clubs and party attendees.

In the unpublished pages, a section oddly written in third person, Ruth pinpointed the age of fifteen when she first heard the call to religious life. She wrote that in 1912, she "became a young woman of prayer and almost daily attendance at Mass, even though she was very busy with high school work.

"Several years later three more children were born: two sisters and a brother. Fairly soon thereafter," she wrote in an abrupt, yet very matter-of-fact shift in tone, "my father became ill and died and that changed the entire outlook of the family. We older three siblings had to work as well as study, for we had to contribute to our maintenance with but a small pension to provide for the total family."

In Arthur's letter to Sister Mary, he wrote that Ruth worked in the office of Harlem's historic St. Philip's Church. Ruth only mentioned having one job in the unpublished pages. She wrote that she began part-time work at the age of seventeen for the American Society of Mechanical Engineers (ASME). ASME in the early 1900s was most noted for its advocacy and activism for devising safety codes for boilers and boiler steam pressure vessels used in building heating and power systems. These were the very systems that her father stoked as a fireman to support his large family. In the published version of *In Wisdom Thou Hast Made Them*, Ruth made no mention of ever working for the parish where she was confirmed, nor her father's death, nor any of the family's misfortunes, except her own childhood illness.

Despite her father's death, daily attendance at Mass, and her schoolwork, Ruth did make time for social activities, as noted in the *New York Age*. During the summer of 1915, she organized a celebrity fan club for the London, England–born Samuel Coleridge-Taylor. Before his untimely death at the age of thirty-nine in 1912, Coleridge-Taylor was a much-lauded, racial-barrier-breaking classical music composer of "mixed-race heritage" and, by many accounts, a pan-African activist who worked with W. E. B. DuBois.

"The Coleridge-Taylor Club has been organized by Ruth Blaine [*sic*] Younger. The officers are as follows: Ruth Blaine Younger, president; May Edward, treasurer; Ida Radford, corresponding secretary; Edele Burnham, recording secretary; Carmen B. St. Clair."[9]

Two years following her father's death, another notable mention in the *New York Age* for Ruth Younger was a February 3, 1916, graduation party for Miss Frances Mulford, "the only colored graduate of the class of forty" from Bayonne high school. Among the attendees of the party along with the eighteen-year-old "Miss Ruth Younger of New York City," was "Paul Robeson of Somerville, N. J."[10] More

---

9. *New York Age*, page 8, https://www.newspapers.com/image/33453627/?terms=%22Ruth%20Blaine%20Younger%22&match=1, accessed May 14, 2023.

10. *New York Age*, page 7, https://www.newspapers.com/image/33454224/?terms=%22Ruth%20Elaine%20Younger%22&match=1, accessed May 14, 2023.

likely than not, that Paul Robeson was the same Paul Robeson who graduated from Somerville High School and went on to international fame as a singer, professional football player, stage and film actor, and civil rights activist. Later that year, the *New York Age* reported that "Miss Ruth Younger and Miss May Chinn of New York City were the weekend guests of Ms. Frances Mulford of 70 Andrews Street in Bayonne, N. J."[11]

While I was often frustrated by my inability to reconstruct a detailed, research-based chronological accounting of Ruth's early life, the *New York Age* tidbits provided me some latitude to conjure up a mythical profile. Ruth took on more mystical qualities after I read that she had circulated in the same orbit as Dr. May Chinn and Paul Robeson, both of whom became trailblazers who rose to prominence at the height of the Harlem Renaissance. Ruth's other news clippings—the formation of the Coleridge-Taylor fan club and a leadership position in a women's auxiliary group supporting the segregated African American infantry regiment deployed to France—offered proof that she closely identified with and cared about her community, the Black community of Harlem. She also served as the assistant recording secretary and on the entertainment committee for the Women's Auxiliary of the Fifteenth Regiment, New York. According to the New York State Military Museum and Veterans Research Center, the regiment was "New York State's first segregated African American National Guard unit, formally organized in 1916."[12]

The *New York Age* news briefs were the only documented evidence that the young Ruth had the normal social life of a teenager and young adult. In both Ruth's unpublished and published peek into her life before entering the convent, she almost exclusively focused on her gravitation to religious life, writing that as a teenager, her life was dedicated to daily attendance of Mass and her relationships with notable White Episcopalians.

---

11. *New York Age*, July 27, 1916, page 10.

12. "New York State Military Museum and Veterans Research Center," NYS Division of Military and Naval Affairs, https://museum.dmna.ny.gov/flags /infantry/369th-regiment-us-army/369th-regiment-us-army-regimental-color -c-1920, accessed May 22, 2022.

She wrote in the unpublished pages, "My life was filled with interest in the Church, especially the Cathedral on the hill at 110th Street, where I began to attend Mass daily. There I became interested not only in the growing, developing building, but more especially in the life of the young women who lived at the nearby Deaconess House and attended Communion daily." Throughout the first decades of the twentieth century, the Cathedral Church of St. John the Divine was under construction. To this day, the cathedral remains unfinished, with several missing architectural features including a steeple, transept, and tower.

In Ruth's storytelling, the absence of meaningful and notable Black Harlem figures and St. Philip's parishioners (such as W. E. B. DuBois and later poet Langston Hughes), where she attended during her early childhood, was perplexing. One person who received quite a bit of acknowledgment in the book was a White woman who was an officer of St. Hilda's Guild, Harriet Bronson, "an expert in embroidery for the Church." She and the guild members designed and maintained church vestments and altar linens. Ruth's friendship with Harriet received substantially more attention in both the unpublished pages and the final book than her own family members. Her actual childhood friendships with May Edward Chinn and Carmen St. Clair were omitted altogether in the published book. It was solely Miss Bronson's friendship for which Ruth provided an in-depth description of her secular-life relationships, writing in both the first and third person:

> She was an Associate of the Community of St. Mary at Peekskill. She satisfied me very much as a person since she was a devout woman of prayer and she produced such beautiful work for the altar as well as other embellishments for the Church. [Embroidery] was a very attractive occupation as was also the happy friendship with Miss Bronson, who daily attended St. Luke's Chapel, in Greenwich Village, New York. The friendship between the two, far apart though they were in age and background, grew so that confidences were exchanged.[13]

---

13. The Reverend Mother Ruth, CHS, *In Wisdom Thou Hast Made Them*, 3.

Their acquaintance would extend into the years during which Ruth entered her first convent, the Sisterhood of St. John the Divine in Toronto, but soured decades later as Bronson turned against Ruth and attempted to sabotage her later efforts to establish a religious order in New York.

I was confused by the fact that the Rev. Mother Ruth did not provide any detail about her friendship with Dr. Chinn or her socializing with Paul Robeson. Despite her brother Arthur's assertion in his letter to Sister Mary that written correspondence was exchanged with his sister, as I sifted through hundreds of documents in the vast files in the CHS archives, it was apparent Ruth did not retain any letters from family. By contrast, volumes of personal letters from a variety of non-religious acquaintances from all over the United States, Canada, and England—about significant as well as mundane chronicles of life, teas, luncheons, books, and concerts—were preserved by Ruth over her lifetime dating as far back as 1925.

* * *

Much of my work to reconstruct Ruth's biological family life was relegated to the computer screen and the file cabinets. But some of my research, as with the meeting with Mother Ruth's nephew Peter, compelled me to drive. And my growing interest in her family life led me to the streets of Harlem. Twenty-two West 134th Street was the first address I found for the Younger family in the 1905 Census. My car's GPS indicated no such location existed. Nonetheless, I continued down 134th Street past descending address numbers and some hallowed Harlem institutions, including the Youngers' family church, St. Philip's Episcopal. I drove as far as West 134th Street would allow me to travel. I reached a dead-end on Malcolm X Boulevard. I had to laugh when my GPS car map indicated I was at the Malcolm X intersection. Over the first year of my research, I had come to ascribe the motto "by any means necessary"—commonly associated with Malcolm X—to this Rev. Mother from Harlem. The phrase thoroughly captured Ruth's tenacity and dogged determination, as described in the interviews I had with those who knew her and letters she had written about her God-appointed mission to create a new religious order.

The storied Lenox Terrace apartments—once billed as Harlem's first luxury apartment building—now occupied the block where the Younger family's home likely stood in 1905. I consulted a scholar on Harlem real estate, Dr. Kevin McGruder, an associate professor of African American history at Antioch College and a former research fellow at the Schomburg Center for Research in Black Culture at the New York City Public Library. He was also the author of a biography on the early twentieth-century Black real estate titan, *Philip Payton: The Father of Black Harlem.*

"22 West 134th Street is part of an area (133rd, 134th, and 135th Street between Lenox and Fifth Avenues) in which the properties were demolished as part of a slum clearance initiative in the 1950s and replaced with Lenox Terrace, six high-rise middle-income apartment buildings," McGruder wrote to me in an email.

From the time young Ruth was two years old until age eighteen, the family moved at least four times. According to McGruder, apartment moves sometimes occurred annually among Harlem's Black families in the early 1900s, especially those with low household incomes.

During my drive through Harlem, I turned left onto Malcolm X Boulevard—also known as Lenox Avenue—and headed the three blocks up to 129 137th Street, another address I found for the Youngers in the 1915 Census records. It was the year after William, the Younger patriarch, died, and the elder Ruth is listed as "Head of Household." The building, constructed in 1910, was still standing. The exterior facade was a medium beige. I don't know if it qualified as a brownstone, but its existence provided me a sense of relief because I concluded that perhaps not all the Youngers' homes were classified as slums. However, with nine people listed in the apartment in the Census, I suspected it may have been cramped and it was likely one of the buildings with shared bathrooms for multiple families, which was common in that era.

The 1910 Census entry for the Younger household by far provided the most intriguing information about the family. During that year, the entire family's race was listed as White. I relied on my own imagination, a little research, and an educated guess to draw my own conclusions. It was up to the Census taker to make the decision on the accuracy of the information provided. A 1910 handbook for the "Thirteenth Census for the United States April 15, 1910" stated in its "Instructions to Enumerators" that they had "a right not only to an answer, but to a truth answer. Do not accept any statement which you believe to be false. Where you know that the answer given is incorrect, enter upon the schedule the fact as nearly as you can ascertain it."[14]

I decided that the door-to-door Census taker ascertained the Younger family was White. It seemed the most rational explanation, especially if Mrs. Pinkie Ruth Younger provided the answer to the survey questions; a woman whose youngest son described her decades later as either "an Octoroon or Caucasian."

This government record, which I found on Ancestry.com in the early days of my research, was a harbinger of the dialogue to come from school alumni, CHS sisters, and others on whether the Rev. Mother Ruth was "passing" as a White woman. Moreover, the Younger family also fit a commonly accepted profile of Black Episcopalians as having light skin. "Colorism" was a dominant sociological element pervasive in the Episcopal Church in Black communities, as many Black church historians have concluded. Some congregations "were identified with light-skinned families known as the blue vein society," the Rev. Canon Harold T. Lewis wrote in his book, *A Steady Beat: The African American Struggle for Recognition in the Episcopal Church*.[15]

Arthur placed the blame for young Ruth "abandoning the family" at the feet of its rector, the Rev. Shelton Hale Bishop, and encouraging her to become a nun. However, documented evidence exists of others whom Ruth consulted—such as the Rev. Florada Howard, the Black vicar of the segregated Manhattan Episcopal mission,

---

14. "Department of Commerce and Labor Bureau of the Census: Thirteenth Census for the United States April 10, 1910, Instruction to Enumerators," Government Printing Office, 1910, retrieved from https://www.census .gov/history/pdf/1910instructions.pdf.

15. Harold T. Lewis, *A Steady Beat: The African American Struggle for Recognition in the Episcopal Church* (Trinity Press International, 1996).

St. Jude's Chapel on the Upper West Side, and the Rev. S. C. Hughson, a superior of the Order of the Holy Cross monastery; the latter she publicly credited for encouraging her to follow her calling into religious life.

In fact, Father Howard's response to the teenage Ruth was less than encouraging. According to a 1981 pamphlet on the history of St. Jude's Chapel, the Rev. Howard wrote in a 1942 newsletter article about counseling Ruth Younger, "Many years ago, a woman just out of high school came to the vicar (the Rev. Florada Howard) for advice about joining a religious order. We do not go in for that particularly at St. Jude but since the young lady was determined she received the best advice. After many years, when the conversation was forgotten she visited St. Jude's again, a graduate of the University of Toronto and devoted member of a Canadian religious order."[16]

Ruth gives credit to two priests who were also monks in Holy Cross Monastery. She writes in the unpublished pages: "I came to know Father [James] Huntington and Father [Shirley C.] Hughson." Fathers Huntington and Hughson were very prominent Episcopalians; Huntington was the founder of Holy Cross Monastery, which was founded in 1884.

As a teenager, Ruth's first step into an avowed religious life came through her admission into the Confraternity of the Love of God, an affiliation of Holy Cross Monastery, which at that time was located in Lower Manhattan. The Confraternity of the God of Love had a stringent rule of life that required prayer multiple times a day, fasting and abstinence, attendance at Mass on Sundays and feast days, and regular reports to the Superior, according to an early 1900s Holy Cross confraternity's rule of life booklet contained in Sister Mary's FedEx package. "I thought the time had come in my late teens when I had the duty of thinking seriously about and deciding upon my life's work," Ruth wrote in the unpublished pages. "I was seriously drawn to the Religious Life in order to live for God and not for myself or for any earthly goal. Increasingly I felt called

---

16. Pamphlet, St. Michael's History, 1981.

to give myself and any ambitions or desires in self-surrender to my Lord, serving Him and His children."

In Arthur's letter, he implied that his sister's desire to become a nun was an effort to avoid supporting the family. If, as Arthur's letter implied, Ruth's sole purpose in becoming a nun was to avoid supporting the Younger family, perhaps unbeknownst to him, it wasn't her only avenue. Ruth had another option to escape the grim and turbulent impoverished home life and their widowed, depressed mother. An opportunity to remain in the secular world, with ties to religious life, came in the form of a marriage proposal from an aspirant to the priesthood. Ruth's immersion in all things of the Episcopal Church led her to cross paths with a young seminarian who expressed a romantic interest in her. Charles Cuthbert Canterbury Corbin Jr. was an immigrant from St. George's, Bermuda, enrolled at the Episcopal Church's General Theological Seminary in Manhattan's Chelsea neighborhood on the Lower West Side. His US selective service registration card listed his address in Harlem at 26 West 131st Street, just a couple of blocks from Ruth's home and St. Philip's Episcopal Church.

In the postscript of her CHS history book, *In Wisdom Thou Hast Made Them*, nearly seventy years later, she wrote about Corbin:

When I graduated from High School in New York, in the presence of a number of my friends, one of them who also attended the same Church and who was graduating from the General Theological Seminary asked me to marry him. I had thought for some time before this request that I had been inspired by our Lord to give myself to Him in the Religious Life. This good Priest was willing to understand that the call of the Lord comes first.[17]

The Rev. Corbin was ordained in 1917, the year Ruth made an unsuccessful application to St. Mary's. He eventually became the rector of the all-Black congregation St. Augustine Episcopal Church

---

17. The Reverend Mother Ruth, CHS, *In Wisdom Thou Hast Made Them*, 23.

in Atlantic City, New Jersey. "He told her if she didn't marry him, then he would never marry," said Sister Mary of another of Ruth's secular life memories she chose to share with her personal assistant. Government records from Ancestry.com appear to confirm he was single his entire life.

Ruth's first application to become a nun was made to the Community of St. Mary's in New York. By many historical accounts, the order is believed to be the first Worldwide Anglican Communion's religious community for women formally and canonically recognized by the church, by the Episcopal Diocese of New York's Bishop Horatio Potter.

According to the 100th anniversary history, "Ten Decades of Praise: The Story of the Community of St. Mary, Its First Century," on February 2, 1865, Potter became the first Anglican bishop to receive and consecrate a religious community since Henry VII's order to close the monastic communities in England. "It was he who had chosen St. Mary as their patroness and the Feast of the Purification as the day of their profession."[18] The institution was held in St. Michael's Church on the Upper West Side of New York City.

In her handwritten addendum to the first draft of her book, Ruth writes about her application to St. Mary's Convent:

> Father Hughson applied to St. Mary's Convent at Peekskill. The report of this encounter between the Rev. Mother, C. S. M., and Fr. Hughson had the following outcome: It would be very difficult to admit an aspirant with a strain of "other" blood because of their Southern Sisters. An application was then made to Mother Dora of the Sisterhood of St. John the Divine who gave her consent. I then prepared to enter the Canadian Community.

It is this handwritten notation with the words "other blood" in quotations that provided the evidence and the beginning of Ruth pre-

---

18. Sister Mary Hilary, CSM, "Ten Decades of Praise: The Story of the Community of Saint Mary During Its First Century," Project Canterbury, https://anglicanhistory.org/usa/csm/mhilary/chapter3.html.

senting herself as a biracial woman, claiming one parent as Black, her father, and her mother as White. From the final edited account published in the book *In Wisdom,*

> Ruth Younger's application was rejected because of a strain of "other blood," which was an unacceptable accommodation at that time to southern members of St. Mary's Community. Thereupon, Father Hughson, OHC made a successful application for her to leave the country and test her vocation in Canada in the Sisterhood of St. John the Divine (S. S. J. D.) She was very uncertain about this unimagined change, but she was finally willing to try, even though the price seemed at the time all but overwhelming.[19]

With an initial visit to Toronto in 1918 and her final move-in year cited by SSJD records as 1919, Ruth Elaine Younger became Sister Ruth, beginning a "new life" as a "religious."

From that point and over the next sixty-five years, Sister and Rev. Mother Ruth snuffed out the life of the woman from Harlem and shrouded her behind a black veil and wimple, white facial powder, and a quasi-British accent known as Canadian Dainty. One former CHS postulant, Elizabeth Pettus Losa (whose great uncle, coincidently, is Edmund Pettus of the legendary Selma, Alabama, bridge), recounted how Mother Ruth spoke of her transition, which began in Harlem and ended some five hundred miles away at the doorstep of St. John's Convent in Toronto, Canada.

"She told us she arrived there on the back of some man's motorcycle." And that moment was the beginning of the end of Ruth Elaine Younger's life.

---

19. The Reverend Mother Ruth, CHS, *In Wisdom Thou Hast Made Them,* 4.

5

LITTLE NUN ON THE PRAIRIE

The First World War and a global pandemic were raging as Ruth Elaine Younger became a postulant with the Sisterhood of St. John the Divine (SSJD) in Toronto in 1918. She wrote that the "sacramental life of prayer, Communion, meditation, and the divine office were familiar. There were many opportunities for kindness and thought for these new people, who took some time to get to know her because of the practice of much silence."[1]

More than one hundred years after the newly minted Sister Ruth SSJD embarked on a life of silence—or, not so much silence as her religious vocation unfolded over the twentieth century—I, too, was about to experience for the first time cloistered convent life behind the monastic enclosure. In 2020, I was forced to leave the Community of the Holy Spirit just weeks before the COVID lockdown began. Underemployed with only a part-time parish communications job, I was fortunate enough to be taken in by another Episcopal convent in their Alongsider program.

Instead of living in their separate guest apartment or retreat quarters as I had with the CHS sisters and other religious communities I visited, the Mendham, New Jersey–based order, Community of St. John Baptist, required me to live under their watchful eye. I was exceedingly grateful not to find myself homeless during the global pandemic. At the same time, as an African American woman inhabiting a space referred to as "a cell" next door to the "Superior" was emotionally taxing. Although separated by a century, it still gave me

---

1. The Reverend Mother Ruth, CHS, *In Wisdom Thou Hast Made Them*, 4.

an empathetic perspective and an unvarnished view of restrictive religious life—InChrist-Ceration was how I referred to it—for the twenty-one-year-old Ruth from Harlem.

Ruth Younger was admitted to SSJD as a postulant on the Feast of St. Michaels and All Angels on September 29, 1918. Her postulancy—known in religious institutions as the time required to see if an individual's calling is real and if they fit into the community they hope to serve—would be the requisite six months. She entered the novitiate and was "clothed" (received her habit) on "Passion Sunday," April 6, 1919. In her writings, Ruth provided very little description of her life in the novitiate. Others who have described it likened the experience to a religious-style boot camp, with its intense focus on training for the strict regimented and disciplined life and long periods of silence and seven hours of prayers, Lauds, Prime, Terce, Sext, None, Vespers, and Compline.

"The sisters who served in the military seemed to have an easier time of adjusting," Sister Mary, Ruth's former assistant at CHS recalled. Even the habit is often described in military terms. From the history of the Community of the Transfiguration: "A habit is a kind of a uniform, which shows that the Sister is in service of Jesus Christ, just as the soldier's uniform shows that the soldier is in the service of our country."[2] Sister Constance, SSJD, another African American woman who migrated to Canada from Baltimore in 1933, wrote in her memoir, "Mother Dora was most meticulous about our appearance, and one soon learned all the small but important duties of pulling the puffs of our caps, of raising one's arms carefully so as not to crease one's collar, and inserting the white cuffs."[3]

When she became cloistered with the Anglican Church of Canada order, it had only been in existence for thirty-two years. Founded in 1884 by the Canadian widow Hannah Grier Coome, the Sisterhood of St. John the Divine was only the second convent formed in

---

2. Sister Monica Mary Heyes, CT, *Women of Devotion: History of an Anglican Religious Community Begun in 1898* (Wilmington, OH: Orange Frazer Press, 2014), 74.

3. Sister Constance, SSJD, *Other Little Ships: Memoirs of Sister Constance, S.S.J.D.* (Toronto: Patmos Press, 1997), 54.

North America as a part of the Oxford Movement that began in the mid-nineteenth century. Before founding the SSJD, Hannah Grier Coome made her life vows in the Community of St. Mary in Peekskill, New York, the very order that first rejected Ruth Younger. Luckily for Ruth, the Rev. Mother Hannah made Canada a promised land for racially discriminated Episcopal Church aspirants to religious life from the United States.

In a 2014 blog article on the SSJD website, titled "Our Black History Heritage": "Throughout its history SSJD has had black Sisters. In the early part of the last century, several came from the U. S. A. where segregation prevented them from joining 'white' orders."[4]

The early half of the twentieth century marked the Great Migration for African Americans fleeing the rural South to Northeast cities seeking job opportunities. Yet, for a few Black women seeking religious vocation in the Episcopal Church, they were pushed to the other side of the border.

For nearly forty years, there was one segregated religious order for Black women in the United States Episcopal Church. Established in 1871, a Church of England order, All Saints Sisters of the Poor, opened a branch house in Baltimore to begin mission work in the all-Black Episcopal parish Church of St. Mary's, according to a history of the order, *All Saints Sisters of the Poor: An Anglican Sisterhood in the Nineteenth Century*. Three sisters from England worked in the predominantly poor and Black inner-city neighborhoods. By 1880, "a Coloured Sisterhood" was created as a separate affiliate of All Saints Sisters of the Poor's Baltimore branch.

The history of the order states that "there were three Professed Coloured sisters and one or two novices. They had charge and worked for the Church of St. Mary's, set apart entirely for the coloured people."[5] The sisterhood was disbanded in 1917. Sister Frances, the re-

---

4. "Our Black History Heritage," http://sisters-of-ssjd.blogspot.com/2014 /01/, accessed May 18, 2019.

5. Susan Mumm, ed., *All Saints Sisters of the Poor: An Anglican Sisterhood in the Nineteenth Century* (Boydell Press, Church of England Record Society, 2001), 45

maining All Saints "Coloured Sister," migrated to Toronto in 1918 to join SSJD, the same year Ruth Elaine Younger was admitted.

The writer of the 2014 SSJD's blog post on their black heritage noted: "Sister Frances and Sister Ruth were both of Afro-American heritage although they both looked white. . . . Regardless of colour, these Sisters were treated like all others and undertook whatever ministries the Community required of them."[6]

As a novice, Sister Ruth's first work assignment was in the hospital pharmacy. In her book *In Wisdom Thou Hast Made Them*, she wrote, "During these war years, it was not unusual for Sister Ruth, who had been Clothed as a Novice, to be told to assist in the Sisters' Hospital pharmacy because of her knowledge of and interest in chemistry."[7] In the unpublished pages, she went into further detail and said of the work,

> One of the special people on the staff because of the war was a young South African (white) chemist who had come to learn something about the approach to men in the American and Canadian armed forces so that the approach to their healing after war wounding could be improved. She asked me to return to Africa with her. I explained my situation in the Novitiate and made it clear that I was no longer "free" because of the Religious Life with its rules and demands. Nevertheless, I asked the Reverend Mother who turned down the request but permitted a substitute one, viz. that I should remain in the Novitiate and go to the University of Toronto to major in Science, for no one could tell how long the war would last, and a degree in chemistry could be used in teaching in the two schools for which the Community had responsibility. The Reverend Mother made it possible for me to attend the University of Toronto along with the early training in prayer, self-discipline and growth in givenness to our

---

6. *Our Black History Heritage*, http://sisters-of-ssjd.blogspot.com/2014/01/, accessed May 18, 2019.

7. The Reverend Mother Ruth, CHS, *In Wisdom Thou Hast Made Them*, 4.

Lord. At twenty-five years of age, I was fully Professed as Sister Ruth on the 29th December 1922.

"Sister Ruth is working hard at the University," the January 3, 1923, SSJD annual chapter meeting minutes notes, about the young student. As Ruth noted in her own writing, she excelled in the sciences. She made quite the impression while at the University of Toronto, garnering the notice of Professor Edmund Murton Walker, an award-winning entomologist and son of a prominent Canadian banker, Sir Byron Edmund Walker. In a 1949 thank-you letter to Ruth following his retirement as chair of the Department of Zoology, Walker wrote, "I found in you a most responsive and appreciative student. I had hoped then that you might eventually teach biology, but I trust you have found happiness and satisfaction in the work in which you now find yourself."

In 1923, Ruth obtained her bachelor's degree in natural sciences and earned the university's Governor General's Silver Medal. It was the award that Ruth gave to her brother, Arthur, who grudgingly held onto it for nearly sixty years until after his sister's death. First given in 1873 and still awarded today, the Governor General's Academic Medals recognized the outstanding scholastic achievements of college students in Canada.

Sister Ruth's life, which had been elevated by academic honors, in an instant would descend into horrors. This Younger family tragedy was captured on the front page of the *New York Times*. Sister Ruth's youngest sister, Loretta, had found a job working for the *Christian Herald*, an evangelical newspaper with ministries that included the Bowery Mission and a children's home in Nyack, New York. On August 9, 1923, Loretta and twelve of her coworkers in the Manhattan office traveled to Nyack to the *Herald*'s children's home. That evening, when the staff began its journey back to Manhattan on "a sightseeing bus," it collided with a "concrete mixer and a steam boiler" on a road undergoing repairs. Eight of the passengers—all women—were injured by boiling water and steam scalding, with one dying on the scene and five dying overnight in Nyack Hospital. The *Times* called it "one of the strangest automobile accidents in recent years." Loretta was among the five that died at the hospital.[8]

It was difficult to read about Loretta Younger's horrific and heart-wrenching manner of death as detailed in the *New York Times* articles. I felt that her spirit surfaced as I continued reading through two most fortuitous and astounding coincidences that, for me, felt like a theatrical epiphany. Immediately, it wasn't lost on me that Loretta lived at 302 Convent Avenue at the time of her death while her sister was living in a convent. That seemed just a minuscule bit of irony. What felt inexplicably beyond coincidence was the fact that ninety-five years later, the CHS convent (the second "Mother House" featured in a 2009 *New York Times* article) was on the same street as the Youngers' apartment at 454 Convent Avenue. The CHS sisters were completely unaware of this bit of Younger historical connection back to their community. What truly left me gobsmacked was after two years of work rebuilding the life of Ruth Elaine Younger and her family, I unwittingly ended up signing a lease for a Nyack apartment that was about a tenth of a mile from the site of the *Christian Herald* children's home where Loretta spent the final hours of her life.

I left the New Jersey convent's Alongsider program after six months and shortly thereafter landed a full-time parish communications job on the Upper East Side of Manhattan. I decided to live in Nyack, and at the end of 2020 found a cozy one-bedroom apartment. At the lease signing, little did I know it was less than a quarter of a mile from the location of the tragic accident that ended her life. When I made the connection a couple of days after moving in, I was certain it was providence, because it was in Nyack, after more than two years of trying, that I succeeded in connecting with members of the Younger family. As a big believer in the power of the Ancestors, I gave credit to the spirit of Loretta for bringing her nephew, Peter Younger, to me. And in turn, it was through me that Peter and his brother Art would learn that they had an aunt named Loretta.

---

8. "5 More Women Dead After Nyack Crash," *New York Times*, August 10, 1923, 1.

* * *

Sister Ruth also obtained her teaching degree at the Ontario College of Education and was sent to the Qu'Appelle Diocesan School in Regina to teach science. The Qu'Appelle Diocesan School for Girls was created, according to SSJD history, "to administer a boarding school in Regina for prairie girls." First located in an empty storefront, the fledgling school opened at the height of the Spanish flu pandemic and an economic depression. With a small enrollment of the daughters of farmers and businessmen, the school always seemed to be on the brink of demise, even in the years following the Spanish flu pandemic when Sister Ruth arrived. The school's operating budget was mainly funded by a wealthy British benefactor.

Qu'Appelle, Regina, was a post that Sister Ruth would serve in two separate tenures, the first being very successful as a teacher in the Qu'Appelle Diocesan School for Girls. In a handwritten November 16, 1950, "Biographical note for Dr. [Roma] Gans," Sister Ruth wrote to her professor at Teacher's College about that time: "I was responsible for the Religious Ed. of three thousand children in the Diocese of Qu'Appelle conducted by a fleet of caravan workers in summer and by an office staff, by post, in winter.... These children are very much isolated—especially in the winter, when they depend on 1) the radio; 2) the infrequent post, interrupted for weeks by storms and blizzards. This administrative work, choice of lessons and (provincial) letters was very rewarding indeed from these [illegible] their parents. I was very concerned about the way to bring functional Xtian [Christian] students into the world."

Sunday School by Post, SSBP for short, was the method for teaching Bible lessons and catechism to children and youth on the prairies and other remote parts of Canada during winters in the early twentieth century. During the summer months, children's religious education was delivered through a religious bookmobile of sorts, known as the Sunday School Caravan, often led by women from England on mission from the Church of England. In the 1922 book, *Across the Prairie in a Motor Caravan: A 3,000 Mile Tour by Two Englishwomen on Behalf of Religious Education*, the author F. H. Eva Hasell wrote, "The caravan was much like a tradesman's van in appearance. It was painted black, with 'Sunday School Mission,

Anglican Church,' lettered in red and gold on one side."[9] These women supported the local clergy and the SSJD nuns in providing religious education to parishioners.

During Sister Ruth's first assignment to the school, she wrote a report back to the Mother Superior in Toronto, comparing youth religious education to the life and landscape of Qu'Appelle: "For it is vast prairie field and there is the preparation of the ground, the sowing; cultivating; waiting—and occasionally, the vision of the 'fields white to the harvest.'" For Sister Ruth the work, like that of the farmers, was all-consuming and onerous. It was here where Sister Ruth established a reputation as a gifted educator, especially in the secular subjects such as the sciences.

After the 1925–1926 school year, Sister Katherine, the headmistress appointed by Mother Dora, wrote in her end-of-the-school-year report,

> Sister Ruth taught Science, Latin, Home Economics, Hygiene, Scripture, Art & Sewing. In the Lower School, she taught Nature Study, Hygiene, Scripture, Divinity, Art and Sewing. . . . Sister also had normal school students' Bible class at the Hostel. Sister Ruth divided the lower forms so that the kindergartners and form one are separated from form 2 and lower three. In addition to Sister Ruth's ordinary daily teaching time-table, she has this year a senior class in agriculture and one in home economics for matriculation.
>
> Last year, Sister Ruth coached a pupil in the evening in senior matriculations chemistry. The girl was successful in her departmental examinations as were all of sister's other pupils.

Although Ruth escaped a life of poverty when she entered the sisterhood, she could not elude more family tragedy. Less than a year

---

9. Frances Halton Eva Hasell and Iris Eugenie Friend Sayle, *Across the Prairie in a Motor Caravan: A 3,000 Mile Tour by Two Englishwomen on Behalf of Religious Education* (London: SPCK; New York: Macmillan, 1922), accessed through https://www.gutenberg.org/files/34447/34447-h/34447-h.htm #CHAPTER_VI.

after taking her vows of life profession, Sister Ruth would be drawn back to Harlem following the third death in her immediate family before the start of the 1925–1926 academic year.

On September 2, 1925, Sister Ruth's youngest brother, thirteen-year-old Arthur, held a mirror up to the nose of his mother's motionless body and found her dead. She was fifty-one years old. According to the death certificate, the elder Ruth was buried on September 6 in Cypress Hill Cemetery. The death certificate also indicated her "race" as "colored." The oldest letter found in the Community of the Holy Spirit's archives of documents retained by Ruth during her lifetime was this September 8, 1925, letter from the Rev. Carleton Morris, the chaplain to the Sisters of St. John the Divine:

My dear daughter,

In a letter received today, the Reverend Mother tells me that you have "lost" (as we wrongly put it) your mother. I don't want to invade the privacy of your sorrow, but I do want you to feel sure of my sympathy. I know how hard it is, & how doubly hard to suffer such a bereavement when we are far away—from my own experience 4 years ago. May our Blessed Lord comfort you and—move you through your grief, into a closer companionship with Him self.

I am sorry that I did not see you before you left for the west, but I trust that all spiritual blessings will follow your work. You have worked hard for your success and I think you know enough to [illegible] a learning all your life. The activity of teaching, coupled with your full obligations as a religious will be a tax upon you at first, but you know that we are never called without His support being given. God bless you in all you do for his sake.

Yours Affectionately in our Lord,
Carleton Morris, Chaplain SSJD

The loss of her sister and then mother did not appear to impact Sister Ruth's commitment to her teaching or religious vocation. The glowing work evaluations continued. Following the academic year of 1927–1928, Sister Katherine again gave a stellar report:

> Sister Ruth's pupils have done exceedingly well in her subjects. This year Sister had senior biology, which means more work. Sister Ruth continues her successful work in the Upper School. The results of the departmental examinations have been most gratifying showing steady growth, the scholastic standards being higher than last year.
>
> Sister Ruth and Novice Francesca are doing excellent work and the staff say they could not have better colleagues and works so happily with them. Miss Crowe says she cannot say enough for the thoroughness and preparedness of their work.

The ethnic background of the Qu'Appelle Diocesan School (QDS) students of the early twentieth century was White and European. In the annual school reports from the headmistress, there were no mentions of any difficulties or conflicts between Sister Ruth and the White families and staff to the SSJD superior back in Toronto. Yet, Canada was not free from racism. In contrast to Sister Ruth's experience, the Baltimore-born Sister Constance, who succeeded Sister Ruth on the QDS faculty nearly ten years later, hinted at subtle racism in her 1997 memoir, *Other Little Ships*. Sister Constance, whose skin color was darker than Sister Ruth's, recounted in her memoir an uncomfortable first encounter with a QDS parent:

> I opened the door. The father was in front, and behind him [were] two frightened little girls, ages about 8 and 10.... Though I, of course, invited them in, he appeared stunned and simply stared at me. Certainly, he was not about to enter and certainly did not allow his daughters to enter either. [He said,] "There must be some mistake, I was not expecting this." He meant me, the coloured nun in full habit.[10]

---

10. Sister Constance, SSJD, *Other Little Ships*, 68.

The story has a happy ending. The girls enrolled in the school, and the father became one of its best supporters. It is evident that Sister Ruth's light skin color—as the SSJD website noted she "looked white"—may have protected her from racist hostility in the predominantly White settings on the Canadian prairie.

Despite Sister Ruth's light skin privilege and Canada's more favorable racial climate, she never forgot the racism she was subjected to by the Episcopal Church back in New York City. After Sister Ruth spent the 1920s proving her skill as a gifted teacher, she entered the 1930s inspired to do more. The memory of the painful rejection and cognizance of the festering racism in her homeland coalesced into a grandiose idea for a new ministry. She made it clear that this was not a mere personal aspiration. As she would tell it to the Sisters of St. John the Divine on St. Joseph's Day 1935 and for years to come, she had work orders that came directly from God. And she would passionately and persistently over the following two decades appeal for the support and help from her SSJD community in carrying out those orders.

6

A MONASTIC MANIFESTO

March 19, 1935, commemorated as St. Joseph's Day in Canada, was a flashpoint on both sides of the border for the native Harlemite formerly known as Ruth Elaine Younger. Sister Ruth chose St. Joseph's Day to reveal to the Mother's Council her plan to address racism in her homeland in the hallowed quiet of St. John's convent in Toronto. In the meantime, back in Harlem, a powder keg exploded. "Police Shoot into Rioters; Kill Negro in Harlem Mob; 3,000 Storm Store After Boy Knife Thief, 16, Is Reported Lynched—Several Shot—Many Felled by Stones,"[1] the *New York Times* reported on its front page on March 20, 1935. For Sister Ruth, it was a tragic exclamation point to her proclamation that she immediately needed to shift her ministry to racial justice work from teaching and the other ministries assigned to her at SSJD.

In both the unpublished and published pages of *In Wisdom Thou Hast Made Them*, Ruth's early teaching career, even with all the documented accolades by the school leadership, received the same truncated treatment that she gave her family life. She wrote, "She had but a short time in professional teaching, because of the pressing need for work in accounting and especially with children in the slums."[2]

After leaving the prairie lands of western Canada, the "slums" of Montréal was Sister Ruth's next assignment following a brief stint

---

1. "Police Shoot into Rioters; Kill Negro in Harlem Mob," *New York Times*, March 20, 1920, retrieved from https://www.nytimes.com/1935/03/20/archives/police-shoot-into-rioters-kill-negro-in-harlem-mob-3000-storm-store.html?searchResultPosition=14.

2. The Reverend Mother Ruth, CHS, *In Wisdom Thou Hast Made Them*, 5.

helping to close the SSJD school Bishop Bethune College in the Ontario city of Oshawa. In Montréal, she worked in St. Michael's Mission House, which still, according to the website, ministers to "men and women who are experiencing food insecurity, homelessness, isolation, mental illness, addictions and poverty." In a 1948 reference letter, the Rev. Canon R. Kenneth Naylor, the rector of Trinity Memorial Church in Montréal, wrote about Sister Ruth's ministry there: "She has a gift for dealing with children and conducted very successful classes for the young toughs who live in St. Michael's Mission in Montréal. . . . She has a passion for serving the underprivileged, and the more races and colours she has in her group the happier she is. She has the most catholic mind I know."

The chair of the Religious Education Council in Québec wrote, "I looked forward to, on behalf of the leaders of children, with real anticipation to your course. My experience was that the realization far surpassed the anticipation. The committee felt the children's leaders were highly privileged, indeed, to have one so well qualified lead them in their thinking, and privileged indeed, to have one who led them to such heights spiritually."

Again and again, more praise was heaped on Ruth for her skill as a teacher, this time in the areas of faith and spirituality. Yet, if the 1986 book is reliable proof along with the anecdotes from people who knew her, Ruth took an enormous amount of pride in her management skills and business prowess. In her unpublished book draft, the one sentence that mentioned teaching greatly contrasted with the full page that Ruth devoted to her administrative duties for SSJD in Toronto. She was appointed a member of the finance committee for SSJD's new convent project and treasurer for St. John's Surgical Hospital. Both positions delved into real estate transactions and building construction, experiences that would serve Ruth well two decades later during the acquisition of real estate for the convents, schools, and retreat house in Manhattan and Upstate New York.

Another position Sister Ruth seemed to relish, which gave her a seat at the SSJD leadership table, was her appointment as secretary for the sisterhood. As secretary, Sister Ruth became a member of the Mother's Council, the leadership body of elected and appointed sisters who served as the community's board of directors and the cabinet for the Mother Superior. Her regular access to the Mother Superior, Mother Dora, laid the foundation for Sister Ruth's strategic maneuvers to pursue what she fervently believed was a racial justice mission that God called her to back in the United States. In 1935, three years after becoming secretary, she chose St. Joseph's Day, a church feast day and Canada's patronal saint day, to present her plan to the council. The moment was captured in the Mother's Council minutes:

Sister Ruth then withdrew from the Meeting, and the Mother presented to the Sisters the following letter from her:

Toronto, Canada,
St. Joseph's Day, 1935

Rev. Mother and Sisters:

A call has come to your Sister to help in our Lord's work among her people in the States.

It seemed at first necessary to found a separate Religious Order for this purpose, but as time has gone on it has become increasingly clear that this would hamper and not help GOD's work.

This appears to be an age for the founding of native Religious Communities in the mission field, the ultimate purpose of which would seem to be the carrying their own people in these different lands a work of teaching and evangelization, the natural fruit of their dedicated lives. The problem of foreign missions would to some extent be solved by these native Religious themselves.

The case is quite different, however with the various peoples who dwell on this continent, and who enjoy citizenship in the several countries which compose it. The colour bar, as such is gradually, albeit painfully, disappearing, in the difficult process of amalgamation of widely differing peoples into one nation. To create a coloured religious community now would retrace the steps of the upward march by many years.

This letter is to make a formal request that this Community of St. John the Divine consider the possibility of arranging for the formation of a daughter house, differing from our present Branch Houses in that it would be autonomous and in time have its novitiate and its dependent branches. Until this new "Congregation" has sufficient members, it is further suggested that two or more Sisters be loaned from the Mother House—to volunteer for this mission service.

I need not address to you, my Superior and Sisters, a word about the opportunity and privilege of this service. It is truly one that the world is pleased to regard as unattractive. But is it not just such service to the least of His brethren that He counts as done indeed unto Himself.

(Signed) Ruth, S. S. J. D.

The minutes continued:

The matter was discussed at some considerable length. The sisters were entirely sympathetic towards this request, and when the word "autonomous" had been altered to "affiliated," the following Resolution was passed upon a motion to that effect and duly seconded:

THAT: so soon as a suitable opportunity for work among the coloured people in the States is presented to it, this Community will establish a House for coloured Sisters, in full affiliation with the Mother House. The Novices of this House will spend a year of their novitiate at the Mother House.

While the Mother Council's motion might be construed as a positive response to Sister Ruth's proposal, in fact, it was the exact opposite of what she recommended. Sister Ruth envisioned a multiracial branch house. She wanted a rainbow-tribe sisterhood living under one roof, a vision shared and achieved two decades later by her contemporary, entertainer Josephine Baker, with her multi-ethnic adopted family living under one roof. Sister Ruth proposed a religious version of that, not the segregated house for "coloured" sisters, which she said in the letter was a step backward. Certainly, another probable point of contention for Sister Ruth was the swapping of the word "affiliated" for "autonomous." She made a subtle indication that she wanted to take charge of this branch house. Looking back on Ruth's earlier life even before her entry into the Canadian convent, one sees clues she yearned to be a leader. That aspiration was evident even in the limited scope of the *New York Age* snippets of Ruth's secular years in Harlem, such as her founding and presidency of the Samuel Coleridge-Taylor fan club and the junior officer roles she held for two other Harlem civic and cultural organizations.

Those early steps in Sister Ruth's journey to establish a new religious order in the United States, which formally commenced with that 1935 St. Joseph's Day letter, became a protracted thirteen-year campaign. Some might have given up after a few years, but Sister Ruth pursued this calling with a "By Any Means Necessary" persistence. In the remainder of the 1930s and throughout the 1940s, Sister Ruth's God-directed journey to a new community evolved into a drama-filled crusade that nearly led to her expulsion from religious life. Accusations of underhanded scheming, secretive deal-making, unauthorized travels, and lies, as some of Ruth's sisters in the community believed, were excruciatingly detailed in the volumes of files and documentation in the SSJD archives on Sister Ruth's exploits during that period.

By May 1935, two months after the delivery of the St. Joseph's Day letter, what appeared to be the first promising opportunity for a US branch house presented itself to the SSJD community in Sister Ruth's birthplace, Harlem. At a follow-up council meeting, Mother Dora read a formal invitation from the Rev. Rollin Dodd, rector of All Souls Church:

> The secretary (Sr. Ruth) had not brought the minutes of the previous meeting, nevertheless she wishes to acquaint the Council with her plans with reference to the establishing of an affiliated House of the Order for coloured women in New York. A further formal invitation had been received from the Rev. Rollin Dodd,

Rector of All Souls Church, for the Sisters to come to his parish to carry on the work there among the women and children of his congregation.

It's logical to deduce that Sister Ruth was likely aware of the "race fight" involving Dodd that took place back in Harlem close to where her biological family and secular life friends resided. Six years earlier, the "race fight," as the *New York Times* dubbed it, that Dodd had been embroiled in received blow-by-blow coverage in the paper over the three years. The social unrest unfolded after the "white vestrymen," despite being heavily outnumbered in the midst of Harlem's sweeping demographic change, attempted to ban the new Black and Caribbean immigrant congregants from attending All Souls. Dodd became a vocal opponent of the lay leader's racial discrimination in his parish. The vestrymen had turned to strong-armed tactics that included the distribution of postcards to Black worshipers that demanded that they not come to Our Souls; the door locks were changed; the main gate was padlocked, and scaffolding was erected in the sanctuary to block access to the altar. The Rev. Dodd was issued an ultimatum that if he did not "ban the Negroes" from All Souls, he would be ousted from the parish. They even resorted to withholding his salary. However, Dodd received the support of the diocesan bishop, the Right Rev. William T. Manning, and the parish was eventually desegregated.

The Mother's Council put forth a good-faith effort to pursue this request from Father Dodd. However, the tone of the meeting minutes, as recorded by Ruth herself as secretary, betrayed a tone of pessimism and the foregone conclusion the idea was already dead in the water:

> it was clearly seen that the decision which the Council had made at its last meeting for the establishment of a definite coloured house for mission work among the coloured people of Harlem, and wherever else the Sisters might in the future be called to minister to coloured people in the States, could scarcely be fulfilled with the limitations which work in one parish such as All Souls would impose, nevertheless the Mother and the Chaplain and Sister Ruth would meet Fr. Dodd in New York and discuss

the matter with him. The Sisters seem to be of the opinion that no decision could possibly be reached until the interview with Father Dodd had been held.

The foreboding tone of the May minutes came to fruition. Not only was Dodd's request flatly declined after the visit to New York, but the Mother's Council also rescinded the original St. Joseph's Day motion to establish an "affiliated coloured house."

After the women's return from New York, Sister Ruth recorded the following in the June 10, 1935, Mother's Council minutes:

> The work, however, would be narrowly parochial and would make the fulfillment of the real purpose of establishing the Religious Life in Harlem a very remote possibility. Mother told her Council that all those with whom the matter had been discussed—both white and coloured Priests and lay people—were of one mind—that for the community to accept Fr. Dodd's offer would frustrate the ultimate purpose of its advent in Harlem.

After the council rescinded the St. Joseph Day motion, a consolation prize of a return trip to New York was offered to Sister Ruth, who would be accompanied by Mother Dora, to deliver a lecture on religious life at the annual meeting for the Conference of Church Workers among Colored People (CCWAP), an organization for Black Episcopalians, mostly clergy. The Conference was created shortly after the Civil War with a mission to eradicate segregation within the Episcopal Church, which institutionally relegated African Americans membership in the church to "Colored Missions" and attempted to bar African American men, especially in the South, from the priesthood.

For much of the remainder of the 1930s, Ruth carried out business responsibilities for the community as treasurer. SSJD's convent was filled to capacity and was also no longer structurally adequate to house the sisters. Similarly, SSJD's hospital building, St. John's, adjacent to the convent had also been deemed insufficient. Founded in 1885, St. John's Hospital was the order's first and primary ministry in Toronto. The sisterhood was widely regarded for its work in women's health care, particularly rehabilitative and convalescent care and nurse training. "I, as Treasurer, formed a small part of the total Committee to try to fund and build a new Hospital and Convent," Ruth wrote in an unpublished draft of *In Wisdom Thou Hast Made Them*.

During my time with the Alongsiders with the Community of St. John Baptist, I had a front-row pew where I watched firsthand how frustratingly slowly some religious communities operated. Much like any organization in the secular world, religious communities were rife with power struggles, organizational dysfunction, and an inability to make important business decisions. So I wasn't all that surprised to read that Sister Ruth was not involved in the completion of either project. After serving as treasurer and secretary, Sister Ruth was reassigned to work as the librarian for the Church Literature Department until 1941.

While the new ministry proposed on St. Joseph's Day 1935 may have been dashed in the official records of the SSJD, for Sister Ruth the issue was not dead and would never be dead. She persisted with her campaign well into the 1940s. Annually, Sister Ruth delivered a letter to the Mother's Council which had all the traits of a manifesto with its declarative tone and its adamancy that God was calling not only her but also SSJD to take up this new ministry:

My dear Mother and Sisters,

Even though you have already considered one important aspect of a subject I have to bring to you, I am nevertheless constrained to lay before you a little more of the matter, as it affects you and me:

Because we are all students of the Holy Scriptures and have followed God's leading of mankind, therein, both under the Old Covenant and in the New, I dare again to address you. I want you to know that always since my childhood, I have been conscious of a special and impelling sense of God's pressure upon me, for something He wanted, and yet wants to do through me. That has been a very steadying and constraining influence all my life. Sometimes, when I have tried to free myself from It, I have known insistence, even intense discipline and often acute suffering and punishment. I tell you all this because it is about God and concerns me only as His creature.

I came to our Convent 30 years ago with this same sense of real mission upon me. I was 20 years of age, not too clear about its full meaning but the years have brought clarity, and now I know unmistakably that God wishes to use me for a special work for His Kingdom in the evolution of the ideal of human brotherhood, and of the essential sameness of humanity, regardless of birth, skin colour or other superficial differences.

When I was sent to St. John's against my own will, but by my Spiritual Director, and returned to test my Vocation, I knew and have known since that St. John's which received me had also a part to play in this plan of God.

Once it seemed that the fulfillment of the plan was in sight, but the Sisters had not then, caught the vision and so there was delay.

Now again, I am pressed by God to fulfill the mission to which He has called me, in my own Country and, as the beginning in the Church in the United States of something it has not known: the possibility of a Religious Family composed of members of the many races that make up its population living as witness, and helping even those who are convinced to the contrary, to see that with God it is possible for consecrated women of many backgrounds to really become one in life and work, is very truth.

I believe God has now, in the fullness of time, raised up the Bishop and Priests who also have this vision. Never before has this been the case. The few non-caucasian vocations in one or two Communities are "permitted" to be in them. This new Community would exist because of them.

But this Community for which God has been preparing cannot come into existence without you. My dear Mother and Sisters, it needs your spiritual blessing, your interest and your full co-operation to bring into being and to maintain it in life for its first few years. I will not and cannot fulfill my vocation apart from you to whom I belong.

I know so well the great difficulties that stand in the way of your playing your part in the final act in this drama, to which we are called. But with God, who has called us, I verily believe all things to be possible. You cannot spare two or three Sisters, nor lend your interest and prayers for three years? Even if God required it at your hand, as I am confident He does? Will He not accept your faith and mine, and immediately make up to you in ways you cannot foresee, for your abandonment to His and your utter trust in Him? Will he not bless you doubly and send you other vocations to replace these He wishes from you?

I do not and cannot ask you to undertake new work in the Community's name when you have decided irrevocably against it. I can ask you, can I not, to complete a work of 30 years standing, which is really a quite different matter.

I believe in your desire to seek the Will of God alone, my Sisters. It is amazing that He uses the most unlikely instruments to reveal His Will, sometimes, isn't it? I have never, in my natural desires wished to have anything to do with this work. I fear it and, the demands it makes upon me. Yet I have always known the pressure of God's Hand upon me, requiring it of me. If any of this came from me, I would distrust it utterly. I believe it to come from God's Good Spirit and I feel the necessity for obedience to it.

I cannot think that you will fail to help me. If you do, it will probably be impossible for me to fulfill the work God has asked me to do. I know you will not fail Him.

Your Loving Sister,
Ruth, SSJD

This letter was the beginning of Sister Ruth wreaking havoc on the SSJD order. The annual letter-writing campaign continued throughout Ruth's time in Canada.

7

REPATRIATION I—DETROIT

Much like the rest of White America, the Episcopal Church attempted to preserve a segregated society at the end of the Civil War and through the twentieth century. The Episcopal Church, especially in the north, cast itself as practicing a more charitable and genteel form of segregation that was more James Crow than Jim Crow. Separate galley boxes in White churches and the founding of "Free African" churches and "Colored Episcopal Missions," such as Harlem's St. Philip and the Upper West Side's St. Jude's Chapel, gave the appearance that Episcopalians were benevolent to the Black community.

Colored Episcopal Missions, formed for African American communicants and clergy, did not have full status in the Episcopal Church and were formally known during that time as Colored Episcopal Missions. Almost all of these missions held second-class positions within both the national church and their local dioceses. Despite petitioning, up until 1853, Harlem's St. Philip's Church (founded in 1819) and its African American priests were barred from fully participating in diocesan conventions. During the early 1900s and into the mid-twentieth century, Colored Mission churches and their African American priests (if they had one) were not given full convention voting rights. The Conference of Church Workers Among Colored People spent much of its existence lobbying to gain equal and full status for Black parishes, priests, and their parishioners.

After the initial St. Joseph's Day manifesto, Sister Ruth went on about her regular SSJD assignments for the next ten years. Albeit she did it on her own terms and made up her own rules. From 1936 until 1941, she was in charge of the Church Literature Department.

In her last year in that role, she wrote in her one and only report to the community, "It is some time since you have a Report of this Literature Department, indeed you have never had one from me, though I have handled this work for six years. I have thought an occasional Report better, perhaps, than a too frequent one since the selling of books is after all a subject which one need not say too much too often."

Other positions she held were on church committees for religious education, including the General Board of Religious Education for the Church of England in Canada. She led training programs for church schoolteachers and religious educators and lectured at diocesan events in Montréal and Toronto. While carrying out all these assignments, Sister Ruth's ambitions to create a multiracial religious community work for church desegregation and racial justice in the United States never faltered. Mother Dora's reign as the head of SSJD ended in 1945, and Mother Aquila became Ruth's new superior. By all accounts, Sister Ruth and Mother Aquila's relationship seemed fine in the beginning. But their relationship, too, would eventually sour.

By 1946, another request came from the United States to the Canadian sisters. This time it was from Detroit, and this request came from the Rev. Malcolm G. Dade, the Black rector of St. Cyprian's Protestant Episcopal Church.

St. Cyprian's began as a "Colored Episcopal Mission" in 1919, established to serve the influx of African Americans who migrated from the Southern states in search of work in the burgeoning auto industry. Although St. Matthew's (another historic and renowned Episcopal parish founded in 1846) served Detroit's Black community on the east side, there were only segregated White parishes on Detroit's west side, all of which refused to admit the new arrivals from the Southern states. The Rev. Dade had become St. Cyprian's rector in 1938 and shepherded it through an era of growth and prosperity. Under his leadership, St. Cyprian's successfully convinced the diocese's building committee that its small, incomplete twenty-year-old structure was inadequate for the growing congregation.

When the Rev. Dade reached out to the Sisters of St. John the Divine for help with the parish youth ministry, the request was for two sisters, according to Ruth's first report: "The Mother asked me to go to Detroit alone to discover what possibilities the work offered, and to report to the Chapter. . . . The Rev. M. G. Dade was, I think, a stranger to us all," Sister Ruth wrote about him. "[Our] work was to be leadership and direction of the parish activities for youth."

In her August 1946 description of the church, Sister Ruth wrote, "St. Cyprian's Parish is a small one, of about four hundred communicants. . . . It attained parish status less than three years ago, after having been a mission for nearly twenty-five years. The Church building and grounds are quite attractive exteriorly, but the facilities of the parish house are somewhat inadequate. The parish is rather nondescript as to churchmanship, being that strange medly [*sic*] of Protestantism in its belief and Catholicism in some of its ceremonial."

Reminiscent of the young Ruth's secular era's media coverage in the *New York Age*, Ruth's arrival at the Detroit parish was heralded by the Black press, but this time in headlines: "Sister Ruth Comes to Church Staff," reported the January 12, 1946, article in *Michigan Chronicle*. Also unlike the New York newspaper articles, Sister Ruth was directly quoted: "In beginning this work, there is hope of establishing a nursery school and possibly a primary school in which the spiritual training of the children will be given due consideration." There was detailed information about Ruth's life and teaching ministries in Canada; however, there was no mention in the article that the sister was an American, let alone a native of the nation's most renowned and thriving African American community, Harlem.

Given the title of youth director at St. Cyprian's, Sister Ruth was put in charge of Church School, acolyte training, confirmation, youth groups, nursery, and kindergarten classes. In all of Ruth's writing about St. Cyprian's—in reports while assigned there and decades later in the unpublished draft and her final book—she conveyed little enthusiasm for her work in Detroit. In the unpublished draft, she omitted her two years of work in Detroit, and in other writing she is critical and even negative about her ministry at St. Cyprian's. In her 1946 report, she wrote, "The Church School . . . presents very many problems. There are few satisfactory teachers, and these need further training, not only in methods, but also in the faith itself." Of the acolytes she said, "[they] have had a rather checkered course of training in the past."

While not mentioned in the 1946 report back to her community, in Mother Ruth's 1986 *In Wisdom Thou Hast Made Them* she complained about her housing situation that forced out another family from a parish-owned home and wrote about the mission:

> She made the effort to do any really helpful and useful and constructive mission work. Nevertheless, it was all most difficult. Fortunately, the children were friendly, responsive and loving, and could be taught. Certainly they were poor and needed as much help as possible with their education. However, the Sister was uncertain about this total situation.[1]

Sister Ruth may not have been enthused by her work in the parish, yet her activities received more coverage in the Black press. Similarly to the *New York Age* articles, the *Michigan Chronicle*'s "Party Line" column captured the social activities of the Detroit community. Sister Ruth's participation in the St. Cyprian's flower guild's annual spring luncheon made the news later that year: "Sister Ruth, SSJD spoke on the relation of the flowers to the seasons of the Church Year." Other articles included the Valentine's Day dinner for acolytes and Christmas activities.

In one sense, the 1984 assessment Mother Ruth wrote about her time at St. Cyprian might have been a bit of revisionist history. The Detroit assignment was a pivotal moment that paved the way for the founding of CHS. Initially, what the repatriation back to the States ignited in Sister Ruth was a boots-on-the-ground mission to establish an SSJD branch house that would fulfill her God-directed calling to build a multiracial religious community in the United States. On the final page of her 1946 report, Sister Ruth wrote, "This little parochial work is but the door opening into a larger room, which it may be that GOD is inviting us to enter." She wrote in the final paragraph of the report:

---

1. The Reverend Mother Ruth, CHS, *In Wisdom Thou Hast Made Them*, 6.

as the only Religious of our Communion ever resident in the Diocese of Michigan—it has been possible to witness for and to teach vocation to the Religious Life among other things, up and down the Diocese, both formally and informally. It has also been possible to act as liaison when required, between white and brown-skinned Americans, who in the City of Detroit, as well as in many other places, but more especially in Detroit, are still living in rather acute tension and seething unrest. These conditions are but surface indications of the deeper troubles— mutual distrust and fear and the rest. Some of these people look to the Church, often perhaps unconsciously, for example, for leadership, and for vision in solving these their social, racial and economic ills and problems, as well as for its spiritual ministry. Here at the moment, and for a long day ahead, is the real raison d'être for Religious in their midst.

Respectfully submitted,
Ruth, S. S. J. D.

Evident in that closing paragraph of Sister Ruth's 1946 Detroit ministry report was that she never lost sight of God calling her to a racial reconciliation ministry. Sister Ruth recognized her light-skin privilege and used it—likely aided by being cloaked in a nun's habit—to "act as a liaison when required" between "white and brown-skinned Americans." Perhaps her most eloquent observation was of the people she ministered to at a time of racial unrest, economic hardship, and social turmoil. All things Ruth experienced in her own life. She could see the expectations and hopes they placed in the church to solve those problems. It was in that reflection she was at her best. In 1946, she echoed the calls of an Ancestor, Sojourner Truth. One might consider Ruth a forerunner to such luminaries as the yet unknown Morehouse College student named Martin Luther King Jr., among many others, all of whom regarded social justice activism as a primary responsibility of the Christian church.

Sister Ruth's report likely had an impact on her sisters in Toronto, reviving her hope that a new community might be established in Detroit.

The Mother's Council's response to Ruth's report combined with feedback from Father Dade and a letter to him from the bishop of the diocese were positive, according to the August 15, 1946, meeting minutes.

> The Mother read two letters from Father Dade dated March 7th and July 25th, appreciating the inspiration of Sister's teaching, saying that St. Cyprian House was being renovated for her residence, and hoping for another Sister to accompany her in the Fall. . . . Mother read a letter from Miss Helen L. Flynn, Chief Psychologist of the Psychopathic Clinic of the Recorders Court, testifying to the value of Sister Ruth's work among "youth" and mentioning the acute state of tension which exists in Detroit among labour groups and negroes.

The minutes continued: "Sister Maribel asked whether it was the desire to have a Branch of our Community for white and coloured people. The Mother answered in the affirmative but said that when Sister Ruth returns to Detroit in the Fall, she will be alone."

While it was not everything Sister Ruth had hoped for—she had wanted other sisters to join her in Detroit—the encouraging words from the Mother's Council was the tacit approval Sister Ruth needed to pursue in earnest what she believed she had been called back to the United States to do.

Sister Ruth's repatriation launched a new era in her religious life. In the Motor City, Sister Ruth began going rogue. She took full advantage of not being under the constant supervision of the Mother Superior. Because she also worked in other parishes conducting retreats and other activities outside of St. Cyprian's, she was able to make connections beyond the African American Episcopal community where she served. One of the most instrumental relationships in Sister Ruth's quest to establish an SSJD branch house in Detroit was with SSJD's associates. Men and women, both lay and clergy, who apply to become a religious order's associates are essentially an auxiliary booster group to the community and live by a Rule of Life developed by the order. Sister Ruth solicited a number of SSJD associates' assistance in campaigning for a branch house.

In the meantime, the Mother Superior had given Sister Ruth permission to open up conversations with other clergy in the United States, specifically the acclaimed Father Samuel J. Martin, the rector of another African American parish, St. Edmund Episcopal Church in Chicago. St. Edmund was founded as a "Colored Episcopal Mission" in 1905, and the Episcopal Diocese of Chicago approved St. Edmund's application to become a parish in 1940. By 1946, when Sister Ruth traveled to Chicago to meet Father Martin, "the church boasted the second largest Episcopal congregation in Chicago, with twelve hundred members,"[2] according to a biographical sketch of Martin by the Schomburg Center for Research in Black Culture at the New York Public Library, which holds the Samuel J. Martin Papers.

"In her last letter, [Sister Ruth] stated that she had come to the conclusion that the work in Detroit is not as worth-while as that in Chicago where Father Martin wishes to establish a nursery school for white and coloured." The Chicago parish was known to attract Chicago's Black social and economic upper class; and at three times the size of St. Cyprian, St. Edmund was likely a much more attractive demographic to Sister Ruth. As a larger congregation, the expectation and needs would be that much greater. "Father Martin asked for four sisters to work in his parish," according to the November 1946 Mother's Council meeting minutes. Follow-up letters from the Bishop of Chicago and the diocese's director of religious education indicated they would welcome having St. John sisters in Chicago.

Evidently, Sister Ruth was so excited by the prospect of the move that she asked the Mother's Council to hold a Special Chapter meeting to decide on the matter quickly "so that she may close out her work in Detroit." However, the urgent demands had the opposite effect on the Mother's Council than what Sister Ruth had intended. The council evaluated the community's overall personnel needs and the staffing shortages in its schools in Canada. If Sister Ruth was so quick to leave Detroit, wouldn't it make more sense to have her return

---

2. Samuel Joseph Martin papers, Schomburg Center for Research in Black Culture, the New York Public Library, Schomburg Center for Research in Black Culture, Manuscripts, Archives and Rare Books Division, https://archives.nypl.org/scm/20592.

to Canada to work in the school? The council not only unanimously passed a motion to that effect, but the sisters also (for the second time in ten years) rescinded an earlier motion to explore opportunities to establish a branch house in the United States. Sister Ruth was now a two-time loser. Mother Aquila wrote to Father Martin to decline his request for St. John sisters to work at his parish. After Father Martin told Sister Ruth of the letter, she wrote to Mother Aquila "saying that she felt much disturbed and felt there was some bad faith somewhere." She followed up that letter a week later "in which she spoke of understanding the difficulty of conveying to the Community in general the vision before her mind and the minds of some others with regard to the great opportunities connected with work among coloured people. She said she herself did not feel clear as to whether Chicago or Detroit should be the center of where work could be established, but begged that the Mother visit Detroit as soon as possible."

Mother Aquila's visit to Detroit was hastened after the discovery of plans of the suburban Detroit's White associates to open a retreat house that would be connected to Christ Church in Grosse Pointe "in the care of the Sisterhood of St. John the Divine." According to the minutes, this move came as a surprise to Sister Ruth and Sister Christabel, the ward of associates. "Needless to say such plans have received no sanction from the Mother or Sisterhood," according to the minutes. After this unexpected proposal, Mother Aquila and the council members began to suspect Sister Ruth of engaging associates to wield their influence and gain their help in engineering unauthorized plans on behalf of the community. As for the retreat house in Grosse Pointe, "the council felt that the proceedings should be stopped as soon as possible." A motion that reiterated an earlier one unanimously passed: "That the Mother and the Council consider the opening of a Branch House in Detroit and elsewhere impossible at the present time and that the matter of a recall of Sister Ruth at the end of the year should be considered."

By January 1947, Mother Aquila had reached out to the Episcopal Diocese of Michigan Bishop Frank W. Creighton to ascertain his interest in an SSJD branch house. She reported back to the council: "He was quite definite that he could not have a Canadian community in his protestant diocese." In turn, she conveyed to Bishop Creighton that the community was unable to support a branch house or new ministry in Michigan. The Mother Superior subsequently sent a letter to Sister Ruth demanding that she terminate any activity or dialogue related to the branch house and ordered her to let the associates know that this was the final decision of the community. According to the council meeting minutes, Sister Ruth pledged to Mother Aquila that she would "do her utmost to make the Associates understand the community's position." The council also decided to send notice to Father Dade at St. Cyprian's that Sister Ruth would likely be recalled to Canada in the spring. Mother Aquila received a letter from Father Martin in Chicago after he made a counterproposal of having just Sister Ruth work in his parish alone. Instead of responding back to Father Martin, Mother Aquila wrote to the Bishop of Chicago Wallace E. Cockling. He replied, "expressing his pleasure of having Sister Ruth to work in the parish with the view of investigating permanent work." Shortly after that exchange, another letter was sent by Father Martin which indicated that the St. Edmund's vestry would consider providing an allowance for Sister Ruth's living expenses in Chicago. With letters from both religious figures responding positively, and with Ruth's living expenses covered, Mother Aquila perhaps saw herself with little choice other than to approve Ruth's travel.

All of these scenarios, especially the withdrawal of Sister Ruth from Detroit only to send her on to Chicago, were met with profound disapproval by the other members of the Mother's Council. Simultaneously, Detroit's Father Dade telephoned Mother Aquila to inform her that he and the vestry were highly upset by the impending departure of Sister Ruth from their parish. The church's warden, Major Morton, intended to travel to Toronto to meet with Mother Aquila personally to make an appeal. Separately, Major Morton sent a telegram to Mother Aquila that said the Bishop of Michigan agreed that St. Cyprian should have two sisters working there.

In a move that could be construed as both defiant and fanning the flames of the mayhem that now ensued, Sister Ruth doubled down on her insistence that SSJD should establish a branch house and send more sisters. According to the February 3, 1947, minutes, she put forth arguments in favour of having two Sisters to work in the U. S. A., and arguments against the Council's decision not to establish a Branch House in the U. S. A. She stated her health would not permit her to continue to work alone, but she was content to go to Chicago as a pioneer, if assurance is given that within a few years, at least, other Sisters will be sent to establish a Branch House. She regrets that the Community is unable to see her vision and to respond to God's call to undertake inter-racial work.

The council had enough. "It was felt by the members of the council if Sister Ruth was allowed to continue her work in the United States, either in Detroit or Chicago, she would bind the community to the establishment of a Branch House by the conditions stated in her letter." The council voted to recall Sister Ruth back to Canada by Easter. Just a week later, Mother Aquila revised her plans. Instead of having Sister Ruth return by Easter, she decided to send the ward of associates, Sister Christabel, to Detroit to work with Sister Ruth on a temporary basis so she could assess the situation. In essence, Mother Aquila decided she needed someone to spy on Sister Ruth. By early March, Mother Aquila notified Sister Ruth that Sister Christabel would arrive shortly and that she herself intended to visit Detroit within a couple of weeks.

When the Mother Superior visited Detroit, she met with Bishop Creighton, who repeated his opposition to a branch house in Detroit but supported the SSJD's work in a parish in his diocese. He also indicated he was unaware of the associates' proposed "Diocese Retreat House." Mother Aquila held meetings with the Detroit associates and explained that the community did not have the resources, both human and financial, to open a retreat house, let alone a branch house. According to the council meeting minutes, Sister Ruth stated in front of Mother Aquila and the associates that she was "in accord" with her superior and her community.

After the Mother Superior returned to Toronto, Sister Christabel remained for three months with Sister Ruth at St. Cyprian's. When questioned by the Mother Superior about how to solve a problem like Mother Ruth, Sister Christabel recommended that "Sister Ruth should be withdrawn from Detroit as soon as possible." She was allowed to complete church summer programs with the youth but by August 1947, she was back in Canada.

Despite the abrupt end to her US ministry, Sister Ruth just couldn't let it go. Her last report on Detroit had both a tone of "what could have been" and even an expectation that a branch house might still be possible. She waxed wistfully, "St. Cyprian's House and its use as a Religious House, which had been suitably appointed and blessed, for even though the work had not the status of a duly constituted Branch House, yet it was a centre—the only centre, indeed, in the Diocese—where Religious were in residence and from which their work was carried on."

Sister Ruth went on in the five-page document to describe in detail how all the necessary elements of a branch house had been donated—complete furnishings for a chapel and oratory where Divine prayers and Holy Eucharist could take place, including an altar cross, linens, a silver chalice and paten. "All of these, and many other gifts are still being retained in safe custody in Detroit until the Priests . . . and others,—who are working on the matter, are able to secure two or three Sisters from some other Community to carry on the work upon the Foundation we have laid. They are unwilling now that they have had Religious Life lived in their midst for the first time, to allow it to lapse. May GOD grant their desire in His good time."

By the autumn of 1947, Mother Aquila sent Sister Ruth back to the very place she began her religious vocation as a teacher, the remote, western prairies of Regina, Qu'Appelle. Despite a distance of two thousand miles, a national border, and the Great Lake of Michigan that separated Sister Ruth from Detroit, heading up an SSJD branch in the city was still in reach as far as she was concerned. From afar, Sister Ruth kept pumping and resuscitated an idea that, from her Mother Superior and sisters' perspective, was dead. She continued to stir the pot while en route to Qu'Appelle. Sister Ruth wrote to the Mother Superior "that her confidence in the Mother had been shaken, as she affirmed that the Mother had not been straightforward or honest and [she] could not understand the condemnation of her life and work in Detroit." She also indicated she felt the Mother Superior had lodged personal criticism in front of all the sisters during a community meeting. In response, Mother Aquila escalated the situation by sharing the letters with the priest who was SSJD's warden. His advice was to ignore the letters. However, Mother Aquila wrote to Sister Ruth and demanded an apology. Sister Ruth complied and sent a letter of apology.

When Sister Ruth arrived in Regina, the Qu'Appelle Diocesan School was under the leadership of Sister Constance, the African American woman from a prominent, upper-class Baltimore family. She had come to SSJD two decades after Ruth. The very woman who endeavored to work toward racial harmony developed an adversarial and acrimonious relationship with the very woman who was not just her SSJD sister compatriot, but also a fellow Black woman.

Mother Aquila had told her council: "Sister Constance wrote frequently, reporting increasing difficulties between Sister Ruth and Sister Evangeline." Without "the permission from the Mother Superior or Sister Constance, the Sister-in-Charge," Sister Ruth ejected Sister Evangeline from the Sunday School By Post (SSBP) office. At one point, Mother Aquila considered calling Sister Ruth back to Toronto. However, the school was short-staffed and relied on a lay SSJD associate as a volunteer to run the school programs. Sister Constance begged Mother Aquila not to issue an ultimatum or remove Sister Ruth, because it could "make a bad situation worse."

However, entering the new year, the problems continued to mount. Sister Constance reported that Sister Ruth complained of receiving letters from Toronto enclosed in envelopes addressed to Sister Constance. She kept the SSBP office door closed and barred Constance, although she was the sister-in-charge, from entering. She asked to have a desk moved into her cell and at one point asked permission from the Mother Superior to pray the morning Divine Office prayers alone instead of with her sisters in the Qu'Appelle Branch House. Sister Constance also relayed to Mother Aquila that Sister Ruth "writes innumerable letters to professors, priests, bishops and others in widely scattered places in [the] U. S. A. and Canada."

By May 1948, matters had gotten worse and the reverberations were being felt as far away as Detroit. "In this letter," Mother Aquila reported from Sister Constance, "she speaks of the grave and increasing difficulties caused by Sister Ruth's attitude, which is affecting the Sisters, the staff and Mrs. Matthews [an Associate]."

While the powder keg that was the Qu'Appelle Diocesan School was about to explode, Mother Aquila had also encountered an associate from Michigan who told her that Sister Ruth had sent "disturbing letters." Mother Aquila told the council that Christina Robinson told her that Sister Ruth had written "confidential letters" that stated she intended to establish a new community in the United States and asked for her assistance. A year earlier, Robinson had visited the SSJD convent in Toronto to discuss her calling to religious life. Mother Aquila told her that her health issues made her an unsuitable candidate for the rigors of religious life. She encouraged Robinson to follow a simple "Rule of Life" and permitted her to work with Sister Ruth in a summer youth program at St. Cyprian's.

"Miss Robinson was very distressed by the letter, not knowing how Sister Ruth intended to leave the community," Mother Aquila told the members of the Mother's Council at the May 1948 meeting. "Miss Robinson remarked to the Mother that there appeared to be signs of mental unbalance in Sister Ruth's letter, which condition she had observed in Detroit." At the meeting, council member Sister Lois added, "Sister Ruth is writing constantly to Associates in Detroit and causing grave difficulties in the ward." The Mother concluded it was time to call Sister Ruth back to Toronto and perhaps send her home to New York for some counseling from the priest who had recommended her to the community back in 1918. The Mother had discussed the problem of Sister Ruth with Fr. Edward Schlueter, who referred Sister Ruth to the community as an aspirant. "He stressed the fact that the problem was not entirely due to colour but that Sister was mentally sick and should see a psychiatrist," it was reported in the minutes. "The Mother suggested that it might be possible to ask Fr. Schlueter to counsel Sister in this way. This suggestion was approved by the members."

During the same meeting, another council member, Sister Francesca, who appeared sympathetic to Sister Ruth, referred to a letter she had received from her: "she feels a pressure that she must fulfill her vocation," she said, then asked, "Is it possible that she may have a vocation to found a coloured community, and that the frustration of this vocation may have brought about this present situation?" And for the first time, the idea is brought up at the same council meeting, that perhaps it would be best "to release Sister Ruth from her vows." Or in other words, expel her from the community.

8

A VEILED THREAT—EXPELLING SISTER RUTH

To release Sister Ruth from her vows sounded as much like a consolation as it was punitive. Sister Francesca shared a draft of a letter with Mother Aquila that "urged" Sister Ruth to "apply for release from her vows" to "fulfill your vocation" and to "go forward in His Strength." First, Mother Aquila decided she would confront Sister Ruth, who was headed back to Toronto before traveling to New York for her "rest time," as vacation was sometimes referred to by religious communities. Mother Aquila told the council that she planned to address all of the issues and allegations that had been lodged against Sister Ruth. Even before the meeting took place, a new accusation had been leveled against Sister Ruth of stealing money. "Sister Ruth had obtained two cheques from the Diocesan Treasurer, amounting in all to $100.00, made out in Sister Constance's name, and had taken the cheques to the Bishop's Emissary for signature; on the following Sunday when Sister Constance was in retreat, Sister Ruth handed these cheques to Sister Dorcas and persuaded her to lend her $25.00 from a Trust Fund belonging to a pupil, which money she took with her when she left the following morning for Toronto."

The sisters in Qu'Appelle had on earlier occasions written to the community's warden, Father Hawkes, complaining that Sister Ruth had a number of "personal possessions." Although none of the "personal possessions" were identified in any of the SSJD records, the sisters accused her of violating her vow of poverty. SSJD's warden encouraged Mother Aquila to take action against Sister Ruth. "[He] was of the opinion that much patience and charity had been shown to Sister Ruth over a long period."

When Sister Ruth arrived in Toronto, "the Mother gave her several interviews, each being friendly and frank talks, with the exception of the last interview." In the last discussion, Mother Aquila revealed to Sister Ruth that Christina Robinson had disclosed her "confidential letters" about establishing a new community, as well as another serious infraction of sending similar letters to the novice at another community. "Sister Ruth was much taken aback," the council meeting minutes reported on her reaction. Her response to Mother Aquila was that she intended to tell her everything once all her plans had been solidified. When questioned about what her plans were, Sister Ruth admitted that she had been in dialogue with the Bishop of Michigan and others about forming a new community in Detroit. Mother Aquila then told Sister Ruth that she should apply for a release from her vows. Sister Ruth said, "No, she intended to ask for a transference" to a newly formed community.

It was at this point that Mother Aquila made her veiled threat when she raised other serious charges. In addition to Sister Ruth's disobedience, Mother Aquila told her she had violated her vow of poverty and questioned her about some private possessions that she brought back with her from Detroit last year. According to the meeting minutes, Sister Ruth grew defensive and hurled countercharges regarding the decisions made by the Mother Superior, such as having her work alone in Detroit; that her only meals there were stale bread; and that she had to take possession of the items from Detroit because they were all intended for use in the convent once a new community was established. The following day after that confrontation, Mother Aquila told the council that Sister Ruth was overly obsequious, smiling and offering exaggerated curtsies as if nothing had happened.

Before Sister Ruth left for New York, Mother Aquila gave her permission to meet with the Bishop of Michigan to continue her conversations about a new community, with the caveat that when she returned to Canada, she should apply for her release from SSJD. Mother Aquila preemptively wrote to the Bishop of Michigan and the Mother Superior of the Society of St. Margaret, warning them that any dialogue they might have with Sister Ruth about a new interracial community in the United States was an independent venture undertaken by Sister Ruth alone and that SSJD would not have any role in it. The Mother's Council also decided that when Sister Ruth returned from New York, she would not be allowed to return to Qu'Appelle. And after obtaining permission of SSJD's warden, a "Special Chapter" meeting of the entire community would be called to decide on the fate of Sister Ruth.

Sister Ruth had an entire month of "rest time." She made the most of it. It was likely during this period that she saw her youngest brother, Arthur, and met her nephew Peter, who, during a 2022 interview, recalled meeting his aunt Ruth when she came for an overnight visit in the late 1940s. What was impressive about Sister Ruth's rest time was the sheer number of connections she made with people not only across the United States and Canada, but even across the pond in the United Kingdom. And many of the people she met were prominent Episcopalians and Anglicans.

One such person, who was a trailblazer in his own right, was the Rev. John Burgess, who became the bishop of the Episcopal diocese in Massachusetts and the church's first African American diocesan bishop in the United States. In 1938, he served as the vicar and resident priest of St. Simon of Cyrene, the Colored Episcopal Mission, started by the sisters of the Community of the Transfiguration. The mission was located in the African American community today known as Lincoln Heights, a suburban village of Cincinnati, Ohio. The Transfiguration sisters opened the mission during the Great Depression to assist the impoverished Black families who lived in Lincoln Heights, which bordered the more affluent, all-White suburb of Glendale where Transfiguration's convent was located. By 1948, when Sister Ruth paid him a visit, he was the Episcopal chaplain at Howard University, the historically Black university in Washington, DC. After her meeting with Father Burgess, at his suggestion, she visited Glendale, Ohio, to meet with the Transfiguration superior, Mother Olivia. He wrote to her in July 1948:

I appreciate you taking the trouble to visit with me and talking over your plans and I hope that I can continue to be of some service to you as these plans develop under God's guidance. I am particularly happy that you were able to go to Glendale and see Mother Olivia.

I have been trying to give a good deal of thought to your plans lately. I am still convinced that you have hit upon an emphasis that must be made within the Religious Life of the Church. Two questions arise, however, . . . one—the addition of another small community to the rather large list already organized within Anglicanism. . . . we find so many of them struggling desperately to maintain themselves, to keep a Novitiate and to secure their future.

A second question also arises. You spoke of your plans for a "strict" body. I wonder if such an idea really meets the spiritual needs of women today? . . . it does seem to me that these forms (of traditional Religious Life) ought to be analyzed thoroughly in terms of modern thought.

He suggested to her that she seek a community to sponsor her idea for a multiracial sisterhood that would eventually bring racial integration to an existing community in the process. However, he encouraged her to continue with her mission and said she should feel assured of his interest and prayers.

She also saw the Rev. Edward Schlueter, from whom Mother Aquila suggested she seek counseling. According to a letter to Sister Ruth, retrieved from her archives in New York City, he said the matter of an interracial branch house had been settled by her community. He discouraged her from her continued quest and even admonished her to practice humility.

During her rest time, Sister Ruth also made her way back to Detroit. She met with the new bishop of the Diocese of Michigan, the Right Rev. Richard Emrich. In a move that might be characterized as brazen, irrational, and hardheaded, while in Detroit Sister Ruth wrote to Mother Aquila about the meeting with the new bishop and stated he wanted the SSJD sisters to come to his diocese. The requests were enumerated in a list:

I.   The Bishop and Executive Council desire to have Sisters in the diocese in eighteen months and they have a house in view.

II.   They desire to have the Sisters settled in the diocese under the sponsorship of SSJD at least for the first two or three years.

III. After that time it might be necessary to be affiliated with an American order.

IV.   The Bishop said it would be necessary for him to write to the Mother, but Sister Ruth assured him that she had permission to discuss the matter fully with him, and she explained the situation regarding the attitude of the Community toward the interracial problem and the establishment of a Community in the United States.

V.   The Bishop agreed that it would be well for Sister Ruth to go to England, which she hopes to do with the Mother's permission. The Bishop is establishing a fund for the purpose.

Sister Ruth followed up that letter with another one in which she reported that she had consulted with Father Schlueter and that he "strongly advises her to spend the greater part of the next eighteen months in England."

Mother Aquila then received a letter from Bishop Emrich in defense of Sister Ruth's actions. He stated that he did not believe she "acted in any way out of order, that any blame in the matter attach[ed] to him," although it appeared he had his own reservations about Sister Ruth. He questioned Mother Aquila about Sister Ruth's mental state and personality. According to the council meeting minutes, "he asked the Mother to give him her candid opinion as to whether Sister Ruth is in personality and temperament qualified to form a Community, as he does not want any difficulty introduced into the diocese."

It was evident by the concluding motion for that June 25 Mother's Council meeting that they wanted Sister Ruth expelled from SSJD. "The Council wished to place on record that Sister Ruth had not been authorized to speak for the Community in her interview with Bishop Emrich and they approve of the Mother's intention to refuse Sister Ruth's request to visit England." It was also unanimously moved that if Sister Ruth applied for release or transfer, such "a release or transfer should be unconditional," meaning all ties to SSJD would be forever severed.

Mother Aquila had again elevated the matter of Sister Ruth. In addition to consulting the priest who served as SSJD's warden, she took Sister Ruth's situation to the order's bishop visitor, the Right Rev. Lewis Broughall, of the Anglican Diocese of Niagara. "The Warden considered Sister Ruth's actions in a very serious light—particularly the matter of the cheques—and believes that it is not possible to change her, and that the outcome will probably be dismissal."

On the other hand, while Bishop Broughall agreed with the warden, he wanted Sister Ruth to apply for release instead of the community booting her out. Bishop Broughall then assisted Mother Aquila in the draft of a letter in reply to Bishop Emrich's query about Sister Ruth's personality.

On July 2, Sister Ruth returned to the convent in Toronto from the United States. She met with Mother Aquila and told her, "Bishop Emrich and his Executive Committee were definitely interested in establishing a Religious Order in the diocese, but they were unwilling to take any definite steps until they knew whether SSJD would sponsor the proposed Community." Sister Ruth had also explained that she met with the Mother Superior of the Community of the Transfiguration in Cincinnati but had not spoken about the new community to her. "Their Chapter had recently agreed to admit coloured women as their Bishop had put pressure on them to do so, but the one Indian woman they had admitted had proved a problem," Sister Ruth had reportedly told Mother Aquila.

Mother Aquila lowered the hammer on Sister Ruth. She denied her request to travel to England and told her she should apply for release or drop her interracial community project immediately and "live as an ordinary member of the Community." She also reversed an earlier decision that would have moved Sister Ruth back to Toronto. She returned to the western prairie.

While she agreed to drop the matter, according to Mother's Council meeting minutes, Sister Ruth persisted. It was evident she was emboldened by the fact that the new Episcopal Bishop of Michigan, a committee of priests, and other prominent Detroit Episcopalians were enthusiastic about having a religious community in the diocese and were in serious discernment. Shortly after Mother Aquila's ultimatum, Sister Ruth asked for a second meeting with Mother Aquila to obtain permission to write to the Community of St. Mary's the Virgin in Wantage, England, to inquire about their interest in sponsoring the community in Detroit. When that request was denied, Sister Ruth wrote two follow-up letters while traveling back to Qu'Appelle stating that she had written to Bishop Emrich urging him to send an official invitation to SSJD. She also asked Mother Aquila "to place before the Council a formal request that three Sisters might be sent to the Diocese of Michigan to open a Branch House and to be responsible for fostering a new inter-racial community for at least three years." The Mother shared all of the correspondences with her council. The council unanimously passed a motion that declared Sister Ruth had not exemplified obedience in her life and that the council was prepared to recommend her "release from the Community" so she could independently "pursue God's Call to her."

There continued to be fallout from Sister Ruth's rest time in the United States. She was accused of providing a false account of the Community of the Transfiguration's efforts to integrate, labeling it a failure. According to Mother's Council meetings, she also circulated a false rumor that SSJD's open "door to coloured women" would soon be closed. The assistant superior of SSJD "had recently attended the Jubilee Celebrations of that Community and had been told by the Mother Superior that this 'coloured' woman (whom Sister Ruth spoke of) had been recalled to the Novitiate and later elected to profession and was proving satisfactory."

Mother Aquila and others were distressed by the rumor that SSJD would no longer accept women of color. As Superior, she made every effort to quash the notion. She personally wrote letters to those who questioned the shift: "our Community has not discontinued the practice of receiving both white and negro aspirants . . . we have received on an equal status those of all races who come to us."

Meanwhile, Sister Ruth continued to bombard Mother Aquila with letters of her own, pestering the superior regarding Bishop

Emrich and Detroit. She also repeated her request to travel to England. She made a request to be reassigned to the "Mother House" in Toronto, where she said she could more effectively carry out her mission. She also asked for permission to write letters to other St. John sisters to solicit their help in establishing a new community in the States. In particular, she was interested in connecting with Sister Edith Margaret, a White woman from Buffalo, New York, who wrote supportive letters to Sister Ruth while she had been working in St. Cyprian's Church in Detroit. An exasperated Mother Aquila declined each and every recurring request.

Once again, as she had done annually, Sister Ruth sent the entire Mother's Council her manifesto, which she first sent to them in 1935. And for the first time in thirteen years, the Mother's Council sent Sister Ruth an official letter in response.

July 22nd, 1948

The Sister Ruth, SSJD
Qu'Appelle Diocesan School
REGINA, SASK.

Dear Sister Ruth,

At a meeting of the Reverend Mother's Council held on July 19th, at which all the members were present, your letter of July 6th was read and the matter of your desire to establish an inter-racial Community in the United States was again given prayerful consideration.

I have been asked to advise you that the Council is unanimously of the opinion that the Community has not received a call from GOD to undertake responsibility for such a work. You state definitely that you know the Community is being called by GOD, but the opinion of one Sister cannot be accepted as the Voice of GOD to the Community.

The members of Council recognize that you believe that GOD is calling you to this special vocation; we have no desire to hinder you from obeying what you believe to be GOD's Will for you, but we are convinced that it is not a call of God to the Community. If you feel GOD's Hand upon you and know unmistakably that GOD wishes to use you for this work, should you not be prepared to go forward in faith and be willing to take the seeming risk and leave the future in GOD's Hands? Should you decide to apply for release from your obligations to this Community in order to "fulfill your mission," the Council is willing to recommend to the Community that release be granted, and you would be assured of our prayers and sympathy; but it must be clearly understood that the Community shall not be in any way involved in the plans, neither provide the Sisters to help in the establishment of a new Order nor accept any responsibility for the maintenance of its life for the first few years, as you request in your letter.

We fail to understand your reference to "the completion of a work of thirty years standing." We are of the opinion that this would be an entirely new work, which the Community, as you know, is not prepared to undertake.

Praying that GOD will guide you to accept this decision in a true spirit of obedience.

Your affectionate Sister in Christ,
Secretary, Sisterhood of St. John the Divine

What the council failed to grasp from the phrase in Sister Ruth's manifesto "a completion of a work of 30 years standing" was a reference to herself as a victim of racial discrimination. When in 1918 SSJD accepted Ruth Elaine Younger, from her perspective, that was the beginning of SSJD's work in racial justice ministry. Consequently, the council's response was met with more defiance. Sister Ruth replied that "the decision of the Council is not valid for me and does not satisfy my conscience as being according to the Holy Spirit." As if she didn't understand the word "unanimously," Sister Ruth even questioned the Mother Superior whether the letter reflected the position of all the council members, or if it was just the opinion of the community secretary, who was the sole signatory. Then Sister Ruth quoted a section from the SSJD Community Statutes and demanded that Mother Aquila call a "Special Chapter" meeting of the entire community. She told Mother Aquila that if she did not respond to the request by August 27, 1948, Sister Ruth threatened that she intended to write to two sympathetic St. John sisters, send them a copy of her "official letter" (the manifesto), and enlist their help in obtaining the required sixteen signatures needed to force the Mother Superior to call a Special Chapter. Immediately in response, Mother Aquila sent a letter by special delivery mail to Sister Ruth in Qu'Appelle conceding that it was Sister Ruth's right to obtain signatures from one-fourth of the SSJD community to call a Special Chapter meeting. However, Mother Aquila pointed out that it was summertime and she would likely have difficulty rounding up the numbers she needed let alone successfully gather the entire SSJD community, as many were on their "rest time." Mother Aquila offered to give Sister Ruth's proposal a hearing at the Annual Chapter meeting in the autumn. And finally, Mother Aquila gave Sister Ruth permission to continue her dialogue with Bishop Emrich and others in Detroit "for the testing of what she felt conscience-bound."

What became another equally obsessive worry of Sister Ruth was the prospect of "losing her vows" as a life-professed religious sister. To address this concern, the Mother's Council began to investigate the rarely used authorization of exclaustration, which allowed a monastic to live outside of their community for a finite period of time but with the understanding they would continue to live under their vows and maintain the order's "Rule of Life." It was typically applied when a Sister needed an extended amount of time to care for an ailing parent.

Once again, Sister Ruth requested permission to visit England and approach the Anglican community in Wantage to ask whether they might be willing to sponsor an affiliated community and send two or three of their sisters to Detroit. Mother Aquila, who was scheduled to travel to England, denied the request again, but promised she would "consult with certain people in England, especially the Mother at Wantage."

Before Mother Aquila left for England, she had forbidden Sister

Ruth to communicate about her work for a new community with the other members of SSJD. Despite her best efforts, the Mother Superior was unsuccessful in scheduling a direct conversation with Bishop Emrich to convey SSJD's inability to establish a branch house in his diocese or to undertake any responsibility for a new religious order. As it turned out, she received word from his staff that he was away on his summer vacation. Subsequently, Mother Aquila sent the letter in response to the bishop's inquiry about Sister Ruth's "temperament" and fitness for leadership and let him know SSJD would not sponsor or provide sisters to help establish a community in Michigan. She then departed for England.

When Mother Aquila returned from England, she recalled Sister Ruth from Regina, Qu'Appelle to return to the Mother House in Toronto. When Sister Ruth arrived in Toronto, Mother Aquila proposed to her two years of exclaustration. Sister Ruth asked to seek advice from the clergy she had been in communication with in the United States. Mother Aquila granted that request.

During the fall, Sister Ruth had exchanged many letters seeking counsel. The two sets of letters from priests preserved by her over the subsequent four decades were from Fathers Burgess and Schlueter. While Schlueter's letters were short and sometimes terse, Father Burgess sent thoughtful missives and initially offered himself as a fully vested ally in supporting Sister Ruth and her mission. In his letters, he commented on the regular detailed accounts from Sister Ruth about her situation. It was likely Sister Ruth also sought his counsel because the Black priest had extensive knowledge of and experience with religious orders after working for seven years with the Transfiguration sisters.

In a September 18, 1948, letter, Burgess expressed gratitude for her last update, which included Sister Ruth's account of "the reactions of others." Despite all that transpired, Sister Ruth still indicated to Burgess her hope that SSJD might reverse their decision if swayed by Bishop Emrich. Father Burgess wrote, "I would question very seriously if your order could ever back your plan. It is hardly logical that a group would be willing to deny itself in order to establish that to which it is opposed." He pointed out that the "St. John Sisters" had a history of "projects begun and abandoned because of insufficient staff. It is hard to imagine the Community going out of the country while Canadian work languishes."

Burgess wrote that he also participated in the same Transfiguration's Jubilee Celebration, attended by the SSJD's assistant superior, who reported back the alleged rumors spread by Sister Ruth. Burgess wrote while there, "I overheard Mother Gabrielle of St. Anne's Chicago say that one of the burdens of being a Mother Superior is the constant turning down of requests . . . and every request is usually preceded by a statement of conviction that it is God's will that it be done." But the most striking part of his September letter was Burgess's belief that Sister Ruth's vision of a fully integrated, multiracial religious community has already been realized by Mother Olivia of Transfiguration. "In the midst of [Mother Olivia's] family, includes Negro, Chinese and Hawaiian women. She is most anxious that the novitiate include them. She is distressed there are no more Negro vocations and is delighted to learn that there is a possibility of a Porto Rican candidate in the near future."

Burgess adroitly attempted to encourage Sister Ruth's efforts while preparing her for failure. He wrote that if she was not successful, "[you] could make this ideal [*sic*] the dominating 'intention' of your prayer life." Then, he closed the letter with, "you can depend on whatever help I can give to get your plan underway." He also invited her to speak to Howard University students and at the "colored parishes" in Washington during her next visit.

Sister Ruth's proposal was not presented at the Annual Chapter meeting in the fall. Instead, Sister Ruth asked Mother Aquila if she could spend Christmas time in Buffalo, New York, and stay with the Sisters of the Way of the Cross. She said it was evident that "sisters didn't want me around." She told the superior she would use the time away for discernment on the exclaustration offer and promised to have an answer to Mother Aquila when she returned to Canada.

SHE SAID, SHE SAID—SISTER RUTH ON TRIAL

True to form, Sister Ruth, who asked for permission to take up residence only in Buffalo, ended up traveling to other places, including Michigan and Washington, DC. Evidently, the superiors of the Anglican and Episcopal communities maintained close ties, because Mother Aquila caught wind of Sister Ruth's other destinations from them. "The Mother has received a letter from Mother Ambrose of St. Mary's Convent, Kenosha, Wis., saying Sister Ruth expects to be in Chicago and would like to see their Sister Lucia (formerly of Detroit). The Mother also received a telegram from Sister Catherine Louise, SSM (Society of St. Margaret), Chicago saying they would be pleased to receive Sister Ruth on a visit. All of these plans had been made without the Mother's knowledge."

Obedience to the superior was sacrosanct, and any violation was grounds for expulsion from the community. Mother Aquila compiled an exhaustive list of all of Sister Ruth's alleged violations of her vows, including the checks, and her failure to ask permission for her many exploits.

The face-to-face meeting that Mother Aquila requested with Bishop Emrich during the summer of 1948 finally occurred in the early winter of 1949. And it appeared that Mother Aquila had arrived in the wake of an earlier visit by Sister Ruth with Bishop Emrich. According to the Mother's Council meeting minutes of January 29, 1949,

He stated definitely that he could not accept Sister Ruth as head of the proposed diocesan Community. This decision was not based on the information furnished by the Mother; the most negative thing was his own experience of her reactions. He had told her that he and the Committee wish to investigate further and approach other groups before making a decision; he did not like her reaction; she appears to him to be most emotional and unsuited to be the Superior of a Community. He would go so far as to allow her to work in one parish of the diocese and, if opportunity arose, later, to build up a small group in the parish. The Bishop agreed to put this in writing and to send Sister Ruth a draft of the letter.

He drafted in a letter in Mother's presence as follows:

(a) That the community is investigating further afield
(b) There are many qualities in Sister Ruth that we admire but we are not sure she has the ability to lead or to get on with others.
(c) That the Bishop is willing for her to work in St. Cyprian's Parish as an individual and it may be that there are some steps (that) might be taken by her independently either in Detroit or Chicago.

The Bishop stated that he will not accept her as head of the Diocesan project and that, considering her belief about herself, he would advise her to accept "exclaustration."

Mother Aquila had written to Sister Ruth at the end of January to let her know that she had met with Bishop Emrich and anticipated a letter with his final decision. A few weeks went by, and an anxious Sister Ruth sent a special delivery letter to Mother Aquila from the United States, questioning why she had heard nothing from her. It was apparent to Mother Aquila that Bishop Emrich failed to send the letter he drafted during her visit to Detroit.

Sister Ruth may have begun to have her own doubts in January, because she sent a letter to Father Burgess at Howard University, according to him, "with enclosures." The enclosures may have been letters from Bishop Emrich and the priests on the committee. It was perhaps their response that Father Burgess responded to in a January 18 letter to Sister Ruth when he wrote, "Father Martin's disinterest and Bishop Emrich's decision are in no way encouraging." Apparently, Sister Ruth was still in communication with the influential African American priest, the Rev. John Martin of Chicago, which explained her unauthorized trips to Chicago. Father Burgess discouraged Sister Ruth from her continued communications, writing, "I cannot see that any good will be served by keeping in touch with Bishop Emrich. He has said quite bluntly that it will be many months before any decision is reached in Michigan."

She appeared to share more detailed plans with another priest she was in contact with, the prominent theologian Rev. Norman Pettinger, who was teaching at General Theological Seminary in New York. He wrote on January 29, 1949, "in view of the somewhat unsettled condition of your plan, it might be better to have your two members complete their postulancy in some English house; then, when you are ready to begin over here, you could have the novitiate for them in the house in Detroit."

One of those prospective members was Kathleen Harper of Rottendean, Sussex, England. On January 25, she wrote to Sister Ruth while she was at St. David's House in Buffalo, "My dearest Sister: Hilda told us when she received your last letter that you hope to get a passage in March." It was a passage to England. "I am longing to see you, as there is so much I would rather talk to you about than write—I hope you understand."

At the Mother's Council February 6 meeting, the sisters unanimously decided to hold a Special Chapter meeting of the entire SSJD community four days later on February 10, 1949, to decide on Sister Ruth's fate as a St. John sister. She was ordered to return from the United States to participate in the proceedings. Word must have gotten back to Bishop Emrich or the committee of priests about the Special Chapter. On the very morning of the meeting, Mother Aquila received a long-distance phone call from a Michigan priest who made an appeal to Mother Aquila to delay the Special Chapter meeting until the bishop sent his final decision. Mother Aquila said it was impossible to postpone the meeting, and it proceeded.

Much of the highlights of Sister Ruth's four decades with SSJD were captured in the Mother's Council meeting minutes and letters from the convent's archives and letters preserved by Ruth. By far, the documents from this 1949 Special Meeting—a voluminous two dozen pages in single-space ten-point type—provided the most comprehensive and blow-by-blow account of a watershed moment in Ruth's life. Attached to the meeting minutes was a transcript that read like a movie script, capturing each and every statement made by the St. John sisters.

Forty of the SSJD sisters, including Sister Ruth and the Superior, gathered at 10:45 a.m. in the "Mother House." Missing from the meeting were the sisters living in distant branch houses, such as Sister Constance out west in Qu'Appelle. However, Mother Aquila indicated that she requested their input in writing. The gravity of the Special Meeting was evident in the numerous invocations of the Holy Spirit on the proceedings and citation of three different Collects from three major feast days during the opening prayer. The Collect from Whitsun Day—the Pentecost, asked for the guidance of the Holy Spirit; the Collect from Quinquagesima (the Sunday before Lent) asked for divine love; and Ascension Day Collect was read, "to remind us of the words of our Rule: 'we are called to live with Him at the Right of God in the Power of the Holy Spirit.'"

Sister Ruth's "call from God for inter-racial work," let alone her exploits, was not widely known by the rank-and-file members of the St. John community. So, Mother Aquila opened the meeting by reading Sister Ruth's manifesto. She then gave a detailed account of everything that transpired since Sister Ruth was assigned to Detroit's St. Cyprian's Church in 1946 leading up to the day's Special Meeting. She explained that she and her council felt that the entire SSJD community should decide on whether their sister should be granted exclaustration.

It was at that point that Sister Ruth interjected and revealed, "I cannot accept exclaustration." She claimed that Bishop Emrich had asked her to wait. Mother Aquila countered that he had supported exclaustration for her. Sister Ruth said, "He had changed his mind." Actually, Sister Ruth's contention seemed plausible, given the fact that a priest called earlier in the morning requesting that the meeting be postponed.

Sister Vera, who served on the Mother's Council and over the years voiced disapproval of Sister Ruth's behavior, interjected that she failed to live up to her vow of obedience. "The Mother is not aware of the activities Sister Ruth is carrying on and the plans she is making."

Mother Aquila confirmed to the sisters that this was the case and told of Sister Ruth's most recent transgression. While she had given her permission to spend time in Buffalo, she learned Sister Ruth traveled to Detroit, Chicago, and Washington without her knowledge. Sister Ruth argued that she did have permission to travel, but Mother Aquila responded, "That's untrue."

Sister Ruth insisted that she was not actively engaged in the work to create a new community and that Bishop Emrich and his committee of priests were the ones developing the plans. At that point, Mother Aquila raised "the confidential letter" from Christina Robinson as evidence that she was actively doing this work. Sister Ruth explained the letter only spoke of a "vision" and that she had disclosed the letter to Mother Aquila. The Superior clapped back at Sister Ruth that she did not volunteer the information about the letter; "it was because I asked you" about it.

The tone of the meeting seemed to vacillate between lobs of accusations against Sister Ruth to a genuine sympathetic search for understanding her and the meaning of community. The St. John sisters delved into what it means to receive "a call from God" and whether it was even appropriate for SSJD as a community to support an individual sister's ministry when it diverges from SSJD's established ministries.

Indirectly, Sister Beatrice confirmed and validated Sister Ruth's claim that her call to racial desegregation work was initiated thirty years ago when she first arrived in Toronto. "When Sister Ruth first came to us, she mentioned this and she had to go away, and then she came back with the clear understanding that there were to be no qualifications [to religious life].

"The Council did send a message to Sister Ruth saying that we were making the fullest allowance to test that call," Sister Beatrice continued. "She believes she had the call, it isn't for us to say she hasn't. It is only for us to put her in her obedience and enable her to act upon it."

Sister Loveday said, "it is a question of vocation, not work. None of us doubt that Sister has this call, but since she has allowed herself to be professed, she is to accept her obedience from the Superiors."

As the conversation kept returning to the vow of obedience, there was a shift in tone from Sister Ruth. She finally acknowledged the gravity of her clandestine dealings and that she may have imperiled her vows and, to a greater extent, sabotaged her own mission.

In a contrite response, Sister Ruth said, "I am a very imperfect person, but I have no conscious[ness] of having been disobedient in this. If I have not been, I have not been consciously so. I am a most imperfect person, but GOD uses even imperfect people for his will. I must beg the Sisters not to let any imperfection of mine stand in the way of seeing this larger thing."

To Mother Aquila, she said, "I have your letter in which you said I might seek help and you did not say where or how or when."

Mother Aquila conceded, "I know I did not make it clear."

Sister Ruth knew, though, that if she was going to win over her sisters, she had to ask for forgiveness. "I have acted throughout, maybe faultily, as I say, this was the permission I had. If I am at fault, I am sorry and I hope you will accept it."

Before Mother Aquila or anyone else had the opportunity to respond to Sister Ruth's apology for "unconscious disobedience," Sister Vera quickly questioned Sister Ruth's vow of poverty.

"Where did all the money for this come from?" she asked.

"Must I answer that?" Sister Ruth answered. "Mother knows where the money comes from."

"Mother," Sister Vera asked, "do you know where the money came from?"

"I know we are not providing it," Mother Aquila said.

"How does it affect the vow of poverty?" Sister Vera said.

"That is one of the things I have been worried about, because

Sister has to ask for the money and I am not satisfied with that at all," Mother Aquila replied.

"The first person who contributed to it is a person here in Toronto that Mother knew about," Sister Ruth replied. "There has been provision made by a deeply interested person. It has been most meager, but sufficient. It has been particularly responsible for railway fare."

"May we ask where that person lives," Sister Lois asked.

"I don't care to answer that," Sister Ruth said.

"But we cannot act independently, and I would like to know where that person lives," Sister Lois challenged.

"It is a person in Detroit, and it is not an Associate," Sister Ruth answered.

After that exchange, the sisters returned to the subject of Sister Ruth's interpretation of obedience. One sister appeared incredulous about Sister Ruth's impending travel to England, which now seemed more likely. "When Sister Ruth goes to England, does that carry out the desire to work with the races?" Sister Mabel asked.

"That is a time for preparation," Mother Aquila said, "and the potential for two vocations."

The women refocused the debate on the topic of exclaustration versus release, with some who indicated they were ready to vote.

"I think none of us are prepared to vote," Mother Aquila said. "Do you wish to resume this discussion?"

"It seems to me we have had the situation from every angle placed before us," said Sister Christabel. "A large part of it has been a revelation to the majority of us. It seems to me we have so much to think over from every point of view. The courtesy of waiting for the Bishop is something that is compelling for us. It seems to me that this is the time now to move that we postpone this meeting or adjourn until after a week from Monday. It should be an all day meeting beginning in the morning."

Sister Ruth responded, "I would ask you to give your opinion promptly, for personally I am concerned and I would appreciate a prompt expression of opinion. It would be such a mercy to me when once the Bishop's word is given, but all does not depend on that. I would be so thankful if it could be settled and I would know what my status is and I would not be in the position I have been in."

"We are making history for the Religious Life in Canada and even in America. We should safeguard every step," Mother Aquila said in conclusion.

The meeting was adjourned, and the sisters awaited word from Bishop Emrich.

THE BISHOP'S MOVE

At 12:30 p.m. on March 3, Mother Aquila told her council that the Bishop's Committee was prepared to make a recommendation to Bishop Emrich that "Sister Ruth be granted Episcopal sanction to establish a religious community for women in the diocese." She told her council that a letter to that effect had been sent to Sister Ruth. The council scheduled the follow-up Special Chapter meeting to vote on exclaustration on March 7.

By the evening of March 3, the entire Detroit deal fell apart.

"Mother received a phone call that evening from Father Bugler, Secretary of the Bishop's Committee. He informed her that at a meeting of the Committee that afternoon, the Bishop decided not to use Sister Ruth in Detroit,—the decision being made as a result of certain reactions on Sister Ruth's part," according to the Mother Council's March 6 meeting minutes. "The Bishop was of the opinion that Sister Ruth should be kept at the Convent to learn humility and obedience."

According to the minutes, Father Bugler said Sister Ruth telephoned and "expressed her intention to go to Detroit the following morning to interview the Bishop. Father Bugler asked the Mother to prevent this visit as no useful purpose would be served."

The next morning, Mother Aquila met with Sister Ruth and "forbade her to visit Detroit or to telephone the Bishop, or to make any further contacts in this connection, until after the Special Chapter. Sister Ruth agreed that Detroit is now closed." Mother Aquila also told Sister Ruth she should forget about Chicago as well because Bishop Emrich had conversations with the Episcopal Diocese of Chicago Bishop Wallace Conkling. Mother Aquila warned Sister Ruth that she would be ignored if she attempted to make any contact with individuals in either diocese.

The March 7 Special Chapter meeting proceeded as planned. With Bishop Emrich's final decision, Mother Aquila withdrew the offer for exclaustration until the community gathered for the March 7 Special Chapter meeting. The sisters first asked for an explanation behind the bishop's decision.

"A letter from the Secretary of the Committee, Father Bugler, . . . said that as a result of a letter received from Sister Ruth, the committee had reversed their decision. This was apparently due to certain reactions of a personal nature on Sister Ruth's part," Mother Aquila told the women. The superior also told the sisters that although she had withdrawn the offer of exclaustration, it does not mean Sister Ruth can't reapply.

As if that were her cue, Sister Christabel, who had expressed sympathy for Sister Ruth, asked to speak first.

> There is a great challenge in the world today for bringing together the many races to bear witness to their unity in the Family of GOD. The course of events during the past thirty years seem to show that GOD has called Sister Ruth to help in this work, and that in her preparation for it He has both directly and indirectly made use of our Community. By many significant signs, He seems to be saying that NOW the "appointed time" for further action has come. Although the door in Detroit has apparently been closed, there are others still ajar. In New York especially, there are priests in sympathy with the project Sister has in mind; she knows of women ready to join her, and of others able to give material support. Of our Community, He seems to be asking that we set Sister Ruth free to explore the possibilities of fulfilling the vocation which lay within the call He gave her thirty years ago.

Two sisters voiced their disapproval because the community had paid for her education to prepare her for work in the community, not to pursue her own projects.

Sister Christabel continued, according to the transcript.

The corporate share of the Community in this work would consist of

(I) Permitting Sister Ruth to put her vocation to the test.

(II) Following her with our love, understanding, prayers and sympathy,

(III) Refraining from making any conditions which would hinder her in carrying out God's will as revealed to her, or to injure her in the eyes of the world.

(IV) Seeing that we do not thwart God's plans by narrowness of vision or lack of love. "If this work be of man it will come to naught; if it be of God it will prosper."

A motion was proposed by Sister Anna and seconded by Sister Barbara that "in order to be fair to Sister Ruth, the Community grant her a period of Exclaustration for not more than two years, with the object of testing this particular vocation."

Before the vote was taken, the usual dissenters, Sister Vera and Sister Lois, raised objections.

Sister Vera said, "Sister Ruth has not shown by her life in the Community that she has the gifts necessary to enable her to weld together peoples of different races into one family. She has failed in Detroit. Will not the same thing happen in New York? If she desires to follow her Call, it would be better that the Community should offer her release."

Sister Lois spoke of "the difficulty in her mind on account of Sister having undertaken so many things without the knowledge of her Superior, interpretations having been put on permission which were not intended."

Sister Vera pointed to the recent blowup in Detroit and indicated that it could be repeated in other places and damage the reputation of the entire SSJD community. Sister Vera "begged the Sisters to consider the good of the Community rather than an individual call to God. As a Community, we do not wish to be involved in difficulties with Bishops and Priests" as caused by Sister Ruth.

Mother Aquila steered the meeting toward taking a vote and stated, "The Sisters are not asked to pronounce a judgment on Sister's fitness but to express their willingness to give her the opportunity to test what she believes is God's will."

A secret ballot was taken, and the motion for exclaustration was granted. Two days later, Sister Ruth mailed her formal request to the Episcopal Diocese of New York bishop to return to New York along with five "Letters of Commendatory" as references from priests and diocesan staff and religious organizations.

9th March 1949

The Rt. Rev. Charles K. Gilbert, D. D.
Bishop of New York,
Old Synod House,
Cathedral Heights,
New York-25, New York.

Dear Rev. and dear Bishop Gilbert,-

I write in connection with some work which it is my desire to begin in New York City within the next year, if you are willing to give me permission to come into residence in your Diocese in order to accomplish it.

I have the permission of my Sisterhood in Toronto to undertake this work. Three or four devoted women, two of whom are English, would like to join me in establishing a Religious House that would be a witness to the essential oneness of people of many skin colours and backgrounds. We would take a small house to begin with in some area near a dilapidated and slum section. We would live the Mixed Form of Religious Life, and we would seek quietly to witness Christian Profession by our lives.

Our purpose to begin with would be to help with any work in which we found ourselves useful in a local parish, and which we might be invited to undertake. Our ultimate purpose of work is religious education, with the immediate hope of opening a nursery school for poor children, and classes for their mothers.

This would be the initial unit in a Settlement house, patterned after Mrs. Simkovitch's great Greenwich House, but conducted by Religious.

Our Sisterhood would be Augustinian in form, and we would be under the supervision of a Priest-Warden, with an Episcopal Visitor.

Our underlying raison d'etre would be to supply the need of a Religious Order in the United States into which suitable women of all colours and classes could enter and find full opportunity for the use of their talents and their ministry. If I may mention a personal matter in this connection: I myself was born in New York, and when my Call came to Religious Life in 1918, I was unable to be received into an American Religious Order, because of a strain of "other" blood. I think I am right in saying that the five sisterhoods in New York do not yet, after 30 years, admit coloured vocations. I feel that one of our contributions would be to supply this deficiency.

Our initial financial support,—for the renting of a house and our maintenance—would come from a small group of friends already interested. We would hope to earn our living by our work as we come established and better know. We would want to begin in true poverty, great faith, and real simplicity.

11

REPATRIATION II—WHITE SAVIORS, WHITE SABOTEURS

Despite the Rev. John Burgess's cautionary advice to Sister Ruth not to model a new religious community after those in England, a trip across the pond to visit those convents remained Sister Ruth's priority. Sister Ruth moved back to her hometown of New York City a couple of days after being granted exclaustration. She took up residence at Trinity Mission House, a Trinity Church–Wall Street ministry that served the poor and was operated by the Sisters of St. Margaret. She was there barely a week when she boarded a steamer headed to England. In a letter that oozed with giddiness and a deluge of exclamation points, she wrote,

> I am sitting at the First Officer's Table, so there you are! You will be delighted, I am sure, when I tell you I have a cabin alone! and it is a very comfortable steam-heated room with running water, a couch, a wardrobe, a chest of drawers, writing space, bed, chair—and rug!! I also have a single cabin for my return passage on 28th of July via SS Manchester City. I am very grateful to our dear Lord for his kindness to me and I praise Him for this continually.
>
> There are, as you know, only 12 passengers aboard and of these only 3 are women including myself! I am the only woman at my table. The men are 9/10 Englishman, and very nice indeed—but not very intellectual!!
>
> We have some rather unusual passengers onboard: four seals!—live and in cages en route to the Manchester Zoo. . . . They are on the passenger deck, so we see something of them!!

The recipient of Sister Ruth's letter was Sister Edith Margaret. Shortly after Sister Ruth's exclaustration was approved, Sister Edith Margaret, a White woman from Buffalo, also asked for exclaustration to accompany Sister Ruth. The initial reaction from Mother Aquila and her council to Sister Edith Margaret's request was suspicion. They thought that Sister Ruth had somehow coerced her into joining her. After all, from the time Sister Ruth was first sent to Detroit to work in St. Cyprian, through all her schemes and attempts to force the St. John's sisters to open a branch house in the United States, one of her constant refrains was her need for "two or three sisters" to help in this new work. Evidently, Sister Edith Margaret convinced the council that as a fellow American, she was also compelled to work with her sister Ruth in her racial justice ministry in their homeland.

Sister Ruth cast a wide net during her years of networking from Canada, and she was able to snag some pretty big fish across the pond. Less than two days after Sister Ruth embarked in England, she not only met the Archbishop of Canterbury but had lunch with him. In a second letter to Sister Edith Margaret, she wrote, "I had a good little talk with the Archbishop of Canterbury. When I told him about our new work, he was greatly interested and spoke beautifully about [Episcopal Diocese of New York] Bishop [Charles] Gilbert."

After the high drama of the last few years, Sister Ruth took full advantage of her newfound freedom abroad. While she worked on her "mission from God," at the same time she enjoyed God's creation. "Yesterday we went to a blue bell [*sic*] woods—wonderful—beautiful beyond description and we found some wild orchids and some (many, really) primroses! Do you know the exquisite, frail, pale yellow English primrose? It is elegant and beautiful beyond description and is of the most delicate shade of yellow. I am having a wonderfully peaceful time here, with a really good rest—and the great joy and privilege of daily Communion."

As Sister Ruth settled into her extended stay in England, Sister Edith Margaret was charged with some tasks Stateside. Sister Ruth inquired about them in a letter to Sister Margaret, saying that she hoped "you have been able to accomplish all the commissions I entrusted to you." Her biggest assignment was fund-raising and soliciting money from wealthy Episcopalians in New York City and its neighboring suburbs of Long Island and New Jersey. In *In Wisdom*, Ruth wrote that the retired New York Bishop William Manning "gave her a list of names from the Social Register." Bishop Manning was known for raising $10 million for additional construction on the Cathedral Church of St. John the Divine. He launched a program during the Great Depression that trained and employed men from the neighborhood as stonemasons.

Sister Ruth first told Edith Margaret "to visit (Father Williams) in Long Island who is a Canadian from Toronto and has always known us. Please give him a happy account of our hopes and plans and say we need $45,000, with which to buy a house. Urge him to help us get at least $10,000 of it as soon as possible, as a down payment to hold the house."

Next, Sister Edith Margaret was directed to send a letter "at once" to Mr. and Mrs. John A. Roebling in Bernardsville, New Jersey. John Roebling was the grandson of the famed civil engineer who designed the Brooklyn Bridge.

Sister Ruth wrote, "ask them definitely for $10,000 and show them the necessity for our work. They are conservative, and so the racial angle cannot be stressed with them." She instructed Sister Edith Margaret to name-drop noted priest and scholar Dr. Cuthbert Simpson and Miss Adelaide Simpson, a Columbia University assistant professor, in her conversations with the Roeblings. Another person Sr. Edith Margaret was told to meet with was Father Grieg Taber, the longtime rector of the Church of St. Mary's the Virgin in Manhattan. She hoped that he would serve as the priest warden for their prospective new community.

There were several other people, both lay and clergy, Sister Ruth asked Sister Edith Margaret to meet with in New York. Yet she also cautioned her to steer clear of nuns from other religious orders and to use discretion in disclosing information to them and certain people.

"I hope you will have a full report for me when we meet," she wrote. Sister Edith Margaret was booked to travel to England soon for her own research and studies on religious life.

Sister Edith Margaret, who was eight years younger than Sister Ruth, entered the Sisterhood of St. John the Divine in 1936, eighteen years after Ruth. It was evident Sister Ruth wielded that seniority. The tone of Sister Ruth's letters to Sister Edith Margaret vacillated from dictatorial and authoritative to maternal and loving. Before Sister Edith Margaret's scheduled departure for England, Sister Ruth wrote to her,

> I hope and trust and pray that you will have a really good voyage. Eat much [underlined twice for emphasis]; drink very little; rest much, but keep out on deck in the good sea air, which is specially [*sic*] beneficial in keeping you fit. It is very important to eat as much as you can on-board [the] steamer. I send you very much love, dearest Sister, may our dear Lord have you in his Holy Keeping. Your very loving Sister in Him.

Once Sister Edith Margaret arrived in London, it appeared the two women did not travel or lodge together over the next two months. Ruth primarily stayed in the home of Kathleen, who, with her husband, operated a boarding school in the coastal town of Seadowne, Rottingdean, Sussex. She was the same Kathleen whom Sister Ruth corresponded with during her last chaotic months in Canada.

Once she arrived in England, Sister Edith Margaret took a course in religious education for children at St. Christopher's College in Blackheath. Meanwhile, Sister Ruth traversed England visiting convents, including the Sisterhood of the Blessed Virgin Mary, the Society of St. Margaret, Community of St. Denys, Community of St. John the Baptist, and St. Peter's Convent. As if her thirty years of living with her St. John's sisters were not sufficient, she wrote about the visits in *In Wisdom*: "there was much to learn, particularly about the corporate spiritual life, the sense of family life, and the private prayer life."[1]

Sister Ruth also made the rounds of other Church of England departments and offices, including the Society for the Propagation of

---

1. The Reverend Mother Ruth, CHS, *In Wisdom Thou Hast Made Them*, 10.

the Gospel in Foreign Parts and the Central Council for Women's Work, both located on the campus of Westminster Abbey.

England was the place where she would have her first encounter with Bishop Horace William Baden Donegan, who at the time was the suffragan for the Episcopal Diocese of New York. As suffragan, Donegan was the second-highest-ranking bishop in the diocese. Donegan, a native of Derbyshire, England, spent a good deal of his summers in England. Upon learning that Bishop Donegan would be preaching at a parish in the Midlands, Sister Ruth popped up there. She described that first meeting (in third person) *In Wisdom*: "Meeting her after the service, he was kindness itself and was interested and attentive to what she could tell him about the two sisters' possible future in New York."[2]

While in England, it was the first time it was strongly recommended to Sister Ruth that she should also connect with another Diocese of New York cleric who would become a central figure in her fledgling new religious life in New York. In the offices on the Westminster Abbey campus, he was simply called "Eddie West." The Rev. Canon Edward Nason West was the canon sacrist for the Cathedral Church of St. John the Divine. Often referred to as a "high church priest," Canon West was both an authority on and the creator of liturgical art. He was the designer of the Compass Rose, the official emblem of Worldwide Anglican Communion. During that time, Sister Ruth was in a futile pursuit of the support of Father Taber, rector of the Midtown Manhattan Anglo-Catholic parish St. Mary's the Virgin, and who she hoped would become the warden of the new religious order. Ultimately, it would be this Eddie West who would fill that role.

A final destination in England—more accurately, a pilgrimage—Sister Ruth was compelled to make her way to Whitby, Yorkshire, home to the revered St. Hilda. Hilda was often credited for helping to establish Christianity in seventh-century Anglo-Saxon England. St. Hilda was the patronal name of Sister Ruth's undergraduate college in Toronto.

---

2. The Reverend Mother Ruth, CHS, *In Wisdom Thou Hast Made Them*, 12.

Sister Ruth's four months of expatriation exposed her to England's hallowed saints (along with Hilda there were Hugh, Aiden, and Cuthbert), whose legacies Sister Ruth would carry back to New York and who figured prominently in her future endeavors. Her visits to the country's Anglican convents and the powerful church connections laid the firmest foundation yet for her new ministries. Those experiences coalesced around a slightly altered plan that differed from the one she proposed to Bishop Gilbert before she left Canada.

When Sisters Ruth and Edith Margaret returned to New York in August 1949, they rented rooms in Morningside Heights near the Cathedral of St. John the Divine. The sisters chose to worship at the cathedral because it placed them in the orbit of Bishops Gilbert and Donegan and the Rev. Canon West. Sister Ruth was most adamant about following up on the advice she received in England to seek out a meeting with Canon West. After they met, Ruth wrote "that the meeting of Canon West was the most important moment of the Sisters' lives on the human side since they left England."[3] Once hearing of Sister Ruth's mission, Canon West, in turn, facilitated meetings with some of the powerful and influential members of the cathedral's congregation, including William Bloor, a financial officer for Columbia University, who would eventually become the university's treasurer and chief financial officer. The other individual who would help Sister Ruth was a St. Luke's Hospital pediatrician named Frederick Wilkie, MD. Those two fortuitous meetings catapulted Sister Ruth's mission from God, outlined in the pages of her manifesto first delivered in 1935, steps closer to reality.

However, eluding Sister Ruth was a meeting with her hero in the settlement house movement, Mary Simkhovitch, founder of Greenwich House, which served newly arrived immigrant children. Simkhovitch's husband, Vladimir, a professor at Columbia, met with her instead. "They had a long talk about the problems involved in putting these kinds of inspirations and ideas into practice, particularly the problems brought about by racial mixtures and international back-

---

3. The Reverend Mother Ruth, CHS, *In Wisdom Thou Hast Made Them*, 13.

grounds," she wrote in *In Wisdom*. She concluded, "man proposes but God disposes."[4]

Sister Ruth still very much visualized opening a settlement house as the anchor ministry for her new community. Dr. Wilke, as it turned out, was intent on opening a school, and he had come to learn of Sister Ruth's years as a teacher in Canada's western prairie town of Qu'Appelle. "[He] had recently returned from the war with the firm decision to do all he could to eliminate war. He was interested in finding a place to begin a school for little children."[5] By autumn of 1949, a small informal committee was organized by Dr. Wilke. Others invited to participate in this group were attorney Richard B. Goetze and the headmaster of the cathedral's choir school, the Rev. Canon James Green. He reached out to his fellow parishioner, William Bloor, who, as the assistant treasurer at Columbia, had responsibility for the university's real estate portfolio. Before long, the group identified a brownstone in the neighborhood, on 113th Street, which was available. Shortly before Christmas of 1949, Dr. Wilke, Bishop Gilbert, Richard B. Geotze, and Sister Ruth formed a group now known as the trustees of St. Hilda's School, and they closed the deal on a brownstone at 621 W. 113th Street for a purchase price of $30,000. It was the site of the sisters' new convent, also christened with the name St. Hilda's, and a new school in the neighborhood. These men, Bloor, Wilke, Bishop Gilbert, and Canon West, men of White European background, ultimately made the decision for Sister Ruth that the ministry for her prospective religious community would be education and not a settlement house. Initially, the school became known among some at St. Luke Hospital and Columbia University as "Wilke Tech." From a hospital newsletter article: "The new school has been affectionately dubbed 'Wilke Tech' [since] the chief of our pediatric services played an important part in the school."

During the property transaction, another small exploratory committee was formed made up of parents from the cathedral, Colum-

---

4. The Reverend Mother Ruth, CHS, *In Wisdom Thou Hast Made Them*, 13.
5. The Reverend Mother Ruth, CHS, *In Wisdom Thou Hast Made Them*, 12.

bia, and the neighborhood. Immediately after the closing, renovations to the brownstone commenced to construct a convent with a chapel on the upper floors and classrooms on the lower ones. By February 2, 1950, St. Hilda's School opened its doors to eight children, nursery to kindergarten; the enrollment increased to twelve before the summer break.

In her book *In Wisdom*, she described the half-day school program as building blocks, story time, and daily chapel with songs and prayers. Sister Ruth was now also enrolled in the doctoral program at Columbia's Teachers College. Helping to support the school were fellow graduate students, who collected and donated toys and furniture to outfit the new school. Some of the students also chose the new school as a site for their academic field work.

Sister Ruth expressed pride that two individuals of color, in the kindergarten and the school's staff, were a part of the new school: "an Indian lady in her attractive sari with long braided hair. She seemed strange to the children, but of real interest nevertheless. The Sisters were happy to have her there with her little girl as a member of the kindergarten, for they were determined that from the beginning suitable children of all origins must be welcomed."[6]

Still not lost to Sister Ruth was God's call to establish a religious community and a ministry to address the "racial problem." Although, between the time she left Canada until the opening of the school, it appeared she tempered that language. One of the priests who may have persuaded her in this new thinking was the Rev. Canon Michael Coleman, a British priest posted in Canada, who supported and encouraged Sister Ruth's mission from the very beginning. He remained in contact with her while she was traveling in England and after her return to New York.

He wrote to her during her summer in England:

I know as you do something of this racial problem in the U. S., and I feel that while a firm stand must be taken in doing the right thing, at the same time it is wise and just to discover the

---

6. The Reverend Mother Ruth, CHS, *In Wisdom Thou Hast Made Them*, 16.

reasons which has caused this ultra-conservative outlook in the Church. . . . Now while you and I realize the answer to this danger is just what you plan to do, we also must be aware that those who live in the situation find it hard to think as clearly. In Canada of course there is no problem of colour, but even here there are very few educated coloured people who can become no more than railway porters, which is again unfair.

Once the school opened, Sister Ruth wrote to Canon Coleman, apparently swayed by his influence: "We have begun our school here near the Cathedral with exactly no mention to our constituency of our convent purposes. . . . after consultation in England and here [in New York] and after much prayerful thought we are saying exactly nothing about the 'races.' We hope to make our Religious House a fait d'accompli [*sic*] of supra-racial life—having an array of its members, if God sends them to us, Chinese, Jewish, Indian and Negro Christians with, if it works out and in God's Providence—a preparedness of the majority group."

Canon Coleman wrote in response, "I think your programme is a wise one over the matter of racial problems, and it is well to remember that the wise course is not always a matter of weak compromise." Canon Coleman also mentioned in his letter that in March 1951 he planned to work on a mission project at Harlem's St. Philip's Church with its rector, the Rev. Shelton Hale Bishop. "I am so interested to hear that you may be working with me at St. Philip's," he wrote to her. Later that year, Coleman became the Bishop of Qu'Appelle, the western Canadian diocese where Sister Ruth began her teaching career.

Interestingly, after Sister Ruth's return to New York, there were only brief and passing documented mentions of St. Philip's Church, Ruth's childhood parish, during her years back in New York. In her request to work in the Diocese of New York, Sister Ruth wrote to Bishop Gilbert that she "was very well known" to the Rev. Shelton Bishop. Understandably, Sister Ruth's decision to settle and become affiliated with the Cathedral instead of St. Philip's was a strategic move that gave her close access to the bishops and other powerful people in the diocese's leadership who could make her lofty ambitions a reality. And after the disastrous and dramatic demise of her efforts in Detroit with Bishop Emrich, it seemed that lesson guided her dealings with the Diocese of New York. Her correspondence with her hometown diocese elicited a tone of humility and compromise that was absent from her Michigan communications.

In the early months of 1950, news of the school and "the two sisters from Canada" spread not only across New York and the nation, but also up to Canada, thanks to the work of the diocese public relations office. Credit, or blame in this instance, was also due in part to a gaggle of skeptics, saboteurs, and outright detractors who begrudged Sister Ruth's work, one of whom was Harriet Bronson. She was the same Harriet whom Sister Ruth spoke highly of as a friend from her youth and secular life in the early 1900s. Now mid-century, it was evident a lot of love had been lost between the two.

Harriet wrote to Mother Aquila on March 1, 1950:

Dear Reverend Mother:

It has been a great sorrow and anxiety to us that Sister Ruth has behaved as she has. I am glad that she has not approached me since she came to New York—because that tells me that she knows I could not approve—and I know full well that nothing I could say or do would have any effect on her now.

In another envelope, I am sending you the folders about the school.

This morning on the telephone, I told Father Schlueter of seeing you. He is sorry that he did not see you. . . . So it was natural for me to tell him of your gracious kindness in seeing us last evening. You would be interested in what he said.

"Does she approve of what Sister Ruth is doing?" I said that you did not and that I was doubly glad that none of us at St. Luke's (Church) had become involved. Then he said "I was brutal—the first time she came to see me, I listened and said I could have nothing to do with it. The second time the same, but on the third visit I told her bluntly that she had no idea of obedience and was so headstrong she could not work with anyone else and I could not approve."

He said it is so strange how all these other men fell for her! Of course, I told him nothing you told me, but I thought his attitude would interest you.

It occurs to me that I could help in this way by sending you whatever I hear of developments—and also if there is anything you wish to know at any time, please write me. It is quite probable that with the telephone, seeing Canon West often and other contacts, I could easily obtain information. Naturally no one knows that I am in touch with you except Father Schlueter and Father Wood. So any questions from me would seem only natural interest.

News of St. Hilda's School seemed to set off Mother Aquila. She wrote to New York's Bishop Gilbert less than two weeks after the school's opening to request a face-to-face meeting with him. Even though a year earlier Mother Aquila sent letters to New York clergy and the Episcopal religious community superiors and to the convents in England to inform them of the sisters' exclaustration, she fired off a second round. Those new letters essentially said the same, with the addition that the Sisterhood of St. John had no ties to the new St. Hilda's School. Mother Aquila wrote to Bishop Gilbert yet again to clarify the reasons and conditions under which the sisters came to New York—to establish a new multiracial religious community.

The seventy-two-year-old Bishop Gilbert sent a letter to Mother Aquila after their face-to-face meeting. He wrote that when Sister Ruth first came into his diocese with the request to start a new community, "I referred her to some of our clergy, but it had been my impression that she found little encouragement." Now that the school had been launched, he wrote that he suspected Sister Ruth might approach him again about the new community. He stated that he would give the request "careful consideration."

Others in New York had a role in funneling information to Mother Aquila, even a few who were proponents of St. Hilda's School and Sister Ruth. One was an Episcopalian who lived in the neighborhood and taught at Columbia, Adelaide Simpson. She was a trailblazer in her own right. In 1921, the *New York Times* announced that "Miss

Adelaide Douglas Simpson, a graduate of Columbia University [was] elected Dean of Women at the University of Virginia, a newly created office."[7] The century-old university had recently begun matriculating women through its professional and graduate degree programs with nineteen women admitted in 1921. Twenty-nine years later, in 1950, when Professor Simpson joined the school's board of trustees, she was an assistant professor of classics at Columbia University, where she had earned her master's degree in classical philosophy in 1917. Before joining St. Hilda's board, Professor Simpson was acquainted with the Sisterhood of St. John and Mother Aquila. Subsequently, she was in regular communication with Sister Ruth's Mother Superior in Toronto. Similar to Harriet Bronson, Professor Simpson wrote letters to Mother Aquila detailing Sister Ruth's activities in New York. However, in contrast to Miss Bronson, as a school trustee, Professor Simpson was a supporter of Sister Ruth. Fortunately, her dispatches to Mother Aquila were provided without the cattiness or ulterior motives. Her letters were often filled with compassion and understanding. In an attempt to present herself as an objective observer to Mother Aquila, she wrote, "I see both points of view." Mother Aquila expressed her gratitude to Professor Simpson for "her loyalty" and noted that she would continue to call her for further help regarding the Sister Ruth "situation."

Professor Simpson—along with clergy in the diocese—received the Aquila letters as part of her second sweeping effort to distance SSJD from Sister Ruth and her work. Exactly a year had passed since the debacle in Detroit, in which the superior and her council came to the conclusion that Sister Ruth misrepresented the St. John sisterhood's commitment to starting a branch house and community in the Diocese of Michigan. On February 9, 1950, Professor Simpson wrote, "Reverend and dear Mother, It was very kind of you to write as you did. You may be sure that I will do my best to correct mistaken impressions about Sister Ruth's present project, and its relation (or lack of it) to your Community."

---

7. "Miss Simpson to Be Dean: University of Virginia Calls Her to Head Women's Department," *New York Times*, June 30, 1921, 13.

By the summer of 1950, Professor Simpson's best efforts could not control the power of the press. On July 23, 1950, the little nursery school with just a dozen enrolled children garnered a small article that made a big ripple across the national border. The *Living Church*, an independent, national news and commentary magazine on the Episcopal Church and Worldwide Anglican Community, reported that "Two Sisters of the Community of St. John the Divine established with the blessing of their Order and the approval of the Bishop of New York, a nursery school."[8] The article also erroneously stated that the SSJD warden, the Rev. Granville M. Williams, superior of the Society of St. John the Evangelist, was providing "oversight" of the school. The Rev. Williams, however, was only providing oversight of SSJD and the exclaustration process, not the sisters' work in New York City. The gossip pipeline from the United States to Canada heaped more fodder feeding the beast of dissension. "Sister Agnes while spending her rest time in the U. S. A. heard a rumour from a priest that our Community was shortly undertaking work in New Jersey and that several sisters will be working there," according to minutes from a June 29, 1950, SSJD Mother's Council meeting.

All of this set off a third wave of letters from Toronto to trustees, donors, and stakeholders in the school, as well as a letter to the editor of the *Living Church*, which was published in the subsequent magazine issue. Mother Aquila justified this latest mass mailing "in view of the campaign for funds for the proposed expansion of St. Hilda's School. I wish to make it clear that the work of St. Hilda's school is being carried on independently of the Sisterhood of St. John the Divine." To emphasize how fraught and tenuous the relationship was between the sisters in New York and their Toronto community, a long multi-page letter from the SSJD warden, Rev. Williams, to Bishop Gilbert followed. It reiterated that the nuns' work was independent of the St. John community. One concern for Mother Aquila and the St. John community was the expectation that it would financially support the fledgling school.

Several of the letter's recipients, in an apparent coordinated tac-

---

8. *Living Church*, July 23, 1950.

tic, lobbed their own letters back to Mother Aquila. Trustee Richard Goetze wrote, "Your letter of August 3rd concerning St. Hilda's School, Sister Ruth and Sister Edith Margaret, has told me little which I did not know. The trustees have not and will not make any statement to the effect that they are in any way dependent upon the Sisterhood for aid in their campaign for funds. To the contrary, we have made every effort to keep clear of any such misunderstanding." In defense of the sisters, he added, "The excellent work being done by the two Sisters for the School speaks extremely well for your Sisterhood. The very nature of your position indicates an intelligent and understanding person and there must have been some reason for your writing at this time."

Mother Aquila also wrote to the administrative head of St. Luke's Hospital, Dr. Lloyd H. Gaston, whose response was, "We realize that this project must of its very nature be an independent enterprise, we do feel that it is one to which the Sisterhood may well be proud to have made such a fine contribution even though it be an indirect one."

Canon West's response struck a tone of exasperation with Mother Aquila. "I am somewhat at a loss to understand its purpose," he wrote. "Since Canadian money is not permitted to leave Canada, you obviously don't mean that anyone could have thought a Canadian Sisterhood financially responsible for work in America." It was obvious that Canon West sensed that Mother Aquila was opposed to Sister Ruth's work, because he closed the letter with, "I must confess that, although the Bishop and I have known all along that this work was being carried on as a special project independent of the Order, I have felt a certain sorrow that the Order's good wishes for an incredibly important work in this great city were not better known."

Dr. Wilke's short handwritten note echoed the others but also added the value of the school to the neighborhood and the community. He went another step further and enclosed the original copies of two letters from parents praising the school and the sisters' work as educators. He concluded the letter by stating, "Mr. Goetz, Canon West and myself feel that the time for striking is right now, so we are proceeding."

In spite of a claim Mother Aquila made to Professor Simpson that Sister Ruth did not provide her with any information, according to SSJD Mother's Council minutes, Sister Ruth had sent letters that provided reports to her superior about her life and work in New York. The July 1950 minutes noted that Sister Ruth's letter provided information about the St. Hilda's School $100,000 Capital Campaign and also enclosed the article from the *Living Church*. True, some letters for the most part were cheerful and upbeat without disclosure of the challenges Sister Ruth faced. The terms of exclaustration called for an independent work with no requirement for reports and accountability. During this steamy summer period of postal volley with antagonism on both sides of the US-Canada border, Sister Ruth sought and received Canon West's review and guidance on her letters to Mother Aquila. His review of her letters to SSJD members, some clergy, and even some of the trustees of the school would be a regular practice she would employ in the years to come.

Professor Simpson also received letters from Toronto at this time; however, hers were starkly different from the others who received identical copies of the mass mailing. To Professor Simpson, Mother Aquila wrote, "Remembering our helpful visit together at the beginning of this year, and also your kind offer to be of whatever help you can to us in the future, I am taking you into confidence at this stage of the journey."

She wrote that the *Living Church* article made her "anxious" and she was most aggrieved by the statement that the nursery had been established with "the blessing" of the order. She wrote that she felt "the Community was being used" for the expansion of the school. She implied to Professor Simpson that the two sisters' mission in New York City would likely be a failure, and on March 25, 1951, "the time will have to come for these two Sisters to return to their own Community." She even questioned whether the New York bishops fully understood the reasons the sisters were first granted exclaustration.

"I shall be most grateful for any information or advice you feel able to give me and, of course, it will be held in strict confidence and you will understand that I am writing thus to you because I feel that I can depend on your fullest loyalty to the principles and the best interest of the Religious Life, as well as your desire to be of real help to our Community."

In response Professor Simpson wrote, "So far as I know the article in *the LIVING CHURCH* was written up by the paper from material Sister Ruth prepared in asking for funds. The phrase 'on leave' was used, and I let it pass because I thought the term 'exclaustration' might confuse seculars." She emphasized in her response to the Mother Superior that the school's expedited expansion plan was not Sister Ruth's idea. "The parents virtually forced it on Sister Ruth." Autumn 1950 enrollment "is complete or exceeded," Professor Simpson wrote. "The school fills a great need in this neighborhood." Similar to her fellow trustee members' letters to Mother Aquila, Professor Simpson also praised Sister Ruth: "her courage, endurance and ability are splendid."

Professor Simpson shifted the topic from the school to the emerging community. In the letter, she noted that she was certain the bishops knew Sister Ruth's original reason for returning to New York was to establish an inter-racial religious order. Expressing sympathy and compassion, Professor Simpson wrote, "Sister Ruth's real loneliness is disturbing."

Despite the fact that little mention is provided about establishing a new religious order in public communications about the sisters' work in New York, Sister Ruth was relentlessly focused on recruiting aspiring nuns who would also serve as the school's faculty. Professor Simpson wrote, "from my point of view the great difficulty is in securing adequate teachers. They exist, but not with the religious vocation, and Sister Ruth is intent on having both in the same person. She has been over-optimistic about several attractive young girls who at first showed interest and then dropped off, and at present she is trying to get mature women."

One of the mature women Sister Ruth set her sights on was Professor Simpson. She sent a copy of Sister Ruth's letter to Mother Aquila. In it, Sister Ruth asked Professor Simpson's help locating an eye doctor and a dentist. However, the dominant theme of the letter focused on her aspirational religious community, even a recommendation of a dressmaker for a "new habit."

"I would like your ideas here, for I believe you to belong to the inner circle of our Community and would therefore like you to have a real part in this aspect of its life," she wrote to Professor Simpson about the habit. "A matter that may appear to you to be entirely fantastic, but I think it wants both prayer and careful consideration. Why aren't you a member of our forming Community? Are you being asked to offer your devotion, your maturity, experience and leadership? I think it possible!"

Professor Simpson in reply recommended her dentist and eye doctor. "In regard to my possible vocation with you, I appreciate deeply the honor you do me, and will consult Father Taber, who seems to me the person best able to judge impartially in the matter. I am sorry I do not know any designer or dressmaker."

It was also in this letter that Professor Simpson gives Mother Aquila this assessment of Sister Ruth's first year of exclaustration and efforts to launch a community:

> Things are going well enough, but Sister Ruth is feeling the strain.
>
> And at present she is trying to get mature women. She told me this idea when discussing Maud Johnson, who seems to be working out very well. This is of course an indication of her own need of companionship, which she has admitted to me. But this is the price she has to pay, or part of it.

Maud Johnson, a St. Hilda's teacher, became a prospect for religious life recruitment. For Professor Simpson's part, to avoid giving Sister Ruth an outright rejection, she allowed Father Taber to make the decision for her. She relayed to Sister Ruth that Father Taber felt she was fulfilling her vocation as a college professor and that because of her age and some health considerations, she was not suited for the strict and disciplined life of a nun.

It was apparent that Bishop Donegan, before becoming the diocesan bishop, wasn't engaged with Sister Ruth or the St. Hilda's School. While he was abroad in his homeland of Derbyshire, England, Mother Aquila sent him the same letter she had sent to the others.

When he returned, still six weeks away from his installation as diocesan bishop, Donegan wrote a very abbreviated acknowledgment of appreciation "regarding Sister *Hilda* and Sister Edith Margaret." With Bishop Gilbert's impending retirement, it wouldn't be too much longer before Bishop Donegan would know Sister Ruth's name.

* * *

Bishop Horace W. B. Donegan's 1991 obituary in the *New York Times* described him as "an early church advocate for the rights of blacks, women and the poor," who "transformed [the Episcopal Diocese of New York's] social consciousness."[9] The article also characterized him as especially outspoken on the Episcopal Church's history of racism and segregation in New York and detailed his social justice work. His most divisive act was diverting funds earmarked for the completion of Upper Manhattan's internationally noted religious landmark, the Cathedral of St. John the Divine, toward the construction of housing and other urban development programs for the economically disadvantaged families in Harlem.

Evidently, in Sister Ruth, a Harlem native who endured dire poverty and hardship in secular life and racism in religious life, Bishop Donegan found an opportunity to symbolically right wrongs from the past. This new champion of Sister Ruth transformed her from a victim of racism who had been cast away from her home church and country in pursuit of a calling from God, to an empowered repatriated religious figure who, in short order, would be elevated in ecclesiastical rank back in her home city.

When Bishop Donegan was enthroned in the autumn of 1950, he assumed the chairmanship of St. Hilda's School board of trustees. There was the matter of Sister Ruth's and Sister Edith Margaret's term for exclaustration ending in March 1951. With the school beginning to thrive and Bishop Donegan advocating for the sisters, the St. John's sisters in Toronto, who once again held a Special Chapter

---

9. Joseph Berger, "Bishop H. Donegan, Episcopal Leader, Dies at 91," *New York Times*, November 12, 1991, 34.

vote, granted a two-year extension when they requested it in December with the school in session.

With first grade now added in the autumn of 1950, St. Hilda's was no longer just a nursery school. That first full academic year was a time of accelerated growth for St. Hilda's with Bishop Donegan at the helm of the board. Students continued to be enrolled throughout the school year, including five-year-old Dana Catherine, who was enrolled at its end in May 1951. At first, Dana's mother erroneously assumed that the school was Catholic when she was greeted by Sister Ruth.

"My mother, being a Connecticut WASPY Episcopalian, was very anti-Catholic," Dana said. Like many cradle Episcopalians, she did not associate nuns in habits with her denomination. "Oh my god it's a Catholic school!" Dana mimicked her mother's abhorrence. "I will be polite and then we will just leave."

However, Dana said that during the meeting, which she described as "very intriguing," Sister Ruth sensed her mother's apprehension. "'Of course, dear, you understand we are Episcopal nuns.' My mother was relieved."

Sister Ruth's pledge to mirror British culture and customs in her new community also extended to the school. "It was very British-centric," Dana recalled. "The closets were called cloakrooms." Having Sister Catherine (the name given to Maud Johnson in religious life) as a teacher amplified that aura for young Dana, who also equated the daily chapel attendance as a characteristic of religious primary and secondary schools that Sisters Ruth and Edith Margaret visited while in England. The priests also did their part to foster that culture, by adopting formal customs and high church Episcopal rituals. In a handwritten note from Canon West to Sister Ruth he wrote, "Sister, we must be sure the children are taught either Sarum bows or genuflexion, Dr. Pike is complaining." (Dr. Pike was the cathedral dean.) Formal ritual and customs—especially tied to Anglo-Catholicism—were the preference of both Sister Ruth and Canon West.

As the school showed signs of success, the saboteurs loomed. Mother Aquila was spurred on by more detractors, this time by Vere

Stuart-Alexander, a war widow from England living on Long Island. She wrote to Mother Aquila alarmed that a friend—likely fellow Englishwoman Maud Johnson—intended to "join the SSJD sisters in New York" as a novice. At this point, the SSJD leadership would do more than disassociate the Canadian community from the school. The new tactic was to persuade the recently installed bishop that a new religious order in his diocese would not be a good idea. SSJD warden and religious order superior, the Rev. Williams, was charged with this course of action. But his effort had little effect on Bishop Donegan, who wrote in response to the Rev. Williams's letter, that he would "look favorably" at having a new order in his diocese if the time was right and Sister Ruth requested it.

As the New York warden to the sisters, Canon West "clothed" two religious aspirants into the nascent community in September 1950. Sister Catherine, the St. Hilda's teacher formerly known as Maud Johnson, became the first novice. According to *In Wisdom*, she was from England, "where she had done extensive mission work."[10]

"She wears a very simple habit and cowl, after our design, and unlike that of any other community. Her cross was designed by Canon West," Sister Ruth reported in a letter to the SSJD warden. The other aspirant was a recent Julliard grad named Zoe Euveraard, clothed and named as novice Sister Elise.

Sister Ruth also disclosed in the letter that she enlisted the help of faculty from New York's General Theological Seminary to provide instruction to the novices: Canadian Rev. Cuthbert Simpson (who, a decade later, would become a professor at Oxford University and dean of the cathedral there) and the Rev. C. Kilmer Myers (who would go on to become the Bishop of the Episcopal Diocese of California). Landing the support of these two future leaders was just another example of Ruth's genius for recruiting and connecting with influential and powerful people, stretching back to her secular youth when she hobnobbed with Black society page names and future trailblazers Paul Robeson and Dr. May Chinn.

There was also interest from a Black woman, she wrote. "We have

---

10. The Reverend Mother Ruth, CHS, *In Wisdom Thou Hast Made Them*, 30.

had an entirely unsolicited application from a young coloured nurse in St. Philip's parish to test her vocation at St. Hilda's. We are at present uncertain of the validity of her vocation, but she is under careful spiritual direction at present."

Through her three decades of persistence, Sister Ruth's mission from God, as outlined in her 1935 manifesto, finally had come to fruition. Throughout Ruth's life, she fervently believed it was the Holy Spirit of God who guided her every action and step. She wrote that her "life's work [was] made possible by the way in which the guidance and permission were given by the Holy Spirit of God. So many things might have been different for us in our response to this interior word from the Holy Spirit of God." It was not surprising that she named the Episcopal Church's newest religious order the Community of the Holy Spirit.

BECOMING THE REVEREND MOTHER RUTH, CHS

In the spring of 1952, the three-year-old primary school had an enrollment of 125 students, and CHS had two novices. It was time for Sister Ruth, along with Sister Edith Margaret, to make their formal applications for transfer to their new community. However, nothing ever came easy for the scrappy Harlemite born Ruth Elaine Younger. Even answering the call from God four decades earlier was fraught with barriers and conditions created by others who, ironically, regarded themselves as servants of God. At fifty-four years old, she was a nun who was also a Teachers College doctoral student; a teacher, a headmistress, and a board member of a new primary school; and head recruiter of a fledgling religious community. Through it all, Sister Ruth persevered even as the forces that permitted her to build these new ministries seemed hell-bent on knocking them and her down. Two extreme measures under consideration by Mother Aquila were the revocation of Sister Ruth's and Sister Edith Margaret's exclaustration or releasing them from the community, which would also mean the termination of their vows.

For Sister Ruth, the latter was something she had made impassioned pleas to maintain over the last decade. She appealed to the SSJD warden, the Cambridge, Massachusetts–based Father Williams: "I can't see my way of jeopardizing my vows in Religion in any way. I cannot cut myself adrift from a Religious Community by requesting a release. As you know, my hope is to be allowed a transfer (as there is abundant precedent in the Roman Communion and lately, our own, St. Helena's Sisters here, the Community of the Holy Paraclete in Yorkshire)."

Fortunately, at this juncture, the Rev. Williams's outlook had changed about Sister Ruth and the new community. Two years earlier, he had written to Mother Aquila that he was surprised that Bishop Donegan was amenable to having Sister Ruth start a community, in spite of his "warnings." This June 1952 letter to Mother Aquila was an about-face, as he wrote,

> I can certainly assure you that the new Community has the full approval of Bishop Donegan of New York. My own feeling in this matter, for what it's worth, is that it certainly would be best to give the Sisters permission to be transferred to the new order.... To terminate the period of exclaustration; and request them to return to the Convent in Toronto, I do not think that this course would be of either material or spiritual benefit to the community or to the Sisters themselves.

Back in Toronto, Mother Aquila's argument against granting transference was based on a technicality. "Community of the Holy Spirit wasn't an order—as of April 1952—that actually existed," according to the Mother Council's meeting minutes. After receiving the Rev. Williams's response, the SSJD Mother Superior decided it was time to bring the matter of Sister Ruth and Sister Edith Margaret to the entire community for a vote in a Special Chapter meeting. It was the same process the community followed for Sister Ruth's exclaustration. The SSJD Mother Superior first solicited written opinions from the sisters-in-charge at branch houses in Qu'Appelle and Montréal. One response that came was evident of the lingering rancor targeting Sister Ruth, and the sentiment that she needed to be punished for the perceived "disobedience" and rogue operating methods.

> I think she should be released, not transferred. In regards to Sister Edith Margaret, I think the same, providing she is acting entirely without coercion and is not in any way intimidated. She is, or was, infatuated. That, we can do nothing about. But can we be sure she is not under any force of coercion and fear[?]

The Rev. Williams responded to that long-held rumor that Sister Ruth forced Sister Edith Margaret to join her in New York, that "[he] had no reason to believe Sister Edith Margaret is not happy at the prospect of transference to the new Community."

Another sister wrote to Mother Aquila: "to be easily transferred from our Community to one of their founding, I cannot appreciate as a call from God. They have not been in favour of our Community, but as it appears [are] making use of it. It seems an easy way of fulfilling their own desires."

Pressured by the Rev. Williams's recommendation and the resolute support of Bishop Donegan, the Mother's Council passed a motion supporting a "conditional" transference. Sister Vera, who had long been opposed to Sister Ruth's approach for fulfilling her calling, wanted a clause inserted: "This transfer being conditional upon the proved stability of this new Community." With that stipulation added, transference was voted on and approved by the entire SSJD community. A jubilant Sister Ruth wrote to Canon West on July 27, 1952, "Rev. and dear Father, I know you will rejoice to see the enclosed letter. It looks as if our Canadian anxieties were now forever removed."

The matter did in some respects symbolize a cross-border treaty of warring religious factions. However, the acrimony never quite went away on both sides of the border during the weeks leading up to the service in the Cathedral, when Bishop Donegan officially received the Community of the Holy Spirit into the Episcopal Diocese of New York. Over the years, the opposition to the new community would surface in other ways.

Even months after the vote, SSJD Mother's Council meeting minutes noted, "The Mother said that the Mother of St. Margaret's Sisterhood and other Mothers had spoken to her in Boston about Sister Ruth. They are troubled by the situation and cannot understand Fr. Williams's advice that the Community of the Holy Spirit should be recognized as a regular. A letter from our Visitor (Bishop Broughall) was read to the meeting in which he remarked 'it provokes the fear that those who have been dissatisfied with their home are not the best to form another Community. It is too like separation in a family.'"

Back in New York, it was now all about vows and veils, rings, and invitations. Preparations had begun for the service in the Cathedral, with certain aspects taking on the air of wedding planning. In addition to liturgical rites and prayers, there was the brand-new dress—Sister Ruth's and Sister Edith Margaret's SSJD habits would be returned, and they would be "clothed" in newly designed habits for CHS. There were certain considerations regarding who should be sent invitations. One was extended to Mother Aquila, who, after consultation with the SSJD warden and bishop visitor, declined. Massachusetts-based Father Williams (SSJD's warden) would be the sole representative of the Canadian community.

In Sister Ruth's handwritten draft of a letter to Canon West, she listed categories of people whom she "suggested" for invitations, which included the Cathedral staff, two members of Columbia University's faculty, priests from the Upper East Side parish of St. James', the Madison Avenue parish where Bishop Donegan served for many years, and Fifth Avenue's Heavenly Rest. Under those two notations, she wrote, "I would like to include a Negro Priest, but I think I know your mind in this manner." Then in another phrase that is crossed out, "you will agree with me that we." On page 2, in regard to the "Negro Priest," she wrote, "that should probably wait for a year or two—until our Life and School are fait accompli."

In that same letter, Sister Ruth provided Canon West a proposed daily schedule for the sisters of CHS. Beginning with Salutation at 5:40 a.m., a list with minute-by-minute times for Divine Office, which included Praise, Meditation, and Holy Communion, followed. All were to take place before breakfast. The schedule she envisioned in St. Hilda's convent made allotments for rest time, private prayer, and recreation in half-hour increments, as well as work at St. Hilda's School. That was how CHS's Rule of Life began to take shape. Sister Ruth drew from her SSJD life and "the Rule of the Oxford Mission to Calcutta, an English missionary order in India," according to the book *In Wisdom*.[1] Letters to Canon West indicated that she had also consulted with Father Williams (the SSJD warden who was the Supe-

---

1. The Reverend Mother Ruth, CHS, *In Wisdom Thou Hast Made Them*, 29.

rior for the men's Episcopal order Society of St. John the Evangelist) and Father Lang, the rector of St. Peter's in Westchester Square in the Bronx.

Once Canon West and Bishop Donegan approved the Rule of Life, Constitution, the liturgies, the Office of Profession, and the service for the installation of Sister Ruth as the Superior and Reverend Mother, the date was selected. On August 27, 1952, the Community of the Holy Spirit would be officially established. The date was timed to Bishop Donegan's return from his annual trip home to England and just before the beginning of St. Hilda's school year.

Along with those who received special invitations, the St. Hilda's School parents, friends, and members of other communities gathered for the liturgy in St. Ansgar's Chapel in the Cathedral of St. John the Divine. The opening words to the service and antiphon for the Introit came from Psalm 27, "Behold the Bridegroom Cometh: Go ye out to Meet Him." For Sisters Ruth and Edith Margaret, the rite was a renewal of vows; with the SSJD warden, Father Williams, formally providing consent to allow for them to transfer to the Community of the Holy Spirit. For Sisters Catherine and Elise, they were taking their vows of life profession: the trifecta of religious life, poverty, chastity, and obedience. Bishop Donegan, calling the women "his daughters," placed a ring on each woman's fourth finger of her right hand, and recited a blessing that began, "Receive this Ring as the token of perpetual fidelity to Him, who is the Bridegroom of the Whole Church."

The bishop took the hand of each of the sisters in a symbolic gesture of admitting them and the Community of the Holy Spirit into the church. A second ceremony began that elevated Ruth, her installation as "the Reverend Mother." Canon West, as the warden of the Community of the Holy Spirit, presented Ruth as "Mother-elect" to Bishop Donegan. She kneeled in front of Bishop Donegan. Of the three verses of prayer he recited to her, one phrase stood out: "Take thou authority to rule over this Community." And as the Reverend Mother Superior, Ruth vowed to do so. For she had ascended to the very pinnacle of what a woman could attain in the Episcopal Church at that time.

Throughout the United States, there were many Black rectors and priests leading Colored Episcopal Missions and all-Black parishes. On August 27, 1952, this new Reverend Mother Superior likely became the first person of color of either sex to become a leader and an authority figure over an entirely White congregation. She not only overcame racial segregation; Reverend Mother Ruth managed to gain and wield power over those born into the dominant class who shared the racial identity of her oppressors.

Apparently in 1952, the founding of a new religious order was considered newsworthy. Stories about the service at the Cathedral and photos of the newly christened Reverend Mother Ruth appeared in the *New York Times* and the *Wall Street Journal*, as well as church publications and newspapers nationwide and even in Canada. A returning narrative of obscurity of origins and background was documented in the press, as the Reverend Mother Ruth was described "as from Canada." This perception would be perpetuated in years to come. Nonetheless, that news coverage, and others over the early years, were critical components in the CHS's vocation recruitment strategy. The other key tactic that the Reverend Mother Ruth took on reluctantly was traveling across the nation to visit Episcopal parishes and Episcopal campus ministries in an effort to reach young women to become aspirants and novices in the new community.

In a 1953 letter to Canon West, she attempted to sway him when she wrote, "It has just occurred to me that it would be infinitely more valuable to us in our efforts to develop our Community if you went across the country instead of me." She went on to compare Canon West to the Church of England priest the Rev. John Mason Neale, who, one hundred years earlier, co-founded the Society of St. Margaret, the Anglican order for women, with two branch houses in the United States. "Please say you will go!" the Reverend Mother pleaded with Canon West.

As an acclaimed iconographer and designer of ecclesiastical sanctuary interiors, Canon West maintained his own busy travel schedule, both nationally and internationally. He often plugged the new Community of the Holy Spirit and even solicited offerings and donations for both the school and convent during his speaking engagements. When it came to a direct recruitment campaign, he instructed Mother Ruth to take on that responsibility. In the first few years of CHS's founding, the Reverend Mother Ruth toured the nation. At the parishes and universities she visited, the Reverend Mother Ruth lectured and conducted retreats in hopes of eliciting interest in religious life. Press releases were issued from parish and diocesan communication offices to local newspapers in the major cities where she visited. Her visits were covered in the religion columns of the *Minneapolis Tribune* and the *St. Paul Dispatch* in Minnesota; the Fort Worth *Star-Telegram* in Texas; and the *Bremerton Sun* in Washington State, along with many others.

What was striking about many of the press releases was the occasional error that she was a Canadian by birth. She was also referred to in one parish newsletter in Oregon as "one of the American Church's outstanding personalities" and "one of the leading educators in the Episcopal Church." After Mother Ruth's arrival, the Rev. C. T. Abbott, rector of Calvary Episcopal Church in Oregon, wrote, "The Reverend Mother is a woman of great spiritual depth and I do hope that you will have a chance to meet her. She is interested mainly in meeting women and older girls who may be interested in religious life as a vocation." That same rector offered to write letters to the area high school principals asking for permission for girls to be excused from classes to hear the Reverend Mother Ruth.

The days and weeks following Mother Ruth's tours would yield a few inquiries from women interested in visiting the convent. The first visit was often followed up with a letter exchange, conversation with the aspirants' clergy, and finally a review by Canon West as warden. This was one of the many areas where he gave final approval of the CHS's and Mother Ruth's decisions. In 1956 he wrote, "I quite agree that Katherine H. should try her vocation. I assume if Elizabeth H. comes to us she will have to go to school immediately. . . . June E, sounds excellent—the right age; the right interests; and on top of that, the right education."

As the St. John's sisterhood provided a college education to Ruth so she could teach in their parochial schools, Mother Ruth was compelled to send CHS novices to college so they could teach at St.

Hilda's. Early on, most of the women who lacked teaching credentials were sent to neighboring Teachers College at Columbia. For Elizabeth H., Canon West asked, "is there any chance of her parish assisting [in] any way in the rather prodigious expense which all this will entail for probably the next six years?"

Elizabeth H. was not among the women who entered the novitiate. In the first three years of CHS's existence, only six sisters lived in the community. While there were many visits to St. Hilda's convent by young women documented in letters between Mother Ruth, Canon West, and Bishop Donegan, the rate of conversions to novices and postulants was extremely low initially. That was a minor and temporary challenge. The recruitment troubles paled in comparison with the most imposing challenge to test Mother Ruth since her quasi-trial in Toronto, when she fought for exclaustration and the preservation of her religious vows.

The woman now known as the Reverend Mother Ruth was about to come under intense fire by the very people who were instrumental in opening the school, which laid the groundwork for CHS's founding. With a familiar echo of charges that were lobbed against her in Canada, the Reverend Mother Ruth's integrity, truthfulness, psychological stability, and leadership would be called into question.

CONFIDENTIAL

It is with profound regret that we find it necessary to inform you that several of the most active members of the Board of Trustees of St. Hilda's School have come to the conclusion that the Headmistress of the School has not adequately demonstrated her fitness for the office she holds. This conclusion has not been reached in haste or pique, but represents the earnest efforts of over a year's length to establish with the Headmistress a good working relationship. All such efforts have proven to be fruitless.

The present situation is one wherein the success of the School is the issue.

And so began a six-and-a-half-page report discovered in Bishop Donegan's files from 1953 in the archives of the Episcopal Diocese of New York.

Mother Ruth, for her part, thought the school was in good shape in 1953. That year, Mother Ruth recounted in a letter, rich and vibrant in detail, a meeting she had with a very appreciative parent, an engineer with the Atomic Energy Commission. He had to withdraw his children from St. Hilda's School because of a job transfer to New London, Connecticut. The headmistress's pride in this family was evident as she relayed to Canon West an accounting from the father of the four-year-old's new prayer life learned at the school. The parent also expressed his disappointment that his children would not be able to complete their primary school education there and mentioned his intentions to write a letter of gratitude to Bishop Donegan. After painting a detailed portrait of this family, the Reverend Mother saved the final detail for last. Like adorning a cherry on top, she concluded the letter, "This is a colored family from the lower fringe of Harlem (125th Street) that attends the Chapel of the Intercession, where the children go to Sunday School. I thought you would like me to tell you about this" (125th Street was one of the Younger family addresses during Ruth's childhood).

By the summer of 1953, things began getting hot around the collar for some of the clergy, businessmen, and the Reverend Mother. An opening salvo began with Mother Ruth signing a $1,500 advertising campaign contract without the knowledge or approval of the trustees. Alden Whitman, a copy editor for the *New York Times* who was also notorious for his high-visibility work and membership in the Communist Party, reached out to Bishop Donegan months before the "confidential" report to express his concerns over the brewing tempest.

Dear Bishop Donegan,

I was glad to learn from your note of your hope that the problems of St. Hilda's School will be discussed again this fall, and perhaps solved. . . .

. . . It is regrettable, for the good name of the school, that there should have arisen a situation in which the trustees felt obliged to disavow Mother Ruth's signature to a contract. This is especially the case, since it could have been so easily avoided had there been communication between Mother Ruth and others who are responsible for the school.

I am a parent of two children in the school as well as a trustee, and I am therefore doubly anxious to work out a solution to our school's problems. It is obvious to me that unless Mother Ruth and the trustees can regain confidence in each other the victims are going to be the children.

> *Faithfully Yours,*
> *Alden Whitman*

Bishop Donegan initially planned to meet with a few of the trustees who were most aggrieved in mid-October. When Alden learned of the meeting, he raised "vehement objections" on two grounds. First, "To delay until Oct. 17 is not to solve the school's problems but only to intensify them. Now that school has opened it is apparent that the core of the Trustees' complaint—noncooperation by the Headmistress—has in fact grown worse."

Alden also opposed excluding others on the executive committee, including himself. He wrote that the lack of representation of trustees who have children enrolled in St. Hilda's was also problematic:

Our interest in solving its problems is, therefore, doubly urgent. . . . Those of us who are active Trustees and those of us who have children in the school want to see positive action taken without delay to clear up what is clearly an impossible school administrative problem, the harmful results of which are reflected most directly as you must know, on the children in the school.

Bishop Donegan acquiesced to Alden's protest and decided to meet with just Mother Ruth and Dr. Wilke. He wrote to Alden,

It is quite clear that the present misunderstandings can be resolved by having a good set of By-Laws defining the duties of each of the Committees and persons concerned. Mr. Edward R. Finch has taken the matter up during the summer with a management consultant and I have now a proper organization chart to present to Mother Ruth and Dr. Wilke. If we can come to an agreement on this then the proper procedure is for the Trustees to accept the reorganization plan with such changes as they may wish to make and for all concerned thereafter to abide by it. In your letter you state yourself that the trouble is really an "administrative problem," and it seems to me that the solution I suggest is a sound one.

Edward Finch Jr., a founding school board member, was a progeny of one of New York's most aristocratic Upper East Side Episcopal church families. The family were members of St. Bartholomew Church, and his father, Edward Sr., was an exalted judge "whose career of making and interpreting the laws of New York extended from the horse-and-buggy era to modern times," according to his September 16, 1965, obituary in the *New York Times*. As his legacy, Edward Jr., a partner in his father's law firm and a heroic World War II army officer, occupied an elevated status in New York society and the Episcopal Church.

Mother Ruth, who had been using a different attorney for the convent's business, was opposed to Edward's role as attorney for the school. Instead of approaching Bishop Donegan, she took her complaints to Canon West about these powerful White men. She wrote in April, "We have not appointed Mr. Finch our attorney. Until now, Spencer Byard of Davis, Polk, Wardwell, Sunderland & Kiendl has acted as our legal advisor, without charge (except costs)."

Earlier, Mother Ruth had taken exception to a letter she received from Mr. Finch that notified her of his submission of an application for a provisional charter with the New York State Department of Education. Finch named Dr. Wilke (board chairman) and recently appointed trustee and vice chairman Mitchell B. Carroll (a well-known attorney specializing in tax and financial law) as "the persons legally responsible for the School." During St. Hilda's early days, Dr. Wilke, head of pediatrics at St. Luke's Hospital, was often credited with the founding of and vision for the school. During the school's first year, St. Hilda's School was referred to as Wilke Tech, after all. It was his idea to form an Executive Committee and select the members among the trustees. A school brochure drafted by Alden further raised Mother Ruth's ire when he wrote that "the Community of the Holy Spirit was responsible for the School under the direction of a Board of Trustees." She wanted "under the direction" replaced with "in association with."

"We are not paid employees of a Board of Trustees who dictate policy for the Sisters to carry out," she wrote to Canon West. "I do not want to have unpleasant or strained relations with any of my associate Trustees but I think these mature men, many of whom are quite new on our Board, would want to give our relationships more care and fairer consideration."

Throughout the upheaval of 1953, Mother Ruth couched the conflict as an "us against them," including the four professed CHS sisters in the dispute, whereas the aggrieved trustees viewed Mother Ruth as the sole source of the dissension and problems.

By the time the Reverend Mother received the bylaws from Bishop Donegan, she complained to Canon West about them and other decisions, such as appointing an accountant, whom she felt she was losing control over:

> All the Professed [sisters] have worked over them very carefully. To us the By Laws reveal unequivocally that at least Mr. Finch has no serious notion of what we are trying to do at St. Hilda's. We are very eager that a secular Accountant, who however expert may be, is a stranger to our point of view and way of working, will not be allowed to divide the authority of the School into financial on the one hand, and the educational on the other. Dualism can ruin us. But if our nominee for Treasurer takes over, even that can be overruled.
>
> I am most concerned about my point VII which states the raison d'être of the School and at least mentions that there is a

Religious Community responsible for it. I couldn't care less who is credited with its foundation!

Things did not improve. Shortly before the December meeting, the six-and-a-half-page confidential letter was sent. These trustees maintained it wasn't a communication or administrative problem that plagued the school. The report zeroed in on Mother Ruth's interpersonal relationships, personality, and mental state:

> We could indulge in generalities to characterize our unfortunate relationship with the Headmistress: mention might be made of her inability to confer in a friendly spirit, of her lack of common courtesy in her relations with members of the Board, her attempts to discredit the character of members of the Board, and her apparent psychological inconsistency in matters of truth.
>
> You will grant that these are generalities not to be taken lightly. Our lack of confidence in the Headmistress is the consequence of a long history of individual incidents whose sum has had a great cumulative effect.

Fifteen short anecdotes of parents and trustee experiences were listed. The most serious charge reported by trustees and parents was "the employment of corporal punishment in disciplining children. This takes the form of slapping, ear-pulling, and similar acts not in keeping with the announced program of the school." Other complaints lodged by trustees and parents were about the qualifications of the faculty, because some students were not performing at grade level. A few examples of questionable spending practices and school finances were also raised. And the final complaint, rounding out the long list: "In addition to the Board members, officers of the Parents Association and benefactors of the School, the Headmistress has unfortunately and unnecessarily irritated a number of influential persons associated with important civic, educational, and religious organizations in Morningside Heights."

The report offered two proposed solutions:

(1) To transfer the present Headmistress to another post outside the School and name another member of the Community of the Holy Spirit, or another person as acting Headmistress. Perhaps a leave of absence for reasons of health, study or other purposes would be possible for the present incumbent; or

(2) To disband the School and sell the property if no other solution appears likely. Because there is what appears ample evidence as to the psychological instability of the Headmistress, we urge that this matter be treated most confidentially. There exists a very real fear on the part of members of the Board and others associated with the School, as both friends of the School and as parents of children in the School, that the attitude of the Headmistress toward their children in the event of a disclosure of the information supplied in this letter would be highly deleterious. Their insistence that this matter be called to your attention is in itself an example of their loss of confidence in the Headmistress to the extent that they consider her capable of petty vengeance.

In ensuing years, "petty vengeance" and retaliation would become a feared trait of the Reverend Mother. Some were convinced she was enabled by her two White saviors, Bishop Donegan and Canon West.

Much of Ruth's life from the late 1800s through the early mid-twentieth century was reconstructed through historical documents. Some of the most damning evidence of the Reverend Mother's many controversies were not uncovered in the convent archives, but the Diocese of New York's extensive archival library located in the Synod House adjacent to the Cathedral Church of St. John the Divine. Unlike SSJD's detailed transcript of Ruth's fight in Canada, the paper trail depicting this New York City scrap with these powerful White men came to an abrupt end. However, it was evident the Reverend Mother emerged victorious. The people causing her the most trouble just disappeared—as happened in this case and in many other instances described by witnesses in later decades. By 1954, there were major changes made to the school's board of trustees. The names of Frederick Wilke, Richard B. Geotze, Alden Whitman, and Mitchell B.

Carroll disappeared from the board of trustees list on the school's letterhead. New names that replaced them were banker Julian Bond (treasurer), Philip F. Robb A. B. (secretary), and most notably, CHS Sister Catherine and the Reverend Mother Ruth. Although she was the headmistress, she was initially not listed as a member of the board of trustees.

The Reverend Mother survived this round of a no-confidence campaign. Though it would not be the last of her fights; more was to come. And always waiting in the wings to rescue her were Canon West and Bishop Donegan.

13

A DREAM DEFERRED OR MISSION ABORTED

In the midst of the tempest with the board of trustees, a Canadian clipper bore down on the Reverend Mother Ruth by way of a letter that cut her to the quick. On October 1, 1953, Sister Lois of SSJD wrote to the woman she still referred to as "Sister Ruth" with birthday greetings, an admonishment, and an olive branch. She wrote,

> I cannot agree with the methods you used to set up the new Community and I am entirely unchanged in regard to its animus. . . . I have felt deeply that there was a breach between us. And now I only want you to know one thing more—whatever agreements or disagreements there may be between us—there is no uncharity in me towards you. All that I want is that you know you are my beloved Sister. Every June I think of your little sister who died from steam scalding on a picnic and there are your great days, always remembered.

> God keep you and bless you, my beloved Sister.

An unnerved Mother Ruth received the letter as an offensive volley. Her first attempt at a response was defensive. She wrote,

> Your letter leaves me puzzled in view of many facts about the past. I prefer, however, to consider the whole matter an entirely closed issue. . . . Who am I to judge you or you judge me? I do not entirely regret the S. S. J. D. experiences of recent years . . . the almost total misunderstandings and the sad misrepresen-

tations were wounding almost to death, and yet there has been the Easter Dawn, and a new day. I hold nothing, absolutely nothing against anyone, nor have I an atom of bitterness in my soul about any of it, however regrettable. Who knows whether it will be you or I that will be called first "to give an account of the things that we have done in the body." May "our faces" not be ashamed before Him in that hour!

Before mailing the letter, Mother Ruth sent it to Canon West and asked for his review. She recognized that the letter was triggering. She wrote, "Father, is this too icy and self righteous? I haven't sent this original yet, for as I read it over it chills me! And yet this icyness has made the courage to go on possible—You understand? Were I sentimental, pious or full of 'feelings' it could all fall apart even now. Your daughter in OBL, Ruth, CHS." Below that handwritten note in black ink, in a red pencil—one that a teacher might have used to grade a paper—there was a postscript. "Please let me know what you think—please return this correspondence. R. CHS."

His answer: "My dear and Reverend Mother, This sounds too much like St. Paul in Galatians. I suggest the Philippians' style. Since it is all in the past, it is better to reflect on the whole matter (in writing) with gratitude, affection and pleasure. EW."

Her second draft did just that. She called her years with SSJD in Canada "an enormous privilege" that prepared her "for the work to which GOD has called me from the beginning." She went on to write, "the opportunities for growth I shall always remember with deepest thanksgiving; they were also blessings of the most treasured kind . . . I have nought but joy and pleasure in recollecting."

Mother Ruth sent a carbon copy to Canon West, asking, "Does this do it?" He wrote at the top of the letter in large cursive script: "It does superbly!" Unbeknownst to many who knew Mother Ruth, she did experience extreme bouts of vulnerability, which were only revealed in the letters she wrote to her clergy, her confessors, wardens, and those she considered friends. When Mother Ruth applied for the Community of the Holy Spirit to have membership in the association of Anglican religious orders in the United States, the superiors of the other orders kept her out by imposing newly created stipulations. A very dejected Mother Ruth complained to Canon West in a letter about these "made-up" requirements after another rejection by the group. She wrote, "I am accepted, but I may be wrong here, but unacceptable."

The Reverend Mother continued her recruitment tours across the nation to places like Peoria, Illinois; Ames, Iowa; New Orleans; San Antonio, Texas; Bozeman, Montana; Los Angeles and San Diego. By 1955, she had appointed Sister Catherine (formerly Maud Johnson from Yorkshire, England) to take on the parish and university recruitment circuit. That left Sisters Edith Margaret, Catherine, and Elise; a newly professed Sister Hilary (formerly Edna May McGuire); and a novice, Elizabeth Daly (clothed and now Sister Francesca). Sister Elise was charged with reporting to Mother Ruth during her travels on activities in the convent and the school. Sister Elise, a World War II navy veteran, mailed detailed reports to the Reverend Mother. One such correspondence was a report on a Black mother interested in enrolling her daughter at St. Hilda's.

Yesterday, a Mrs. Brown came to see about registering her child. They are very black, although good looking and West Indian, I would guess. The child is five but will be six in April. The mother had hopes of registering her in Kindergarten but I said we were unable to accept another kindergarten child (registration is now at 21) and also they live out of our district, etc. The mother then asked about the possibility of Grade I. I said it would not be advisable to enroll her as a beginning pupil in Grade I so late in the year. Then she told me that she had been sent here by Father Temple of the Church of the Crucifixion, who had already discussed this with you, and that you had said for her to come and register the child. Now I am under the impression that you did not wish any more colored children. The outcome was that I told Mrs. Brown that Carol would be put on our waiting list, and that we would call her if a vacancy occurred.

What was most galling about Sister Elise's letter was the uninhibited racist overtones in the description of the family. It was permissive language that the Reverend Mother from Harlem obviously condoned. This was not the first or the last time that a quota on Black students would be revealed. And if racial quotas existed in the school, it was easy to conclude one might have existed for the convent.

Reverend Mother's speaking tours proved to be successful because by the latter half of the 1950s, there was a surge of aspirants visiting the new sisterhood. In 1957, at least eight novices were living in the two adjoining brownstones that housed both the school and the convent. Whether it was a dream deferred or a mission aborted, not a single one of those women identified as Black. Five years after the establishment of CHS, the realization of Ruth's multiracial monastic order described in her 1935 manifesto had yet to be manifested. Although there were no women of color in CHS's novitiate, correspondence and several former sisters reported that at least two Black women came for extended visits as aspirants.

Mother Ruth appeared fixated on luring women from the parishes and universities she had visited on her tour across the country. She tapped a pool of women who were White, educated, and from affluent parishes.

In June of 1957, Elizabeth Winston Pettus (now Elizabeth Losa) came to St. Hilda's convent with the belief she had a calling. More than six decades later, as a married woman living in Peabody, Massachusetts, Elizabeth remembered she was enthusiastically welcomed into St. Hilda's convent.

"When I walked in, I realized I had no vocation to this life. I realized this was a mistake." However, Mother Ruth convinced Elizabeth to stay in the CHS novitiate. Elizabeth stayed for two years. For Mother Ruth's budding community, novice Elizabeth was the perfect package. She already had her teacher's education, which meant the community would not have to pay tuition to prepare her for work at St. Hilda's School as they had done for other novices.

"I and my twin sister (in the novitiate) were the first two sisters they got there who were trained teachers before we went in," Elizabeth said. "They needed us."

In turn, she thought St. Hilda's School would offer her a better teaching experience. "I was two years out of college and I was having a hard time teaching," Elizabeth said. "I thought I would join a religious order. I thought maybe I would have less trouble teaching as a nun."

Known as Betsy Win to her family, she described herself as a young "showoff with a pious attitude." The daughter of an Episcopal priest, Elizabeth said, "my letters home were a picture of a woman/child trying to force herself and prove to both herself and her parents that she might have a vocation."

Elizabeth's mother retained all the letters she wrote from the convent between 1957 and 1959. More than sixty years later, Elizabeth offered the letters as a glimpse into convent life. She was, however, quick to point out that her letters had been screened by Mother Ruth and the novice mistress, Sister Catherine, before being mailed. In the Rule of Life written by Mother Ruth, it states,

> The private life of the Community may never be discussed in letters, nor subject of discontent be mentioned. Novitiate letters must be left unsealed in the designated mailing place at the Mother's Convent Office door. No letter nor message may be received into or sent from the House without having first been brought to the Mother or her representative. The Mother may forbid any correspondence which in her judgment appears injurious to the life of a Sister or Novice.

"We weren't supposed to write anything too detailed or personal about our lives in the convent."

In an August 7, 1957, letter, she wrote to her parents that convent life "is like learning a foreign language while living in a foreign country, this religious life. The thought terrain is so unfamiliar." She did not share the reservations she was having about becoming a nun to her parents. "I put a good face on everything to my family."

Reflecting back on that time, Elizabeth said, "I was trying to be the best nun outwardly that I could be. I was very pious." Over the two years, Elizabeth fought her own doubts about her vocation. Sensing Elizabeth's apprehension, Mother Ruth executed a strategy meant to provide the novice a fulfilled, happy existence as a nun.

The Reverend Mother valued, both for herself and the women in the community, an abundance of intellectual, cultural, and artistic sustenance. "The plays, lectures, and other events to which she sent me were phenomenal," Elizabeth recalled. As she flipped through the boxes of letters, Elizabeth sifted through playbills and opera and concert programs enclosed in the envelopes. Another quality the Reverend Mother placed a high premium on was the sisters' physical appearance. An unexpected fringe benefit for Elizabeth was regular appointments with an aesthetician. Mother Ruth sent Elizabeth, who had hairs on her chin, for electrolysis treatments. At some point, the treatments were abruptly halted. Elizabeth suspected that Canon West or Bishop Donegan might have questioned the sessions' exorbitant expense laid out for a superficial problem by a community avowed to a life of poverty.

Despite the Reverend Mother's benevolence toward Elizabeth, she said she was well aware of her dark side and wasn't entirely shielded from Mother Ruth's wrath. An incident she clearly remembered as emblematic of the Reverend Mother's callous nature involved one of the sisters who was later found to be terminally ill.

> While I was there, a Sister, Francesca, who evidently her lay name was also Elizabeth, got very, very sick and began screaming and yelling. She was professed. She was the youngest professed. As she was screaming and yelling, Reverend Mother said, "don't you wish you could put them over your knee and spank them. But then that is not allowed by the Rule." I heard years later that Sister Francesca shortly after that died of a brain tumor.

Still, Elizabeth was among the favored. And some of the encounters she recalled with the Reverend Mother indicated that. "I was coming down the stairs and she was going up. She was in a hurry. She gave me a soft, feathery, powdery kiss. It took me by surprise and I was a little bit shocked. I wondered if she should be doing this."

Fear of losing a novice with the right educational background, the Reverend Mother did something else that seemed out of character to Elizabeth. "During the Great Silence," the quiet period in monastic life after the final evening prayers when talking was forbidden, "I went to knock on her door. She had said to me, 'you can see me anytime you want.' This was an extraordinary statement." Typically, postulants and novices did not interact with the Mother, only with the "Novice Mistress." Elizabeth had hoped to discuss her unrelenting dreams about leaving the convent. When the opportunity to have a private conversation with the Reverend Mother occurred, Elizabeth said, "we ended up talking about my angst, but not about my leaving."

Mother Ruth then decided that Elizabeth should have a psychiatric evaluation and help. "I was to go over to the cathedral and meet with a Dr. Taylor. It turned out that Dr. Taylor vetted the people who were going for the ministry to be priests to see if they really had a vocation. That was what his position was at that point. We had three meetings." During those sessions, Elizabeth came to the conclusion that she could not take vows of life profession and had to leave. She hoped to discuss this with Mother Ruth and made several attempts to set up a meeting. Unbeknownst to Elizabeth, the Reverend Mother also received that very report from Dr. Taylor, as she had for other novices and sisters she had referred to the psychiatrist. Instead of making herself available to talk, the Reverend Mother avoided her.

"She was too busy to see me," Elizabeth recalled. "This was the contradictory nature of the woman." Sister Catherine, the novice mistress, made excuses for the Reverend Mother's failure to respond to Elizabeth's multiple requests for a meeting. Months later, long after the end of her sessions with Dr. Taylor, Elizabeth found herself in a face-to-face encounter with Mother Ruth.

Mother Ruth came to the door to say good-bye to Elizabeth and other sisters who were departing for a trip to the country for rest time. "I looked at her with tears streaming down my face, because I realized she wasn't going to talk to me." Elizabeth walked out the door and joined her sisters in a waiting taxicab. Still shaken and upset that Mother Ruth ignored her, when the cab stopped at a traffic light, Elizabeth jumped out. She walked down Broadway as her perplexed sisters cried out in shock after her. It was the beginning of her act of rebellion that would lead to her liberation. "This was a major disobedience," Elizabeth recalled. She was deeply hurt and wanted to have the conversation with Mother Ruth about the decision she made for herself. Elizabeth eventually made it back to the convent, although not before stopping by one of the Episcopal parishes along the way to call the convent to see if she would be allowed to return.

Once back in the brownstone, Elizabeth said, "I waited for her and waited. She finally would see me. And the first words out of her mouth were, 'we've known for some time that you have no vocation.'"

This further upset Elizabeth. "She wouldn't let me say it. She said it. She had to say it. What I had done, when I got out of the cab, I was saying to myself, I'm not going until I have talked to her. But I never did get to talk to her." That afternoon, the Reverend Mother sent her back to her cell and kept her isolated there. In a final authoritarian act she imposed on Elizabeth, Mother Ruth contacted Elizabeth's family to make the arrangements to have her picked up from St. Hilda's convent.

Mother Ruth, for her part, likely felt she was acting within her authority as outlined by CHS's Rule of Life. "The Sisters may never leave the Convent without the Mother's knowledge and permission."

Sixty years after that encounter, Elizabeth said, "I'm mad at myself now that I didn't break in and say, 'Why didn't you let me say that?' She needed to be an authoritarian."

The interviews with Elizabeth Losa occurred first via emails and then face-to-face in her apartment at the sprawling retirement community where she lived in Peabody, Massachusetts. It was over dinner on my first night in Peabody in her development's formal dining room—my voice recorder and notebook then absent—she railed against Mother Ruth's failure to acknowledge her agency.

After I returned to New York from Massachusetts, Elizabeth sent a follow up email: "I worried because some (but not all) of my encounters with the Rev. Mother cast her in a dictatorial light but her role encouraged that part of her personality; basically she was a loving and hard-working woman."

Many of the current and former sisters who came into CHS talked of experiencing the dichotomous nature of Mother Ruth's personality, which led to conflicting feelings—both loving and loathing her. Another young woman who entered the novitiate during the same period as Elizabeth was J. T. Baumet. She credited Mother Ruth for her "happy life" after she was driven away from CHS by her "meanness."

J. T., who became Sister Joan Theresa, completed the novitiate and took the vows of life profession three years later. Before her entry to the convent as a postulant, J. T. came to know Mother Ruth as a child at a diocese summer camp where the CHS sisters worked. "She was strange to me," J. T. said was her initial reaction to the Reverend Mother. "I had never seen a nun before."

Later, as an older teenager, J. T. was given a part-time job at St. Hilda's School. "I let the kids in the door before school, so the sisters would not be disturbed during the morning office and breakfast. I would return for nap-time and I sat with the sleeping children."

Similar to Ruth Elaine Younger, J. T. had a youth and childhood riddled with hardship. "My mother was a suicidal alcoholic and I never knew whether she would be alive or dead when I got home from school. So, I quit school to be home to take care of her. Indeed, I talked her off the roof once."

Perhaps the Reverend Mother felt an affinity for the teenaged J. T. because of her own troubled family life and a mother who wanted her at home to support her instead of following her calling to become a nun. J. T. credited Mother Ruth for changing the course of her life and helping her achieve what she sacrificed while caring for her alcoholic mother. "The Reverend Mother gave me my high school education, my college education and made me a teacher," she said. After J. T. earned her high school diploma, Mother Ruth sent her to Western Connecticut University in Danbury, and she completed her degree at Fordham University at Lincoln Center.

As life-professed Sister Joan Theresa, she would have a lot more contact with the Reverend Mother. And in short order, she found life under Mother Ruth's rule as traumatic as her childhood home:

My biggest memory was just the constant meanness. We would have daily conferences. If someone had done something wrong, she would rant and rave at the person in front of everyone. There was only one opinion—hers. There was one time I was lambasted by Reverend Mother over a very long period of time, perhaps over a month. It was extremely stressful. As stressful as it was, I don't remember what the cause was.

One year after being life-professed, Sister Joan Theresa left CHS and returned to being J. T. Baumet. "In spite of life inside of CHS, my life since has been great. I owe her a great deal."

1957 was a banner year if press clippings alone were the measuring stick. For the third time in five years, Mother Ruth's photo would grace the (Sunday) *New York Times*. The headline, "School Unites Races and Faiths Under Episcopalian Sister Here," of the January 13, 1957, article, which described Mother Ruth as "neat and petite," proclaimed, "Mother Ruth in Seven Years Attains Goal She Set in Founding St. Hilda's."[1] That article was followed in August with a photo spread in the national magazine *Look*. Mother Ruth was portrayed as the visionary of St. Hilda's School with "children of many faiths and races."[2] The *Look* photo essay had twelve images mainly with brief text and two paragraphs about a loving and joyful Mother Ruth. The longer text described her as a hands-on educator who preferred time spent with children over her administrative duties. Most of the copy was descriptive phrases of each photo.

Children Love Mother Ruth was the caption of a photo of children jauntily following behind her as they exited the front doors of the school. The photo spread depicted the playful Mother Ruth, on a basketball court refereeing a game for a group of boys from the school; the contemplative Mother Ruth, walking in Central Park, extolling the virtues of quiet meditation; and a three-picture mon-

---

1. Stanley Rowland Jr., "School Unites Races and Faiths Under Episcopalian Sister Here," *New York Times*, January 13, 1957.

2. Ernest Dunbar, "Mother Ruth's Children," *Look*, August 8, 1987.

tage of the educator Mother Ruth that quoted her telling students to become "friends" with their books. There was one headline-grabbing nugget, that probably best captured the publicity strategy behind the magazine article. A solitary photo of Headmistress Mother Ruth in the school was captioned, *After the staff tea, she reflects on the school's future and how $3,000,000 might be raised to build a new St. Hilda's.*[3]

As the school ended its first full decade after its founding, the adjoining brownstones on 113th Street reached capacity as enrollment grew. The school trustees had even purchased a third brownstone to accommodate the increasing enrollment and the growing community of nuns that the buildings also housed. Then a fourth building was acquired on Riverside Drive, which was given the name St. Hugh's Charterhouse, after a nineteenth-century monastery in West Sussex, England. One of the many Roman Catholic saints also venerated in the Anglican Communion, St. Hugh is the patron of the sick, cobblers, swans, and the Roman Catholic Diocese of Nottingham, England. Charterhouse became known as the "Upper School" for the junior and senior high school grades.

By the end of the 1950s and into the 1960s, the reputation of Mother Ruth, in tandem with the school, had also grown in prestige. Her Teachers College dissertation, a study on the educational performance of religious schools, widened her collegial circle of religious school educators. In particular, CHS had built a partnership with the Roman Catholic Sisters of Notre Dame de Namur, at the time a 150-year-old teaching order. The Reverend Mother, who now dispatched Sister Elise and other sisters for recruitment tours, entered a new international lecture circuit in Europe. Both the diocese and Columbia University issued press releases announcing a four-stop speaking tour at Oxford and Leeds universities, King's College of the University of London, and the Ecumenical Institute in Geneva, Switzerland.

Media attention on the Reverend Mother, the community, and school also continued. Betsy Deekens, the women's editor of a na-

---

3. Dunbar, "Mother Ruth's Children."

tional biweekly magazine called the *Episcopal Churchnews*, wrote in a 1957 letter to Mother Ruth, "It seems to me that you are making quite a contribution in the field of education, one that our readers would like to know about." She cited Mother Ruth's national study of religious schools as evidence of her heightened prominence. A likely proud moment for the Reverend Mother was an invitation to return to England to speak at a university conference on schools run by religious orders.

"She was so progressive as a teacher back then," recalled Dana Catharine, whose Connecticut-born mother had mistaken the SSJD Sister Ruth for a Catholic nun. "I was in sixth grade in 1956 and 1957, when rock and roll really hit. Mother Ruth used to let us dance to it in the cafeteria. That was amazing when you think about how many adults reacted to rock and roll as the music of the devil at that time. But she let us dance to it."

Yet and still, ever the fervent Anglophile, Mother Ruth liked to project the school's image as an elite, high-toned British private school. The lay teachers were even required to wear black academic gowns while working at the school. Because of that, Dana said years later, "I used to tell people I went to Hogwarts," Harry Potter's fantasy boarding school from J. K. Rowling's youth fantasy series.

Dana recalled as the school added upper grades, "the curriculum that she proposed was high level. I would say that we were on the equivalent of any top British school. Which had its immense disadvantages and drawbacks, because when I graduated, I had no other knowledge of literature from any other country in the world. I can recite the names of the Kings of Great Britain from 1066 to 1603, but I'm not quite sure of all the presidents of the United States."

Even the school's very first brochure was an ode to England. The long opening paragraph was both a profile of the school's namesake Hilda and a travelog of "Old York" and "the journey eastward in Yorkshire to Whitby on the seacoast." The brochure copy was reminiscent of a letter Ruth wrote about her own travels through Yorkshire and Whitby in 1949. As Sister Ruth the teacher in Canada's western prairie lands, she spent quite a bit of time with the British women who were missionaries with the Sunday School Caravan. Even stretching back to her secular life, the young Ruth Elaine Younger created a whole fan club around the British biracial composer Samuel Coleridge-Taylor. Even after moving back to the United States, the Reverend Mother continued to use British spelling in much of her writing as well as words and terms, preferring "cloak room" to "closet." But her most outward projection of her Anglophilia, and by many accounts most memorable, was her speaking voice.

It was very evident the woman born Ruth Elaine Younger took great care in curating her image as the Reverend Mother. It was perhaps why she allowed the misperception that she was "from Canada" to persist and she spoke with an accent that a few sources humorously mimicked; one person described it as a fake British accent. Most likely it was Canadian Dainty she acquired during her thirty years in Canada. Toronto linguist Jack Chambers told the CBC in 2017 "the quasi-British pronunciations were a marker of the elite" that took hold of the country in the nineteenth century. He said that the vernacular custom stretched into the early twentieth century. Schoolchildren were taught to say "tomahto" (tomato) and "shed-yool" (schedule).[4]

In 1957, when the *Episcopal Churchnews* women's editor wrote to the Reverend Mother to request an interview, among the list of questions she asked were about her hometown and life before becoming a nun. In her six-page letter in reply, she avoided those questions. Instead, the Reverend Mother gave this explanation: "I will answer the questions that you put to me as far as it is possible for me to do so, within the limitations my Community Rule and the principles of religious life impose. If therefore, any of the questions are left unanswered, I hope you will understand."

In one of the early versions of the CHS Rule of Life from the 1950s, it does not explicitly state that those who enter the convent are forbidden to talk about their secular life. That Mother Ruth felt

---

4. Lakshine Sathiyanathan, "Some Canadians Used to Speak with a Quasi-British Accent Called Canadian Dainty," CBC.ca, July 1, 2017, https://www.cbc.ca/news/canada/toronto/canadian-dainty-accent-canada-day-1.4167610.

the revelation of her hometown was a violation of religious life and the Community Rule was her interpretation of being a religious.

Her detachment from her birthplace of Harlem and the acquisition of the Canadian Dainty accent were a part of the ruse that obscured her racial background. Upon meeting the then Sister Ruth in 1951, Dana and her mother were oblivious to her racial background. "We did not know that she was a person of color," Dana said. "My mother told me much later that she suspected it, but we didn't know."

The made-up word "incognegro" was first uttered in the 1990s by a corporate management consultant, the late Richard A. Orange Jr., during an AT&T management seminar for Black public relations managers. Orange, a leadership trainer who was African American, used "incognegro"—a term which he had planned to trademark before his untimely death in 1998—to describe a Black person in predominantly White corporate America who tried to hide their Blackness. This term easily applied to the woman who described herself as having a "strain of other blood."

Her hair roots were not as easily hidden as her Harlem roots. The sisters in the community who saw the Reverend Mother when she wasn't wearing her veil said they immediately knew by her hair that she had "Black blood." Others zeroed in on her nose. One former sister, who feared she would be labeled racist and asked that she not be identified, said, "One day I was staring at her and kept looking at her nose. I thought her nose looked like a Black person's nose." Another former novice recalled that, during recreation time at the convent in the 1950s, Sister Lucia, an artist, was drawing a picture of Mother Ruth. It was the depiction of her nose in the drawing, the former novice said, that was like an ethnic epiphany.

Another former sister, who was also among the first students at St. Hilda's School in 1952, said Mother Ruth's brothers did show up at the convent. "I heard from [a sister] that more than one of her brothers showed up and they were blackmailing her. They would reveal that she was their sister, and therefore Black."

By the 1970s, Mother Ruth's racial heritage became an open secret among Black clergy and some African American families. Another St. Hilda's alumna, Karen Watson, said, "Almost everybody thinks she was passing. Some of the Black parents knew she was Black. At least, some of them did." During an alumni reunion event decades later, Karen remembered a conversation with Sister Elise. "I was talking about the Reverend Mother and how she was a Black woman and how she faced discrimination. And Sister Elise corrected me and said she was one-eighth Black. She was very defensive. And I said, 'Well, she still faced discrimination.' And Sr. Elise agreed, yes, she did. I thought it was an interesting exchange, because she wanted to parse out how Black Reverend Mother was."

Some current and former sisters believed she was pressured by Canon West to conceal her racial identity. Theories, rumors, and speculations about the racial identity of the Reverend Mother Ruth continued to persist some four decades after her death. One thing was clear, the Reverend Mother used her light skin privilege and her nun's habit to accomplish big things, such as business and real estate deals. By the end of the 1950s, the Reverend Mother Ruth had secured the purchase of a second property for the sisters in the affluent Brewster enclave in Putnam County, New York. Three-quarters of a century later, it was the same place I hoped to begin my "lay vocation" in a farm ministry reentry program for women of color intended to honor the legacy of Mother Ruth in the twenty-first century. Christened by Mother Ruth as Melrose, after the medieval abbey in Scotland, the manor home that became a retreat house for the sisters was named St. Cuthbert, after the Anglo-Saxon bishop who served as the prior and abbot of the monastery.

The Brewster real estate acquisition was the culmination of the 1950s for CHS and marked a period of prosperity. As the sisterhood entered the 1960s, challenges to racial segregation in the South and the Civil Rights Movement were in full swing. Quietly, in the state of New York, the Reverend Mother Ruth, a woman of color, pulled off a feat that was unthinkable at that time. On April 17, 1960, Dr. Martin Luther King Jr. appeared on NBC's *Meet the Press* and declared Sunday morning at 11:00 "the most segregated hour in Christian America." As he uttered those words, a woman of African descent led a Christian congregation of all White women seven days a week and twenty-four hours a day. Also at that time in the Episcopal Church, Black men who were priests were still relegated to serve in "Colored Episcopal Missions." Perhaps it was her racial ambiguity or her portrayal of only being alternately biracial or one-eighth Black that made her acceptable in this predominantly White institution. Whether unwittingly or knowingly, dozens of White women in the 1950s and over three subsequent decades fell under the command of this Reverend Mother from Harlem.

14

THE KIDS OF ST. HILDA'S & ST. HUGH'S

The era of long hair and short skirts had entered. The young St. Hilda's & St. Hugh's School children who enjoyed Mother Ruth cuddles in the 1950s were now the teenagers of the 1960s. They steered clear of their diminutive school headmistress in the imposing black habit.

"With respect to Mother Ruth the dominant emotion I remember was always fear," said one alumnus, who was sixty-five years old when he made that statement.

While credited with permitting cafeteria dancing to rock-and-roll music and Beatles songs played on the piano in chapel, Mother Ruth drew the line at high hems, high afros, mop tops, and crop tops. Some fifty years after graduating from the school, a few alumni—now well over sixty years old and some into their seventies—still harbored a deep-seated resentment over the harsh treatment the Reverend Mother meted out to them when they were teenagers during the hippie era.

In 2018, one provided a list with bullet points of grievances from his teenage years that still languished over the decades:

- girls kneeling on the gym floor to make sure the hem of their dress touched the floor while boys were inspected to see if their hair was over their shirt collar.
- girls rolling up their skirts at the bus stop after school.
- being sent home to get a haircut as were other boys (I know one who wore a wig to school to try and avoid this).

That list came from David Pyle, who was enrolled as a seventh grader in 1966 by his parents, the late Alice Parker, famed choral arranger, composer, and musician, and the late singer Thomas Pyle.

"Most of my memories of Mother Ruth are disciplinary related," said David, who, along with his four siblings, attended St. Hilda's & St. Hugh's. "Reverend Mother brooked no nonsense and held everyone to a very strict standard which sometimes seemed too strict. Some of my favorite nuns ended up leaving the convent and I always thought that might be why they left, though I'll never really know.

"I could never really forgive her for not allowing me to run for student body president because of the whole kerfuffle over the Junior Class Yearbook page."

That incident involved a teenage prank gone awry that reached the desk of Bishop Donegan. More than fifty years later, David is reluctant to talk about the incident. His consolation prize for exclusion from the student body election was a starring role in the school's much lauded Christmas pageant.

"I always felt that I was picked to play Joseph in the pageant my senior year, in part to make up for that," David said. "At that point my hair was not long enough to be sent home to get it cut but it was still a concern so they made me wear a ridiculous hat. I'm pretty sure I was the first and perhaps only Joseph to wear a hat!"

"Despite all of the above," David wrote, referring to his grievance list he sent in email, "I very much enjoyed my time in high school and wouldn't trade it for anything. The school kept us all grounded in a turbulent time and I met many wonderful people. Sister Mary Elizabeth was a great history teacher and I always liked Sister Mary Christabel who made the school library a very welcoming place."

David's younger brother Timothy did not fare as well. He lasted only two years at St. Hilda's & St. Hugh's, to the chagrin of his mother, Alice. Mother Ruth decided that because of his disciplinary problems, he was not suited for the Manhattan day school. Timothy ended up at a boarding school in Massachusetts. "I remember Mother Ruth well as I spent too much time in her office as a student," he said. "But she always had my best interests at heart!

I have fond memories of my two years at St Hilda's that certainly shaped my future."

One diametrically opposing sentiment of Mother Ruth was expressed by Alice Parker, the mother of David and Timothy. "For the kids, she was a constant source of friction. But I absolutely loved Mother Ruth," she said. Alice died on Christmas Eve in 2023 at the age of ninety-eight. Five years before her passing, Alice was able to give me two extensive interviews about the Reverend Mother and wrote a number of emails that described her relationship with her. Out of the dozens of people who knew the Reverend Mother while she was living, only Alice felt she truly understood her.

"I considered Mother Ruth to be a friend and advisor, and she was warm and affectionate with me," she said. "I just always found it so very easy to talk to her and to communicate with her. She impressed me as being very much like my Mother: a forceful, competent and visionary woman."

Alice was herself a "visionary" in the world of music. A renowned choral music arranger, conductor, and composer, she spent twenty years working and collaborating with the famed Robert Shaw and his Robert Shaw Chorale. In her obituary for the *New York Times*, E. Wayne Abercrombie, professor of music emeritus at the University of Massachusetts Amherst, said, "She is a giant, was a giant in the field of choral music."[1]

Alice even composed a song for Mother Ruth in 1982 to celebrate the sixtieth anniversary of her teaching career. Before even meeting Mother Ruth in 1966, she was already in awe of her. "In the same year, she founded a school, a community and was getting her doctorate. Doing any one of those things would have been plenty for the average person."

About Mother Ruth's authoritarianism and the fear she instilled in both her students and the CHS sisters, Alice said, "I had a mother that I feared. There's a lot to be said about keeping a tight rein, because there is respect with that fear."

---

1. Adam Nossiter, "Alice Parker, Composer Who Heard Music in Poetry, Dies at 98," *New York Times*, January 10, 2024.

Alice said she was not a fan of educators and school leadership who presented themselves as friends to the students. Instead, she said she appreciated "the tradition of a much more formal relationship" that Mother Ruth and the teachers had with the students. "I loved that the students stood up when Mother or one of the sisters entered the classroom. All of those types of little things that the students fussed about, I just thought they were wonderful."

She found St. Hilda's & St. Hugh's a safe harbor, as heavy drug use among teenagers sailed in during the swinging '60s. However, according to several alumni interviewed, the halls of St. Hilda's & St. Hugh's School were not immune to rebellious youth and the drug scene. "She had no sympathy at all for a kid who got involved with drugs," she remembered. "They were just out. There was no crawling back."

A lot of the quirks in Mother Ruth's personality many people complained about and got her into trouble both in Canada and the United States were the very traits Alice commended. "She was extremely strong minded, independent. If she set out to do something, she really didn't care much about people's feelings that she was dealing with. That's the only way she could have possibly done what she did. Forging through like an icebreaker. If it's solid ice, you just go right through it. Other people would get very frustrated by her; a lot of the sisters would get very frustrated because they couldn't figure out where she was coming from. I could always figure out where she was coming from."

One place she was coming from, Alice strongly believed, was the dark and hurtful trauma of racial discrimination. "That awful rejection when she was younger fueled Mother Ruth's determination. I can totally see it. You had to blow your way through it." However, despite the "friendship" that Alice characterized as her relationship with Mother Ruth, she too, until her interview for this biography, was in the dark about Reverend Mother's birthplace, family, and racial background. She indicated that she initially learned of Mother Ruth's racial identity as a "rumor" from the CHS sisters.

"There were rumors that she had one parent that was colored," Alice said, adding, "and that she was from Canada." Decades later, it was of little consequence to Alice. She expressed pride in the ethnic and racial makeup of the school and knew that it was an intentional design by the Reverend Mother to create a multicultural community. "She believed in teaching across the color lines." Mother Ruth was insistent that the school reflected New York City and the Morningside Heights neighborhood, which Alice described at the time as being "one-third white, one-third Black, and one-third Puerto Rican."

"The school was a mini-UN [United Nations]," said Alice, who was also known in the musical world for composing two pieces of work to honor Dr. Martin Luther King, first after his assassination, and ten years later marking the anniversary. Alice recalled the ethnic identities—Ukrainian, Japanese, and Chinese—of her daughter Molly's friends. Along with Alice, for many of the alumni who attended St. Hilda's and St. Hugh's School, it was this attribute about the school that most stood out and made the school beloved, in spite of Mother Ruth's wrath.

Alice, who said she "was practically living at the school" as a parent volunteer, also spent time at the convent and earned the nickname Sister Lasagna, after cooking supper for the entire community.

"I felt so close to the sisters, especially Sister Elise, she felt like a sister to me and Sister Mary Christabel. I had such a good time with all those gals. They were just so much fun to be with."

She credited Mother Ruth and the community for helping her get through the untimely death of her husband Thomas in 1976.

While Alice was already a prominent figure in the arts when she enrolled her children in the school in the 1960s, another St. Hilda's mother would shoot into literary stardom while teaching at the school during that decade. Her name was Madeleine L'Engle.

15

MOTHER RUTH AND MADELEINE L'ENGLE—
KEEPING UP APPEARANCES

"Four years ago this January, Hugh and I came into Charterhouse on a cold, raw day and talked with you about admitting our three children into St. Hilda's & St. Hugh's School right in the middle of the school year. We hadn't been with you for very long before we both knew that this was where we wanted our children."

This was how Mrs. Hugh Franklin, as typed in the closing of the November 11, 1963, letter, recalled the very first moment she entered the world of the Reverend Mother Ruth. The year was 1959, when the woman known then as Madeleine Franklin, along with husband Hugh, resumed a New York City–based quest for fame and fortune. The couple had decided to return to New York after living for ten years in Goshen, Connecticut, where Madeleine pursued her floundering writing career. Hugh's goal was to resurrect his acting career, which he abandoned a decade earlier to run a family grocery in the quaint New England village. In 1960, one year after their return, Madeleine was hired by Mother Ruth to teach English at the school. During Madeleine's teaching stint at St. Hilda's & St. Hugh's, she also lent her creative writing talent, most notably her adaptation of Jesus's nativity for the Christmas pageant. Hugh also provided his theatrical coaching to the pageant, which elevated it to a Broadway caliber production. It is still the single most enduring legacy of Madeleine's contribution to the school and to the community.

The Christmas production, even before the Franklins' arrival, was the school's signature event. "The pageant became massively important," said Dana Catherine, who recalled the simpler show of the early 1950s when it was performed in the chapel of the brownstone schoolhouse. Over the years, it moved to the chapel at Columbia University and then a few years later to the spectacular Cathedral of Saint John the Divine's main altar.

"It grew in beauty. It wasn't little kids in bathrobes. In spite of the fact we grew to be sarcastic cynical adolescents, nobody ever messed with the pageant; nobody made fun of the pageant. It became a holy sacred thing to us. And some time after Thanksgiving vacation Reverend Mother decided who would be Mary and who would be Joseph."

Under Madeleine's and Hugh's direction, the production's notoriety grew to the point that the Franklins attempted to get it televised on ABC, where Hugh was cast in daytime soap operas, according to Dana, who was also Madeleine's goddaughter and lifelong friend.

"Imagine the main altar at the Cathedral; the choirs singing in that space. The three kings approaching in the back of the cathedral and they are in these gorgeous satin robes and bejeweled turbans," said Dana. "It was an extraordinarily beautiful thing. That was Madeleine."

In 1962, Madeleine also immersed herself in the life of the religious community.

"Madeleine came to full blown Christianity in the middle of *A Wrinkle in Time*," said Dana. "She grew very close to the convent and her kids were there at the school, so it was kind of home to her."

Madeleine became a CHS associate at the same time she received word that her children's novel, *A Wrinkle in Time*, would be published by an imprint of Farrar, Straus and Giroux. In 1963, the woman now known to the world as Madeleine L'Engle received one of the highest honors for children's literature, the Newbery Medal. After all of that, she now coveted a special place in the convent. Her relationship with the Reverend Mother Ruth took on more significance and urgency. Even the archival files of CHS mark 1963 as the beginning of the documented and complicated relationship between Madeleine and the Reverend Mother. Volumes of folders contained several dozen letters, postcards, and notes from the popular children's and spirituality author.

Over the next twenty-three years, even in the years when Madeleine still worked in the same building as Mother Ruth, there was frequent written correspondence between the women. Clearly, if the folders were any indication, the letter writing appeared to be one-sided, as most came from Madeleine. There were few carbon copy replies stapled to Madeleine's letter, as with other archival files of the Reverend Mother's correspondences. Although letter writing was customary in the early and mid-twentieth century, even with those living and working within close proximity, it seemed as if Madeleine's letter writing was a campaign of sorts.

"To Mother, she presents a life that is chaotic and she seeks some semblance of sympathy and is solicitous of prayer," Dana said. She provided Mother Ruth reports on her family, her work—both as a teacher at St. Hilda's and her writing and newfound celebrity. In many letters, there were requests for prayers. For her daughter, Josephine, she wrote, "May I ask you, please to continue your prayers for Jo's eye? The doctor says that he has never had such trouble with this kind of infection."

In her first report to Mother Ruth after joining the confraternity, Madeleine emphasized her appreciation for her admission with an underlined thank you. She wrote that having "The Rule of the Confraternity" was a comfort and joy. In the letter, she indicated that it was through the confraternity that she was first introduced to Canon West. In subsequent years, she developed a close relationship with him and identified him as her exclusive spiritual advisor. "The single most important thing stemming directly from the Confraternity has been being sent (and the way it happened it does seem to have been direct Intervention) to Canon West for my Confessor. It would be impossible to tell you in words how much this has meant and the difference that it has made. He has turned me completely around and set me on an entirely new path." Canon West was the inspiration for Canon Tallis in L'Engle's books after *A Wrinkle in Time*.

As Madeleine's literary fame increased, it appeared she sought to curry favor with Mother Ruth. During the early 1960s, the school and the convent entered a period of prosperity with the acquisition of Melrose property in upstate New York, the influx of new vocations, and the school's expansion to include high school grades. In many of the letters, Madeleine referred to Mother Ruth as if she were her own mother; she shared some details about her life and from time to time, she fawned with adoration. However, Madeleine's goddaughter cautioned her not to read too much into the letters.

"This is me speculating, but I think Madeleine was doing those things because it was necessary. I think keeping Mother Ruth apprised of what was going on with the family, is the way you keep a good and important neighbor apprised."

Madeleine went to these great letter-writing lengths to secure her place in the convent and community. Through bolstering Mother Ruth's ego with what may have been feigned praise and adoration, Madeleine ensured that she had ready access to the convent.

"She kept the relationship going with Mother Ruth in order to stay close to the convent, which was more than Mother Ruth herself. It was a safe place. She looked to the community for support, both spiritual support and creative support," Dana said.

When *A Wrinkle in Time* was (for the first time) optioned for a movie, Madeleine requested to spend two weeks living in the convent to write the script. It was only the Reverend Mother who was able to grant permission. "Mother Ruth was like royalty, but not always benevolent royalty," Dana said about the process of gaining the Reverend Mother's approval for a request. "I think the important thing was, no matter who you were, you had to butter-up Mother Ruth to maintain the relationship."

For the Reverend Mother's part, as the Franklins' stature grew—Hugh landed an important Broadway role—she, too, understood the value of maintaining the relationship. As Madeleine shot to fame, Mother Ruth was keenly aware that having her on the faculty and as a CHS associate helped cultivate potential donors, helped with the school's enrollment, and even helped attract new vocations to the convent.

The Franklins, and even Madeleine's mother, became important new donors for a capital campaign for a new school building. Mother Ruth and the trustees were ready to consolidate the lower school (still being taught in the brownstones adjacent to the convent) and the upper school (in the Charterhouse) into one building. At that time, as Bishop Donegan was sending donor solicitations letters to the most prominent businessmen in the country who were Episcopalians, including Eli Lily Jr. and Harvey S. Firestone Jr., Mother Ruth made the most of courting and stewarding the Franklins.

"What a delightful and lovely thing you did from our point of view," Mother Ruth wrote at the end of 1963 in a letter addressed both to Madeleine and Hugh. "We are so happy to have the check to deposit in the school building fund." Then she added that a new brochure about the school featured Hugh and Madeleine's daughter Josephine.

The Reverend Mother extended her favor to Madeleine's children and took a special interest in them individually. In the same letter, after she expressed her gratitude for the monetary gift, she added before closing, "I want you to know that I have appointed Josephine as Assistant Editor of the Touchstone [the school yearbook]. Marina Torneansky is the Editor. I hope Josephine will find that she can work with Marina and that together they can produce a first-rate book. I hope this will not take too much time in her senior year for there are so many other things to do, too, and scholarship should not suffer because of extra-curricular activities! Now let me close and say I look forward to seeing you on the 29th and hope that perhaps you can bring Josephine with you." The twenty-ninth was the clothing of a novice.

When a check arrived from Madeleine's mother, Madeleine Camp, it sent the Reverend Mother over the moon. "I imagine you have heard from your dear mother that she has most generously given the school a large gift for its building fund. Indeed it is the largest single gift we have received from any one individual. I have written her at once to thank her and to send her a receipt for income tax purposes. I think it is marvelous that she should want to give to our school. She says 'because it means so much to my daughter and my son-in-law and my three grandchildren.' Isn't it a lovely compliment which I accept on behalf of you all?"

While Madeleine's literary prestige was on the upswing, Hugh bounced from supporting roles in theater to short stints in television network soap operas, such as *Love of Life*, *The Dark Shadow*, and *As the World Turns*. Madeleine had written to Mother Ruth about her prayers for acting roles for her husband. "Hugh is up for something very good which would keep us in New York all summer, as against something not nearly so good which would take us all out of town.

I am praying very hard that it will be God's will to say 'Yes' to this prayer, since He has seen fit to say 'No' so often to my prayers about Hugh this past winter. Three interesting plays have been snatched, as it were, right from under his nose because of small conflicts with T. V. or other commitments."

Eventually, Hugh landed what appeared to be a plum co-starring role in the Broadway play *Arturo Ui*, alongside Christopher Plummer of *Sound of Music* fame. On October 4, 1963, Madeleine wrote,

Of course, I will be happy to be present at Sister Mary Michael's First Profession on Saturday. Unfortunately, Hugh's hours again make it impossible for him to be there, but this time for a happy reason, as he will be in rehearsal for the new Bertolt Brecht play, [The Resistible Rise of] Arturo Ui, which David Merrick will be presenting on Broadway in November. After a dry period, he found himself having to choose between several plays, including a musical which will probably run longer than the Brecht; but I think Hugh has made the wise choice, as the Brecht gives an important message. It is often, alas, not easy for an actor to find an honourable [*sic*] engagement. Do you think you might possibly find time to go with me one evening?

Lovingly and faithfully yours, Madeleine.

Mother Ruth replied, "I think you know that I practically never go out socially. This is not because I don't enjoy these occasional experiences, for I do. The truth is that I never have time. But I shall take time to go and see this play with you, and see your husband take his part. This will be not only a duty but also a real privilege. How delighted I am that there is this new provision and that Mr. Franklin is actually able to choose among performances. This is as it should be and as it probably will be from now on." She went on to praise Madeleine for her "invaluable work" in the upper school.

After the Franklins' gift and the large one from Madeleine's mother, it appeared that Mother Ruth made an attempt to respond to Madeleine's volume of letter writing. And while Mother Ruth couldn't keep up with Madeleine's correspondences, when she did, she engaged in a bit of celebrity fawning.

Mother Ruth wrote to Madeleine at Crosswicks, the family estate in Goshen, Connecticut. "My dear Madeleine: I have just re-read all of your recent letters and I have been so glad to see more clearly and continuously your real point of view and way of working. You do have a genius exact and disciplined and hard work, don't you?"

Aware of Madeleine's interest and love for the convent, the Reverend Mother made sure to keep her updated on the growth of the community. In fact, in the few letters the Reverend Mother wrote to Madeleine, she included invitations to the clothing of novices and the services for life professions of new nuns. With cautious optimism about vocations in the 1960s, Mother Ruth wrote to Madeleine, "We've had ten or eleven Professions during the last twelve months, it is certainly to be expected that we will have a leaner time succeeding this very fat one!"

While it appeared that Mother Ruth was Madeleine's confidant, because of the long letters that disclosed the intricate ups and downs of her life, her goddaughter, Dana, reiterated that the letters were also part of a strategy of paying respect to a powerful and influential person.

"She didn't have any illusions of Mother Ruth and who she was. I'm saying, she was playing it safe, in sending those letters," said Dana. She also referred to Madeleine as a "master manipulator," who was equally skilled, like Mother Ruth, in obtaining what she needed from people. Ensuring that it worked on Mother Ruth meant staying on her good side. "She was a powerful woman who Madeleine felt it was important to stay in her good graces. The Reverend Mother could be intolerant and unforgiving."

There were many similarities between the two women, as both were hypervigilant in creating a carefully crafted public image. To differing extents, faith and spirituality were the main undergirding of their images. Madeleine received some criticism of *A Wrinkle in Time* from evangelical Christians and fundamentalists. In Mother Ruth, it appeared that Madeleine sought validation and approval to buffer the assaults on her work.

Dana said it was Canon West who served as Madeleine's sole spiritual advisor, not Mother Ruth, despite what was contained in her letters. Still, Madeleine, as a member of the CHS confraternity, wrote to the Reverend Mother about maintaining the Rule of Life as an associate. In much the same way religious orders instituted a Rule of Life for their life-professed vocations, lay associates were expected to adhere to a modified version for the secular world. Associates' Rule of Life might include worshiping on major feast days on weekdays, regular sessions with a spiritual director, and individual confession with a priest. As for praying all the parts of a religious order's Divine Office, associates might only be required to recite Morning Lauds and Evening Compline prayers. She sought Mother Ruth's understanding when she wrote of the challenges of maintaining the CHS Confraternity Rule of Life as she traveled on book tours to places such as Chicago, Cleveland, and Portugal.

"The Confraternity has been to me only a comfort and joy. I will have it in the various writing trips I must take this summer. I am held up by the strength of discipline." Then she expressed concern about staying disciplined and how her life as a celebrity book author and travel with family affected making regular confessions to Canon West, receiving Holy Eucharist, and other requirements of confraternity. It was as if she used these correspondences as a way of offering a mea culpa and seeking pardon for her failure to stick to the Rule.

In addition to Madeleine's teaching stint and financial donations, which included redirecting her speaking fees to the school and the convent, Madeleine contributed in other ways: she was known for her writing circles and writing retreats, for the confraternity associates and other adults, as well as highly sought-after classes at the school. Several of St. Hilda's School alumni said Madeleine offered one-on-one mentorship as a writing coach and invited them to come to the cathedral, where she was an artist in residence.

To Mother Ruth and Sister Elise, Madeleine also sent poems. Two were early drafts of unpublished works. One titled "Love Letter Addressed To:" was longer than the version eventually published in her 2005 book, *The Ordering of Love: The New and Collected Poems of Madeleine L'Engle*.

Love letter addressed to:
Your immanent eminence
Wholly transcendent
permanent, in firmament
holy, resplendent
Other and aweful [*sic*]
incomprehensible
legal, unlawful
wild, indefensible
eminent immanence
mysterium tremendum
mysterium fascinans
incarnate, trinitarian
being impassible
infinite wisdom
one indivisible
king of the kingdom
logos, word-speaker
star-namer, narrator
man-maker, man-seeker
ex nihil creator
unbegun, unbeginning
complete, but unending
wind-weaving, sun-spinning
ruthless, unbending

    Eternal compassion
    Helpless before you,
    I, Lord, in my fashion
    love and adore you.

She shared one unpublished work with Mother Ruth:

Fast on Friday
How do I fast today? What does it mean?
Lobster bisque in a fine tureen?
Shrimps succulent in cocktail sauce:
A gorge-ous fast free from remorse?
(If I must fast, a little fish
Or egg will do upon my dish.)
Let me not think today on food:
My appetites are noisy, rude.
Show me the fast that does not feed
My self to assuage my hunger's need
(Comfort of food when the need's for love).
You feed me, Lord. I've no food to give
For the larder's bare. Feed me today
The food you will. Help me obey
And eat the bread of adoration:
Not easy, Lord, since on each occasion
I just break the mirror of vanity
Before I can see through self to thee.
Fast me on pain if it be thy will.
Fast me endurance. Help me be still.
Feed me on love, your love, not mine.
If I may not have your bread, your wine.
This abstinence does not prevent
Your feeding me in sacrament.
Abstinent, absent, I am able
To be filled by you at your holy table.
Lord! You deny me food, yet feed
And nourish all my starving need.
Come now to me with what repast
You will for me: teach me to fast.

After receiving the latter, Mother Ruth wrote, "Thank you for your poems which Sister Elise and I have shared. To verbalize the deeps of one's spiritual experience and feeling is surely a great and enviable gift. Thank you!"

THE NICE BLACK FAMILIES

In the early 1950s, when Dana Catharine was a young primary school student, the self-described "WASP from Connecticut" pointed out to her mother that one of her classmates, "Joannie Pringle," was Black. Admittedly, Dana said she grew up around family members who engaged in various forms of prejudice. "My family was Republican, WASPY, racist, anti-Semitic," she said. Dana's mother almost rejected St. Hilda's School because she thought it was run by Catholic nuns. Ultimately, Mrs. Catharine felt it was more acceptable for a Black Episcopal nun to educate her daughter than a White Catholic nun. Dana's mother assured her it was okay and gave her approval of the Pringle family when she told her daughter, "They are nice Black people."

The Pringles, the Watsons, the Kelseys, the Adamoras, the Rhones, and many more were some of the "Nice Black Families" Mother Ruth vetted for enrollment in St. Hilda's & St. Hugh's School.

"You could tell Mother Ruth really didn't want anyone from the 'hood,'" recalled Kris Watson, an alumnus from St. Hilda's & St. Hugh's class of 1977. That may have been partly true. Other factors, such as membership in the Episcopal Church, came into play. In building her Rainbow Tribe, like her contemporary in the entertainment world, Josephine Baker, Mother Ruth insisted that St. Hilda's & St. Hugh's enrollment diversity go beyond the dichotomous Black and White.

Kris's older sister, Karen, who graduated in 1975, said four decades later at a school reunion, she and her fellow alumni marveled in hindsight at the formula used to achieve diversity at St. Hilda's.

"What a multiracial, multicultural, multi-ethnic group of students we were," Karen recalled and indicated it was a dominant conversation at the reunion. "We started talking about how that was not an accident. Mother Ruth had kind of carefully constructed that at the school. Although the school was mostly White, she made sure no one race did not have another racial companion, so as not to feel isolated. She kind of built a mini-UN, within the school." It was at that same reunion where Karen recalled having the conversation with Sister Elise about Mother Ruth being "only one-eighth Black."

"She was ahead of her time in creating the multicultural environment," Kris said.

Even Dana credited Mother Ruth and St. Hilda's for her rehabilitation from a family steeped in bigotry, racism, and anti-Semitism. "I became a diversity leader, who cared about [fighting] racism. I learned to care about people. The fact that I went to school on the Upper West Side and my classmates were from all over the world prepared me to be okay with people who were different from me. I didn't learn any of that from my family. It was St. Hilda's."

Kris said that diversity also came with an ugly side: "There was elitism there, too."

Some alumni, parents, and one prospective faculty member indicated that Mother Ruth engaged in many forms of "respectability politics." The origin of the term "respectability politics" is associated with the groundbreaking Harvard University scholar Evelyn Brooks Higginbotham. A professor of African American religion and the Victor S. Thomas Professor of History and African American Studies, Dr. Higginbotham's *Righteous Discontent: The Women's Movement in the Black Baptist Church, 1880–1920* captured the very era that the woman formerly known as Ruth Elaine Younger was born into and came of age in. Although Mother Ruth was thoroughly Episcopalian, as a secular young person she carved a similar path as the Baptist women Higginbotham studied. The teenage Ruth immersed herself in church life as well as Harlem's cultural and civic groups and with Black society. Where Ruth's path diverged from Higginbotham's church ladies was that she sought her status and social acceptability directly from a White patriarchal institution, the Episcopal Church. Still, Ruth, both secular and religious, was an adherent to a racial equality path of the Black church ladies of that era. Like them, Mother Ruth subscribed to a strategy of dismantling negative stereotypes and images, which would enable Black Americans to gain acceptance in White America through achievement, physical appearance (such as clothing and hairstyles), and a pull-yourself-up-by-your-bootstraps mentality.

There were accusations by parents that Mother Ruth discriminated against Black families. And as Sister Elise's early 1950s letter to a traveling Mother Ruth about a "very black colored family" suggested, there was more evidence that this was true. One was documented in a full-throttle Mother Ruth letter. When one family leveled that charge to Suffragan Bishop Charles F. Boyton back in 1958, Mother Ruth went on the offensive, first by discrediting the couple:

Without being rude, I wonder if you have some friends living at East 223rd Street in the Bronx to whom these adjectives could apply:

aggressive	*pushing*
conceited	*rude*
insulting	*suspicious*
personal, though a stranger	*trouble-making*
political	

I think if there is one way of making it impossible for educators or any others to want children of minority groups, it is to use the tactics of somebody called Mr. and Mrs. H. We had a most unpleasant session with them and the "gentleman" ended by saying that he was one of your friends!! Since he means to have a talk with you about our refusal to admit his child living on East 223rd Street since we are a school for poor old dilapidated Morningside Heights, let me say that Sister Elise who is our admission officer used her consummate tact with these people through two or three letters. A half dozen or more telephone calls, and a final threat to publicize our "discrimination" by taking it to the state authorities, and the newspapers, have been made by Mr. H. This kind of behavior is, as far as I am concerned, most unsupportable. In the language of youth, it is most 'orrid. Please choose your friends with greater care, Sir!!

So in 1968, when Olive Kelsey met the Reverend Mother Ruth to apply for admission to St. Hilda's & St. Hugh's School for her daughter Holly, she had some concerns. She suspected that her family might have been turned away if they hadn't projected a refined background.

"If I had been an ordinary African American, or Negro or Colored or whatever we were calling ourselves in those days, she may or may not have considered me," said Olive, who still lives in the Manhattan Upper West Side neighborhood a few blocks from the school.

She and her husband were indeed far from ordinary. In 1968, Olive's husband, thirty-one-year-old Everett N. Kelsey Sr., an Ivy League–educated, racial barrier–breaking bank executive with Chase Manhattan, was a scion of the Black elite. Everett's father, the Rev. Dr. George Kelsey, was a much-lauded professor and mentor to the Rev. Dr. Martin Luther King Jr. when he was a student at Morehouse College. The elder Dr. Kelsey, a Morehouse alumnus who earned his doctorate at Yale, convinced the young King to pursue a career in ministry because it would provide him a platform for becoming a social and racial justice activist. Similarly in 1918, more than ten years before Martin Luther King Jr. was even born, Sister Ruth of Canada wanted her ministry in the church to focus on "the problems of the races" in the United States, as she wrote in her manifesto.

Mother Ruth likely saw in Olive and Everett, who earned a master's degree from Columbia University, the model Black family for her St. Hilda's rainbow. "We did have a unique background. After we earned our masters' degrees, we lived in East Africa." Everett was a Ford Foundation Fellow in the Africa-Asia Public Service Program in Tanzania.

When the couple met Mother Ruth, the family of four, which included three-year-old Everett Jr. along with eleven-year-old Holly, had returned to New York after living in Paris, France. "We had selected St. Hilda's because it had been recommended to us by Everett's parents," Olive said.

"Both Everett and I met Mother Ruth in her office," Olive said, when Mother Ruth informed them that Holly would be admitted as well as Everett Jr., when he was ready for kindergarten. "We were a little bit different. I don't know for sure if that was a factor."

For the Kelseys, the deciding factor for St. Hilda's was the French language teacher. Holly had spent three years in a French-speaking school in Paris, and the family wanted to ensure that she maintained her ability to speak French. When the family returned to New York, "Holly was speaking more French than English," Olive said.

A few short weeks after Holly was enrolled in school, Everett Sr. unexpectedly and tragically died, succumbing to a rare bacterial infection in September 1968. The widowed Olive, who was a stay-at-home mother at the time, realized she needed a job.

"I composed a letter to the Reverend Mother and sent it by mail," said Olive, who received her undergraduate degree in education at Kean College, then known as the New Jersey State Teachers College. "I identified myself and I said I was a rusty teacher, but I'm a good one. She hired me and I became a third-grade teacher."

Olive said work at the school enabled her to be close to her grieving children and their home. During this time, Olive said she experienced a lack of empathy by Mother Ruth for her situation.

This was ironic, because while a teenager still in school in 1914, Ruth's own father died, leaving her mother widowed and financially destitute.

"Public school teachers were making twice as much as what I was making. I was a widow, with two children, and I paid full tuition for two children, while working at the school," Olive said. "I never asked for a break on the tuition. However, I think a sensitive person would have said, 'You are a widow and you are a single mother and you are working for us. We will give you a break, maybe half the tuition.'" But that never happened.

This contrasted greatly from the charity Mother Ruth extended to Alice Parker after her husband Thomas Pyle died in 1976, eight years after Everett's death. Mother Ruth saw to it that tuition for Alice's daughters was covered. "I didn't pay anything," Alice said.

On top of the burden of one income and the private school tuition for two, Olive was greatly appalled when Mother Ruth imposed a twenty-five-dollar fee to cover the costs of hiring a substitute teacher when she was absent from school. She found out about the fee when she attended a teachers conference, one which Mother Ruth asked Olive to attend.

"She sent me and another teacher—one of the nuns who later left the order—to a conference at Haverford College," Olive said. "Even though she was the one who asked me to go, I still had to pay the $25 to cover the substitute teacher. When my little boy got sick, and I had to stay home with him for two days, I had to pay the school fifty dollars. I know I did a good job and was a valued teacher. But where was the empathy?"

No longer an ordinary St. Hilda's parent, Olive's relationship with Mother Ruth was identical to most students. She avoided her. "The Reverend Mother was not an approachable person," Olive said. "I didn't feel you could knock on her office door and go in. I always smiled and kept it moving." Like Alice Parker, whose daughter Molly was also friends with Holly, Olive was privy to the rumors about Mother Ruth.

Olive remembered an afternoon when a man, purportedly one of Mother Ruth's brothers, showed up at the school. "I heard he was Black and Mother Ruth had him removed." That incident sent a shock wave of gossip through the faculty, staff, and sisters. The man who came to St. Hilda's was unmistakably Black, according to others who recalled the visitor, who blew Mother Ruth's "incognegro" cover.

However, Olive said she steered clear of that incident and other gossip prevalent among both faculty and parents. Actually, when Olive and her husband first visited the school, they were completely oblivious to Mother Ruth's race. "We were so focused on finding a school with a French teacher for Holly," Olive said. "Honestly, I really didn't pay much attention or it just never occurred to me to pay attention as to whether Mother Ruth was Black or white."

"She was clearly a Black woman," said Kris Watson. "There was no question in my mind that she was a Black woman. The white kids didn't think she was Black. They just thought she had olive skin. I think it was because they never thought it would be a Black woman leading this type of institution."

The Watson sisters, who attended St. Hilda's School beginning with kindergarten, recalled their parents having a conversation with them about Mother Ruth's race. "I didn't think about her race, because it wasn't until late in my tenure there, that my parents talked to me about her being Black. They told me she was passing," Karen said.

After that, Karen took a much closer look at her. "She was light skinned, with a nose that could have gone either way. Her lips were thinnish, not thick. In a different era, she would have been referred to as a high yellow. Because she wore the habit, her hair wasn't visible. But sometimes some strands of her hair would peek out the wimple, and you could see that her hair was kind of nappy."

What came as a surprise to both Watson sisters was discovering more than forty years after they had graduated from the school, that Mother Ruth was from Harlem.

"Harlem!?" Kris's voice rose in disbelief after being told of Mother Ruth's birthplace during her 2018 interview for this biography. "Whenever I talk about St. Hilda's, I've been telling people all this time, for years, that I was educated by a Black-Canadian nun. I didn't know she was from Harlem." Also during their interviews, both sisters mimicked the Reverend Mother's voice. Their comic imitation, a mid-range pitch that was contralto, had flecks of a British accent, consistent with Canadian Dainty.

Mother Ruth's "Respectability Politics" spilled over onto the Watson girls and other students of color. As a teacher, Olive recalled, one student in particular, a Hispanic boy from a low-income family, was also a constant target of Mother Ruth's respectability offensive. While Mother Ruth inspected boys for their hair length, the Black students were checked for the height of their afros. Unlike the White boys, whose shirt collars served as the demarcation line of hippiedom, for many Black students, the measuring stick was Mother Ruth's unpredictable whims.

"It was the late 1960s and 1970s. The years of the big afros. Holly and I had big afros," Karen said. "Mother Ruth had a pet peeve about the hair and she made me cut my hair. She did not like any radical looks."

Kris and many of the students recalled that Mother Ruth was also virulently opposed to the demonstrations and civil unrest taking place in the 1960s and 1970s. Being nestled on the Columbia University campus, it was difficult to avoid. The punishment for being spotted participating in a demonstration or protest was harsh: expulsion from St. Hilda's & St. Hugh's.

The Watson family was anything but radical in New York Black society. Still, their parents were political. "My mother went to school with Martin Luther King," Karen said. "My Dad was close friends with Malcolm X. The Civil Rights Movement was a daily part of our lives."

Like the Kelsey family, both the Watson sisters' parents and their grandparents were trailblazers with an elite pedigree. Their grandfather, James S. Watson, in 1930 became one of the first of two African American men elected to serve as a municipal court judge in New York City. Their father, James L. Watson, followed in his father's footsteps serving on the bench. In 1966, President Lyndon Johnson appointed Watson to serve as a federal judge in the US Customs Court. He was the first African American judge to preside over trials in Southern states, including Georgia, Texas, and Florida. Before that, he was a New York City municipal judge and served for nine years, from 1954 to 1963, in the New York State Senate.

About their parents' relationship with Mother Ruth, the sisters indicated their headmistress might have been intimidated by them, in particular, their mother, D'Jaris Watson. D'Jaris had risen to a level of prominence in the political world in her own right. President John F. Kennedy appointed her to serve on the Equal Employment Commission. She also worked in administrative positions for three New York mayors: Robert Wagner, Abraham Beame, and John Lindsay.

"Mother Ruth met her match when she met my mother," Kris said. "My mother was a Scorpio, she would cut your knees off and smile in your face with her Southern charm. She was also an educator. She could read people like a Dick and Jane book and she did not play. She came to the school and told Mother Ruth, 'don't mess with my kids.'"

Karen and Kris's mother was part of a new generation of Black women that Father John Burgess, the former Episcopal chaplain to Howard University, warned the then-Sister Ruth of SSJD Toronto about in the late 1940s. Sister Ruth told Father Burgess she had in mind a "strict body" for her proposed new, multiracial community. He cautioned her that the Black female students he encountered at Howard would not put up with any manner of draconian treatment.

Although "Mother Ruth did not mess with my parents," Karen said it was obvious the couple respected her. They used their influence to help the school. "I know whatever my parents could do, they did help Reverend Mother because they valued the quality of the education that we were getting at St. Hilda's and because it was close to home," said Kris, who followed in her father's footsteps and became an attorney. She later became an ordained minister in the United Church of Christ.

In spite of the fact that Olive Kelsey leveled some criticism against Mother Ruth and St. Hilda's educational quality, especially for putting nuns in the classroom who lacked teaching degrees, still, she supported the school. "I brought other children to St. Hilda's." When Holly graduated from St. Hilda's in 1975 and was accepted to Middlebury College to study French literature, Olive decided she needed a higher-salaried job to pay for Holly's college tuition. Olive went on to work in the corporate sector, landing a job with Chase Bank, where her late husband had been employed. She withdrew Everett Jr. from St. Hilda's, and he ended up attending the Choir School at St. Thomas Episcopal Church on Fifth Avenue. He completed high school at Forman, a Connecticut boarding school for students with dyslexia.

A 1973 graduate of St. Hilda's & St. Hugh's School, the late Dr. Adaora (Ada) Alise Adimora, MD, came to discover forty years later, in hindsight, that perhaps the Reverend Mother Ruth may have cared about her. Dr. Adimora died of cancer at the age of sixty-seven on

January 1, 2024. The daughter of a physician and a nurse administrator, Ada and her family lived on the Upper West Side and attended All Angels parish on 80th Street and West End Avenue. After graduating from St. Hilda's, Ada earned a bachelor's degree at Cornell University in 1977 and received her MD in 1981 from Yale University School of Medicine.

For a little more than two months, she refused to talk about the Reverend Mother Ruth. After a dozen emails, voice mails, and conversations with an administrative assistant at the University of North Carolina at Chapel Hill Medical School, where Dr. Adimora was the Sarah Graham Kenan Distinguished Professor of Medicine, she relented. The acclaimed epidemiologist's research work as a physician, infectious diseases and public health advocate, and scholar received international attention. She was renowned for her research and advocacy work to close racial and gender health care disparities heightened during both the HIV-AIDS epidemic and the COVID pandemic. When she finally returned the call on a September 21, 2018, afternoon from her UNC office, she admitted it wasn't her busy work and family life that prevented her from returning the calls.

"Mother Ruth didn't even like me," Ada said during the first phone call. When asked if St. Hilda's & St. Hugh's School or if Mother Ruth, who received accolades in college for her research and studies in the sciences, was instrumental in steering Ada to a career in medicine, she answered with a blunt, "not at all."

After I explained to Ada that Mother Ruth's longtime personal assistant, Sister Mary, recommended her as an interview source for the biography, she was still reticent and cagey with her answers and asked why.

"Sister Mary Winifred said you were a St. Hilda's success story and Mother Ruth thought you were brilliant. She was very proud of you." I then further explained that I thought because of Mother Ruth's love for the sciences and as a Black woman from Harlem, that she might have taken a special interest in her. Those responses left Ada more confused and elicited a bewildered, emotional response.

"She was Black? I had no idea she was Black. She was from

Harlem? Wait, are you also telling me she went to St. Phillip's in Harlem!?"

Ada said during that first phone call that all the new information was a lot to digest. She explained that Mother Ruth had done something to her for which she had never forgiven her. Yet, she promised to participate in a formal, recorded interview the following evening from her home.

"Mother Ruth fired me from my position as president of the National Honor Society," she said. The reason she was fired—uniform violations. "She told me I was not representing the school properly." As president of the National Honor Society, "it wasn't a big deal inside of the school, but it was a position that meant something to me."

Up until that moment, Ada, a high school junior who had attended St. Hilda's since kindergarten, considered herself a well-behaved and high-achieving student. With the exception of accidentally flooding the girls restroom as a fourth grader, which resulted in a traumatizing punishment, Ada believed she had successfully spent most of her eleven years at St. Hilda's & St. Hugh's out of Mother Ruth's crosshairs. Or so she thought.

Ada recalled the firing incident, which took place forty-eight years earlier, as if it happened last week. On that 1971 spring afternoon, she was about to exit the school building to head to an event with her classmates. Before stepping out the door, the teenaged Ada unbuttoned the collar of her uniform blouse and pinned up the school skirt, often described as dowdy and frumpy, to the outer world's 1970s mini-length standard.

"Her door was open and she was sitting there, so she saw me and she called me in," Ada said. "Oh. My. Goodness," she paused after each word. "She went off! She was soooo angry!" The uniform violation escalated into a felony-level criminal indictment of Ada's last ten years at St. Hilda's that veered into a full-scale attack on her entire character.

"She said she found me suspect, because I flooded the school. Mind you, now I was in the tenth or eleventh grade, so the flood happened six or seven years earlier. She remembered that and brought it up as if I had done it on purpose. I clearly had not."

The girls' bathroom flood had also risen to the level of an extreme disciplinary action that, for a nine-year-old Ada, left an emotional scar. It was 1963 or '64, the school was still in the 113th Street brownstone. The three adjoining buildings that housed the convent and the school were constantly plagued by structural problems, in particular, the faulty plumbing. When the flood was discovered by the school's staff after the students returned from recess in the park, Ada actually outed herself and readily admitted that she had been the last student in the bathroom and struggled with the problematic valve.

"At home, if I admitted to doing something wrong that wasn't intentional, my mother would have understood. So, I stupidly assumed the same would have occurred here because there were always problems with that bathroom sink. But instead, what they did was give me a pink slip. The pink slip was signed by Mother Ruth. I remember being devastated, because I was good. I was an incredibly well behaved young child. I was never disciplined. The pink slip, that was something that only happened to bad boys and bad girls. I was absolutely devastated."

So during Ada's dressing down over the uniform violation, Mother Ruth brought up the flood and other unrelated incidents that to Ada were benign and insignificant. "She told me you need to straighten your hair," Ada said, then joked, "Well, maybe she was right about that. My 'fro did look bad!"

But what was most astonishing, Ada said, was that Mother Ruth even made accusations against her mother. "On that day when the Reverend Mother was bawling me out," Ada began, then she dropped her voice an octave and launched into an imitation of Mother Ruth's voice: "And your mother called me up and she attacked me! Your Mother was attacking me about the German class!" As an aside Ada said, "I'm sure you heard about her speaking voice. She had this very odd speaking voice that, frankly, sounded very affected."

The academically gifted Ada had asked her mother to obtain a dispensation from Mother Ruth to permit her to take two foreign language classes simultaneously. "You have to understand, my mother was a reasonable person and she was a force of nature herself. She was pretty savvy and knew how to talk to people. So

I asked her to talk to the Reverend Mother so I could take both French and German."

When Ada reported back to her mother what Mother Ruth had said, she was completely shocked. "My mom said, 'Is she crazy? What is she talking about? I wasn't antagonistic toward her. I very politely asked her if it would be all right for you to do that.'

"So now you understand why I didn't want to talk about Mother Ruth, because I always got the sense that she didn't like me," Ada said.

"Holding these pretty minor behaviors on the part of a child and holding them in her head for all those years, I also had to wonder, what is wrong with you [Mother Ruth]?"

Mother Ruth's recapitulation of the St. Hilda's incidents that involved Ada, all fabricated with the intention of making her look like a bad seed, encapsulated five decades of animus.

The hour-and-a-half conversation about Mother Ruth and Ada's time at St. Hilda's & St. Hugh's brought to the surface some suppressed memories. In one case, she had a very positive memory of Mother Ruth coming to the rescue of the Adimora family. When Ada's mother had to travel to Cape Cod for a family funeral during the school year, she arranged for ten-year-old Ada to spend the week in the convent.

"Sister Penelope was this very young nun who was very pretty and very nice. All the kids loved her, certainly I did. She took care of me during that week. She would eat dinner with me. I stayed over one weekend, and she took me to the opera to see *Carmen*. To this day, I remember it being a kind thing that they did. Clearly, Reverend Mother Ruth approved it. I couldn't imagine they would allow a student to be in the convent that she didn't know about."

Although Ada initially claimed during the first phone call that she did not know Mother Ruth was a person of color, on the second phone call she had a breakthrough in her memory. She recollected overhearing a conversation among some students who speculated that Mother Ruth was Black. "I heard the other students talking about Mother Ruth being Black. I think my reaction was I didn't believe it or really, I just didn't care one way or another."

Although Ada was removed from her school leadership position, she still emerged as a dynamic change maker and student activist. Ada went after the very rule that led to her downfall—the dress code. In this case, she was victorious.

"That uniform," she sighed. "I proposed a liberation day, one day a year that we didn't have to wear the uniform. And they went for it. It was the 1960s and '70s, the rigidity of the dress code was just so obnoxious. It was an unfortunate and unreasonable source of tension."

After spending a considerable amount of time talking about some of the painful experiences, Ada shifted her focus to happier times and concluded that St. Hilda's was a great place to go to school. "I do look back on it fondly," Ada said about her years at St. Hilda's. "It wasn't super strong in math and sciences, but it was a great school for the arts. We were always doing plays or musicals or concerts." In 1968, the school's glee club performed with Duke Ellington and his orchestra as part of his Sacred Concert at St. John the Divine cathedral.

The dress code aside, "ironically, there was more intellectual freedom in some ways in that school, than there was, as far as I can tell, in many public schools today. My memory was that for the intellectual things you wanted to do, we had extraordinary freedom. Even at chapel, I remember being allowed to play Beatles songs on the piano. I played 'Let it Be.' People would read poetry and I remember someone read something from Ingmar Bergman's *Seventh Seal*.

"Sister Mary Christabel encouraged me to read anything and everything. She was the one who introduced me to *Catcher in the Rye* in the sixth grade."

Also, Ada was among the few chosen to participate in Madeleine L'Engle's extra-curricular writing club. "This was after she became famous."

St. Hilda's enrollment surged during the turbulent 1968 New York City Public Schools teachers strike that left one million students without a place to attend school.

"There was no question that it was better than the New York City public schools. That was the reason I was sent there. It wasn't the elite sort of deal, like Nightingale-Bamford or Brearley, it was more affordable."

Also, what stood out for Ada about St. Hilda's was the level of diversity that didn't exist at the elite private schools. "There weren't tons of Black students in the school. But I remember, in the sixth grade, a fair number of Jewish people because some of my friends were leaving class to go to Hebrew School. Out of my class of twenty-three, four of us were Black."

Ada, along with the Watson sisters Kris and Karen, and other St. Hilda's alumni, credited and praised Mother Ruth for St. Hilda's many positive attributes. As some tried to rationalize Mother Ruth's most irrational behaviors, many attributed it to the racism she endured over the years.

Karen Watson wondered whether "she must have been internally conflicted and maybe even traumatized on some level."

Kris summed up Mother Ruth this way: "She was a mixed bag."

RUNAWAY NUN

Throughout the 1960s and picking up steam in the 1970s, the convent cloister was more like a turnstile. For every aspirant who walked through the St. Hilda's convent door, another two departed. "My favorite nuns were always leaving," David Pyle, the alumnus who was relegated to play Joseph in the Christmas pageant, lamented. "I'm amazed that she is still sane," the former Sister Julian said about the former Sister Mary Winifred, who spent twelve years working as Mother Ruth's personal assistant. Sister Mary's predecessor, the former Sister Clare Marie, who served for a relatively brief stint in that role, was not okay. "She just left," said Sister Mary, now an independent religious who dropped "Winifred" after leaving CHS in 1994. "She walked out."

In some respects, the mid-1960s through the 1970s appeared to be a golden age for CHS, for the schools, but most especially for the Reverend Mother Ruth. The Charterhouse property on Riverside Drive enabled an expansion that added the upper school, "St. Hugh's." By 1965, the foundation stone for a new school, which would bring together the upper and lower school under one roof, had been laid. Ever the Anglophile, Mother Ruth was effusive that the cornerstone from St. Hilda's Abbey in Whitby, Yorkshire, had been given by the Mother Prioress of the Holy Paraclete Community at Whitby in North Yorkshire.

Melrose, the branch house convent and retreat center in Brewster, New York, also expanded with the purchase of the house across the road from the larger manor house. The modest two-story bungalow was christened St. Aiden's and, in short order, became the site of the

Melrose School, CHS's second school. The community and its educational ministries—for children and adults alike with spiritual retreats for the confraternity associates and arts activities led by musician Alice Parker and writer Madeleine L'Engle—added real prestige to the community. When the new seven-story school building opened in Manhattan's Morningside Heights in January 1967, at the dedication dinner, Bishop Donegan awarded Mother Ruth the Bishop's Cross. The Reverend Mother from Harlem, now sixty-nine years old, became the first woman to receive the highest honor in the diocese, which recognized outstanding contributions in the community and world as well as to the Episcopal Church.

Outwardly, everything flourished. Beneath the carefully honed reputation and adeptly crafted images, life behind the monastic enclosure and in the classrooms of the gleaming brand-new multi-storied school building was anything but "wholesome" (as proclaimed in one piece of marketing collateral).

All the accolades and notoriety only emboldened the Reverend Mother Ruth as she became more secure in her power. Her caustic, ingrained stubbornness, and an even worse mental and physical antagonist—aging—brought Mother Ruth to a new level of ugly tyranny that would traumatize some of her school students, but most notably and with more lasting effects, demoralize the sisters of her community. The young CHS sisters, without the buffer of parents (although some attempted unsuccessfully to rescue their daughters from convent life), descended into the depths of a dark and collective dysfunction.

For the late Shawn Matteson Dutch, who became Sister Clare Marie, both conscious and subconscious memories of Mother Ruth triggered nightmares. "It took me years and years and years to get over the nightmares," she said. "It has taken me a very long time to actually work through all that stuff." Even in 2018, Shawn said she still dreamed about the Reverend Mother. On January 25, 2024, Shawn died at the age of seventy-five.

Born November 13, 1948, Shawn Matteson grew up in rural Kirkville, a suburb of Syracuse. She received "the call" in the mid-1960s as a teenager. "I really felt God's call on my life." She also admitted later that the film *The Sound of Music*, which came out the year before Shawn entered the convent, also had a big influence. "It romanticized convent life."

Eventually, Shawn acted on that calling. "What I did was I sent out a bunch of letters to different communities. And Mother Ruth responded. It was the way she responded that kind of drew me to that Community," Shawn said. "She was interested in me. She sent me a Rule of Life for aspirants."

However, her parents were against Shawn, who was in her mid-teens, taking life vows as a nun. So when Mother Ruth sent Shawn the Rule of Life for aspirants, she kept it from her parents. "All of this had to be done very hush-hush." Eventually, her parents relented and drove her to Manhattan to visit and later begin her novitiate.

"I entered in '66. It was actually Feast of St. Nicholas, December 6, when I entered as a postulant," she said. "It was a big shock, culturally. Coming from living in the country to being thrown into New York City. That was Harlem. It was a real big thing. There were so many things I saw, things that I didn't understand. Steam coming out the grate in the road and those little cone shaped buildings on top of buildings, the water towers. So many things that were foreign."

After serving out her postulancy, the young woman, really still a teen, became Sister Clare Marie. She was now in the novitiate and became truly cloistered, which was another cultural shock to her system. "We couldn't read newspapers. There was a TV, and we did get to see the men walk on the moon. There were a lot of things that happened, like the Sharon Tate murders. Robert Kennedy's assassination. Things were going on that I had no idea of."

Over the summer, Sister Clare Marie was sent to the Berkshires to attend a teaching seminar. "A workshop on using a method of teaching math, the Cuisenaire rods. The following September, I found myself teaching first grade. I had not gotten my bachelor's. I was fresh out of high school. I was practically the same age as some of the seniors in the high school. It was difficult. Telling kids my own age not to run down the stairs.

"I remember feeling panicky. I hadn't gone to college; I hadn't had any education classes. It was challenging. But I did at least know more than a first grader." Still a novice, she decided that religious life and teaching wasn't something she wanted to do. "I didn't really feel like there was a way to get out," Shawn said. Looking back at that time as an adult, Shawn said she was too immature to realize she could have just said no and walked away. She ended up living the life of Sister Clare Marie for six years. "I felt trapped. I struggled with it because I thought this is what God wanted me to do."

But what was also brutal was being cut off from family. "My grandfather died and my uncle died while I was there and I was devastated by that," Shawn recalled, who was prohibited from attending the funerals. "I wasn't even allowed to talk to my family. I really, really wanted to be there with them."

She tried to communicate her feelings of homesickness and isolation to her family, but her unhappy experiences she wrote about in letters never reached her parents. "I didn't find out until after I left that a lot of my letters were blacked out with a marker."

Like all the young postulants and novices, Sister Clare Marie experienced bouts of homesickness. And like many novices struggling under emotional distress, the typical method of response by both Mother Ruth and the novice mistress Sister Catherine was to schedule a counseling session with the community's therapist or chaplain. In these situations for the religious novices, confidentiality agreements were nonexistent. Similarly to Elizabeth Losa's experience twenty years earlier, everything Sister Clare Marie confided to the chaplain made its way back to the Reverend Mother. "I realized he was going to divulge everything I told him to Mother Ruth. After that, my trust level went down," she said.

During her time there, the school was also trying to seek accreditation. Subsequently, Sister Clare Marie (who was already working as a teacher) was sent to Barnard College to obtain a bachelor's degree. While at Barnard, she befriended a classmate who was going through a difficult period. On one occasion, as Sister Clare Marie left the campus to head back to the convent, the student confided in the nun. She invited the young woman to accompany her on her walk back to the convent so she could continue to unburden herself. When they arrived at the convent, Sister Clare Marie instructed the young woman to wait for her in the foyer until she retrieved what she came for and then the two would depart and continue their walk.

"I got in trouble for that," she said with bitterness still in her voice. "I was not supposed to bring her into the convent. But she was confiding in me. What is the point of being a nun if you can't help people, counsel people?"

As with most novices, Sister Clare Marie had little to no interaction with the Reverend Mother, unless she got in trouble. But all that was about to change. First, Sister Clare Marie became the school secretary and finally—her last job in the convent as a nun—the personal secretary to Mother Ruth. Or more accurately, she was Mother Ruth's housekeeper, chauffeur, and overall lady in waiting. "That included bringing her breakfast to her office in the morning or anything she wanted me to do. I also used to drive the Reverend Mother where she needed to go."

And with that change, things would go from bad to worse. But through it all, Sister Clare Marie found that the most trying of situations only made her stronger. "It was having that job that gave me the impetus to leave," said Shawn.

She described what appeared to be minor transgressions, unintentional mistakes, and even completely unknown misdeeds mushrooming into major incidents that ended with Mother Ruth's notorious explosive and scolding tirades. "Sometimes, you never quite knew what you did wrong. But you knew you were being punished for it." In some of those instances, Mother Ruth preferred to use the silent treatment or cold shoulder, as she had also done years earlier with the novice Elizabeth Losa, as she tried to withdraw from the novitiate.

Sister Clare Marie drew the line when Mother Ruth's direct orders violated her personal relationship with God. Before entering the convent, Sister Clare Marie had been raised in the Anglo-Catholic tradition of the Episcopal Church steeped in the rituals of the Roman rite, so she was accustomed to going to individual confession with a priest. At the Community of the Holy Spirit, she did not have the opportunity to go to one-on-one confession and receive absolution from a priest and wanted to do so before receiving Holy Eucharist. Mother Ruth insisted it was unnecessary for her to have a private confession because corporate confession is a part of the service, which is the standard practice for most mainline Episcopalians.

"I didn't go to Communion for a few days because I hadn't gone to confession," Shawn recalled. She believed receiving "the Body and Blood of Jesus" without confession and absolution was a sin. However, the Reverend Mother tried to force Sister Clare Marie to take Communion. "In my heart, I knew it was morally wrong. How can she order me to go? I am the one who has to stand before God. Obedience only goes so far, here. But I continued not to go to Communion." Things came to a head when the community gathered weekly for "Chapter of Faults." A traditional meeting in religious orders where monks and nuns publicly confess their sins or some type of moral failing to the entire community and the superior. When it was Sister Clare Marie's turn to tell her faults for the week, when she did not mention her failure to go to Communion, Mother Ruth intervened and mentioned it, as if she forgot.

"I did not go to Communion when I was told to," she said to Sister Clare Marie.

"I'm sorry, I cannot confess that," Sister Clare Marie responded.

Mother Ruth hit the roof. "She was just indignant," Shawn said. "She told me to leave the room. So I left, and I went up to my cell and waited for the shoe to drop. And sure enough, as soon as Chapter was over, Sister Lucia came up and said Mother Ruth wants to see you. I don't remember all of the conversation, Mother Ruth got really angry with me. She went to slap me across my face and her hand stopped right by my cheek. I think she realized, had she hit me, she knew I would have been out the door right then. Either that, or I would have hit her back. It would have been one or the other. That was the beginning of the end."

Sister Clare Marie found the strength to challenge and stand up to Mother Ruth. It was something of her swan song, before leaving for good. "On one hand, she liked it," Shawn recalled. "On the other hand, she hated me for it, because she saw it as disrespectful. But nobody else did it. Even her Counsel of Sisters, there was Sister Elise,

Sister Mary Christabel, and Sister Lavinia. There was a small group that was supposedly her inner counsel, but they all were her yes men as well. I would only take so much. I'd tell her what I thought."

It was 1972, when she planned her first escape while working at the school. "One of the things that I did was I worked the switchboard, the old-fashioned phone switchboard at the school. I knew how to use it. I went over to the school and called home. My father wired me money, and I left. I got a ride to the airport and came home." It was obvious that Mother Ruth may have respected Sister Clare Marie. Otherwise, why would she have sent Sister Elise on a four-plus-hour drive to the Matteson home to persuade her to return to the convent?

"Sister Elise just sat outside my house. My parents told me to ignore her. They did not want me to go out there, but I said I had to do this. I went out. We went out to lunch, I think. She basically talked me into coming back." Sister Clare Marie returned for "just a couple of months" before she left the convent for good and returned to being Shawn Matteson.

No one from the convent ran after her this time. Instead, Shawn was deeply singed by an act of vindictiveness Mother Ruth was also known for. "Mother Ruth wrote a scathing letter to my Dad and also to my priest. I heard from my priest. I kept that letter [to my father] for forty years. I kept it in the drawer of my vanity. Every once in a while, I would take it out to read it."

The letters said that Shawn had made promises to God and she had broken those promises. "She didn't say I was going to hell. But, it was very strong language. That took me a very long time to work out."

Her priest took Mother Ruth's letter very seriously and heaped scolding on Shawn. "He was putting pressure on me. He said, 'you made these vows. This woman has paid for your education, blah blah blah.'" Shawn ended up leaving the Episcopal Church. She became a Roman Catholic.

After holding on to the letter into the twenty-first century, Shawn realized that letting it go was part of the process of not only healing but also forgiveness. "I got to the point and said I'm never going to heal if I keep reading this thing. I finally ripped it up and threw it away.

"It has taken me a very long time to actually work through all that stuff," she said. "Now I am able to appreciate the good. It wasn't all bad. She did do a lot of things to develop us culturally as well. We were always going to Gilbert & Sullivan, light opera.

"I can now see really what a remarkable woman she was. And how she had to be strong to be able to do the things she did." Shawn said it never occurred to her that Mother Ruth was a person of color until years later after leaving the convent and connecting with other former sisters.

"I should have realized, it was very obvious from her nose that she had Black features. I knew she used face powder to cover up her skin," she said. "It never dawned on me. It wasn't until after I left. Then I started hearing stories, like when her brother came to the school."

The nightmares of Mother Ruth and the life in the convent were well in the past. The nocturnal appearance of Mother Ruth in the slumbering Shawn has now been downgraded to plain dreams. "It's gone from nightmares to dreams. Well, that took—I'm seventy, I went into the community when I was eighteen—fifty-two years. It's an interesting progression."

In fact, a few nights before her phone interview for this biography, Shawn had a dream. "It was Marilyn [another former CHS nun], and Mother Ruth and I. I don't know where we were, but we were sitting having a glass of wine or something. Mother Ruth was just in civvies. She was just laughing and having fun. And I thought, oh my gosh what a change. And I'm not afraid of her anymore."

18

MIDDLE SISTER—ALONG COMES MARY

It wasn't just the students of the 1970s aggrieved by some of the rules at St. Hilda's. The parents, like the board members twenty years earlier, organized an attempt to oust Mother Ruth as headmistress. During the 1970s, as a woman in her seventies, Mother Ruth's competency on many levels came under question. Even her friend, Alice Parker, acknowledged during that decade, "she was out of touch with what was going on around her."

In 1974, parents distributed letters to other parents with their concerns and began to organize. The letter reached Bishop Donegan and board members. The parents complained that the 1970s board members didn't include people who had children currently attending the school.

Mother Ruth discovered the campaign, because leaflets were circulated in the school. True to her nature, Mother Ruth fought back. Time and again, and even at age seventy-seven, the Reverend Mother Ruth felt completely confident and secure in her authority. She attempted to shut down the parents' campaign. She enlisted the help of the Mother's Council when it was suggested by Bishop Donegan that the letters should be "studied." The Mother's Council wrote a letter to Bishop Donegan that defended Mother Ruth:

> We feel very strongly that such a study of the parents' documents, if it should be undertaken, should be done without any kind of circularizing of the parents to let them know that one is taking place.

Furthermore, we all do feel that such a "study," done even for the acknowledged purpose of proving the contents of these documents false, would result in too much pain for the Rev. Mother.

The letter also asked for the bishop's help to identify "the instigator"; Mother Ruth believed the letter to be the work of one mother.

In February of 1974, all of St. Hilda's parents received a letter from Bishop Donegan. He stated, "I write to advise you that I do not reply to any anonymous communication! If the 'Concerned Parents' identify themselves I will meet with them. . . . As you know the School exists only through the dedicated leadership of the Headmistress and the devoted Sisters of the Community of the Holy Spirit. The Headmistress has my firm support and that of the Board of Trustees."

But that didn't stop the parents. Another unsigned memo claimed that some of the ninety-two families who wanted to meet with the trustees had "25 years of association with both the school and convent." Similarly to the board revolt against Mother Ruth in the 1950s, these parents also feared reprisal by Mother Ruth that might be directed against their children for airing complaints.

While the majority of the complaints focused on the administration of the school and Mother Ruth's behavior, the parents' tactics shifted and zeroed in on the fact that she was aging. An April 17, 1975, memo, again unsigned from "The Concerned Parents of St. Hilda's & St. Hugh's" to the "Board of Trustees," stated, "We implore you to request a full medical report on her health from Bishop Donegan who is fully aware of her serious medical problems."

One of the people closest to Mother Ruth, Sister Mary, the CHS sister who served as her personal assistant, conceded that by the mid-1970s she was in decline. "When I first came to the convent in 1969, she was always present, totally in charge at school and at home," she said. "But that started to slip."

In 1977, Mother Ruth turned eighty, and she struggled to keep a tight rein of control over both the school and the religious order she founded. The latter, the Community of the Holy Spirit, had a constitution that ultimately forced her to step down as the order's superior. But not before an amendment was made to the original constitution that gave her a third term as the superior (since she was the founder), then a new role as the Reverend Mother General, with sisters elected as convent and branch house "Mothers." Finally, by 1980, Mother Ruth was forced to step down when the universally beloved and respected Sister Mary Christabel was elected as the Mother General.

Mary Christabel was both the ideal and obvious choice as she had proved herself to be a good lieutenant to Mother Ruth. She was also Canadian, whose mother was close to Ruth while she was with SSJD. Born Mary Dawson, she came to New York as a postulant in 1956. Mother Ruth enthusiastically wrote to Canon West about her arrival. "Mary is the daughter of an old friend of mine in Montreal and is a young woman of high cultured background, a graduate of McGill, and is in her 30's. . . . I think if she can give her all to God she will make a most superb religious."

By all accounts, from current to former CHS sisters, Mother Ruth held Sister Mary Christabel in high regard and trusted her completely. Still, Mother Ruth, as the "Reverend Mother Foundress," did not relinquish control or cede power to her handpicked successor and duly elected new superior.

The person caught in the middle was Sister Mary Winifred. "When Sister Mary Christabel was elected Superior, it was really no better. Once when I complained to Canon West, our confessor, that I was in a terrible place he said, 'yes, you are caught between Scylla and Charybdis'" (referring to Homer's metaphoric "between a rock and a hard place").

The assistant's allegiance and loyalty were to the Reverend Mother Foundress. And that loyalty meant ensuring that Mother Ruth continued to appear to be a competent leader.

But that was far from the truth; mistakes were mounting as Mother Ruth advanced in years. "She wouldn't; she couldn't say that she couldn't do something." Instead, new assignments were foisted on Sister Mary Winifred as well as others she trusted.

Four decades after Mother Ruth's death, Sister Mary is still protective of her and her legacy. Early on, Sister Mary, along with the Younger family, was one of my most desired face-to-face interviews. While she was this single spectacular source for the most fruitful, groundbreaking research information providing an invaluable list of people to interview, she refused both a voice-to-voice and face-to-face interview with me. She requested that I send questions through email.

On February 11, 2019, I emailed her: "At this point, the very best help you can give to me is a face-to-face interview. You can provide a balanced, holistic, full-person, human perspective that I am not getting from other people. I am finding it very difficult to communicate with you solely through email."

From the beginning of our email exchange on June 29, 2018, it would be exactly nine months to the day, March 29, 2019, that I would first hear her voice. I drove five hours from Brewster, New York, to Salisbury, Maryland, to meet her. It was the most profound of all my meetings, because instantaneously I understood that I was in the presence of someone who was deeply and emotionally close to the Reverend Mother Ruth. Most of the current and former nuns I interviewed commonly referred to their former religious superior as "Reverend Mother" or "Mother Ruth." Most especially during this in-person meeting, to Sister Mary, the Reverend Mother Ruth was more often than not simply "Mother." And after nine months of two to three typewritten sentences to the questions I posed (and in many cases, "I don't remember"), face-to-face, the floodgates opened.

Known in CHS as Sister Mary Winifred, Emily Shepherd had been courted and charmed by Mother Ruth since she was an eight-year-old child in Houston, Texas. "My first introduction to Mother Ruth was in the article in *Look* magazine—she was with the school children and laughing and I thought it would be very wonderful to be just like that! I was about eight when I read the article and only discovered later who she was."

About ten years later in 1968, while that magazine article was long forgotten, Emily, as an eighteen-year-old, knew she had a calling. As a student at Texas Christian University in Fort Worth, Emily met Sister Elise and soon after became a CHS associate. As an associate, she began to receive brochures about both the community and the school. "That was really my first introduction to Mother Ruth—she had a very serene and loving face."

Shortly after that, Emily wrote to Mother Ruth to let her know of her interest in becoming a nun. Emily was thrilled to receive the response from Mother Ruth, which led to a one-year letter exchange. Mother Ruth had a real knack for wooing women from afar and luring them to her convent in Manhattan.

"You will know what is best and it is your vocation that the Lord has given you," Mother Ruth wrote to Emily in March 1969. "I have no desire to press you about it, but I do want to encourage you and to let you know that I think of you prayerfully and lovingly and hope that reasonably soon you will feel that you must put this vocation to test."

Unfortunately, Emily received substantial resistance from her family. And while many lay people may have had little inkling that Mother Ruth was a person of color, clergy and others in the church world who knew the former Sister Ruth SSJD certainly knew. Emily was unaware until the TCU Episcopal chaplain questioned her selection of CHS.

"It was the chaplain at TCU who asked me why I would go to a community led by a Black woman. I just asked him who cares," Sister Mary wrote in an email exchange. "Mother had written to me, and even though I had her picture, I didn't know or care what color she was."

By the summer of 1969, Emily had moved to New York to become a postulant. Three years after moving to New York, Sister Mary Winifred's parents had accepted her decision and wrote to Mother Ruth. "It is easy to see that our daughter is very happy in the life she has chosen, and we are happy for her."

Soon after her arrival, with only two years of college education and more classes at Fordham to finish her degree, she failed as a kindergarten teacher. "I was teaching as a novice in the kindergarten classroom. I had a white veil, I remember I got grape juice poured all over me. I didn't think I was that big of a failure, but I was sent to work in the admission office."

When Sister Clare Marie abruptly bolted from CHS and her role as Mother Ruth's personal assistant, Sister Mary Winifred was tapped to take the place of the runaway nun. She was thrust into the role of handmaiden to the Reverend Mother. "I was told by the novice mistress, 'you can't do anything, so Mother is going to take you on.'"

"Everyone who worked for her left," Sister Mary Winifred soon learned. At that time, Sister Mary was still in the novitiate and had not taken her final vows of life profession. "I was always afraid I would not get elected to life profession." So Sister Mary Winifred was poised to do a good job, because she had flamed out as a school-teacher. "I was thinking maybe they'll get rid of me. But I was told that Mother would give me a chance."

Sister Mary Winifred polished Mother Ruth's shoes, made her bed, and cleaned her cell and bathroom. "[I] took breakfast to her, got her mail, and then eventually, when she didn't walk to school anymore, I had to drive her to school. It was just around the block, but Mother wasn't able to walk that long anymore."

Although Mother Ruth no longer joined the sisters for breakfast, she almost always came to dinner, which was the time she held court. Decades later, Sister Mary marveled at all the customs, formalities, and reverence Mother Ruth demanded of the sisters.

"If you ever watched *Downton Abbey*, the postulants and novices were like the downstairs staff, and the professed sisters were like the upstairs family," she recalled. They were given specific chores to reflect their lower-level status.

"We all ate together. But when Mother was finished, everyone was finished; a little like eating with the Queen!" One former sister recalled that if a nun was late to dinner and didn't have an approved excuse—such as working at the school—she would not be allowed to eat at all.

While Sister Mary Winifred's parents thought their daughter was happy when they were allowed to visit that first year, that happiness would be short-lived. "There were certainly wonderful times, but I was exhausted physically and emotionally most of the time," Sister Mary said about her life as the Mother's assistant. She was also upset that her connection to her family while in the novitiate had been severed. When cousins and other family members came for visits to New York, she was forbidden to see them.

Admittedly, Sister Mary Winifred said she was naive when she entered the convent. "I was a very young twenty-year-old." The fantasized portrayal of convent life, depicted in 1960s Hollywood—the *Sound of Music* and the *Flying Nun*—was a far cry from the world Emily Shepherd found herself in. And the carefree, playful, and laughing Mother Ruth that an eight-year-old Emily idolized in the *Look* magazine article was also evidently fiction. Through it all, Sister Mary Winifred was committed to being a successful assistant and a good nun.

"I bought into it, hook, line and sinker," she said. "This is what you are supposed to do. God wanted me here. I was twenty, but a young twenty. I lived a very sheltered life."

As Mother Ruth's personal assistant, Sister Mary Winfred's most demanding, and at times, unscrupulous responsibilities were chief apologist, shield, and buffer. "I had to cover for her; she would tell someone she would be somewhere at a certain time and wouldn't show up for whatever reason. I would meet the public and cover for her. I would have to smooth things out.

"She was tired and not at her best and she had a very mercurial personality," Sister Mary said, describing the aging septuagenarian. "She still had brilliant moments and became a tyrant if anyone crossed her. She was always loath to share responsibility, but it got to be too much, physically for sure, and later emotionally and intellectually."

Mother Ruth had unrealistic expectations, meaning the rest of the world had to conform to her standards. "She had to have the mail by 8 a.m., so I would have to call the post office to make sure that happened. She always wanted to have new dollar bills and specific denominations—100 singles, and fives and tens only."

On many occasions, Sister Mary Winifred wasn't certain she was cut out for life in CHS, let alone as Mother Ruth's personal assistant. She was close to her family and the separation was painful. Mother Ruth committed one of her most callous and heinous acts—a dramatic gesture intended to display the severed ties between daughter and parents—right in front of Sister Mary Winifred's eyes. One morning after she retrieved the bundle from the post office for Mother Ruth to sort through, the assistant excitedly awaited to receive her mail, which included a new subscription to a science magazine that her parents sent as a gift. When Mother Ruth looked at the magazine and who it was addressed to, she held it up and tore the magazine in half and threw it into the garbage can.

"She didn't say anything to me or why she did it," Sister Mary said. "Everything became a balancing act."

The community, as a whole, walked on eggshells around Mother Ruth. Three decades under Mother Ruth's heavy-handed, authoritarian style of rule began to take its toll on the CHS sisters. The constant pummeling had a splintering effect on the community. Suspicion, harshness, coldness, high crimes, and misdemeanors. The Reverend Mother Foundress's personality and worse character traits had infiltrated the culture of the entire community.

"It was stressful being in CHS," Sister Mary said. "No one said anything to each other in fear it would get repeated back to Mother. It was always safest in the convent to reveal nothing, certainly no weaknesses or doubts or joys. Anything like that could and would be used against you."

Sister Mary's predecessor Shawn Dutch said, "I never felt like I had a family. Everybody was spying on everybody and reporting you if you ever did things that they thought were suspicious. It was kind of like living with the KGB. A very not happy situation."

This was the community that Mother Ruth created, that in the last two decades of her life was a simmering cauldron of a community in dysfunction.

19

RESISTANCE—CHALLENGING A RUTHLESS REGIME

In much the way 1968 was a watershed year for the United States—the assassinations of Martin Luther King and Robert F. Kennedy, the Vietnam War, and raging protests—the year marked the entry of at least one radical into St. Hilda's convent and the school. It was also a time of major breakthroughs for Black women. Diahann Carroll became the first Black woman who starred in a titular role television show depicting a woman who wasn't a maid. Shirley Chisholm of Brooklyn, who attended Columbia University Teachers College during the same year as Ruth, was elected to Congress, succeeding a White woman. Her first year as a member, she began her campaign for the presidency, becoming the first Black and first woman to run for nomination in a major party. Like Shirley Chisholm, who occasionally was labeled mercurial and endured criticism and ostracization by Black and White alike, Mother Ruth was in that same league of Black women who challenged the status quo of White male entitlement. And like both women, the road to the top was littered with bodies they stepped on along the way.

Enter center stage in 1968, Regina Christianson. Regina had shopped around before literally knocking on St. Hilda's convent door. She had visited and spent time with three other Episcopal religious orders. Mistakenly, she thought that the Society of St. Margaret would accept her as a postulant. She had not only visited the St. Margaret's sisters at their convent in Boston, but she worked with the order's New York City sisters at Trinity (Wall Street) Church's summer camp.

"I was discouraged," she said, about the St. Margaret sisters. "They told me that they didn't think I had a vocation."

Regina, who is also a musician, had hoped to be a teacher. In 1968, the Society of St. Margaret had one school in Haiti. Initially, Regina did not know there was another Episcopal order of nuns with a school right in New York City. That was until the dejected aspirant attended a service at the Cathedral of St. John the Divine. It was there she found out about the Community of the Holy Spirit. So Regina showed up at the brownstone convent on 113th Street without an appointment or an inquiring phone call or letter, as other aspirants typically did before a visit.

"I knocked on the door," she said, and told the sister who answered, "I think I'm called to be a sister." Within minutes, she had an interview with Sister Elise and within weeks she was in the novitiate. Like the Reverend Mother, Regina was able to keep her secular name and became Sister Regina in 1968.

"We had such fervor and such idealism," said the former CHS sister, who is now an Episcopal priest. "I thought I was a part of something that was the new beloved community. Then I was shocked to find I wasn't."

Like all novices, she had little to no interaction with Mother Ruth. Once she became life-professed, she employed the strategy of the students she taught at the school. "I tried to avoid her," she said of Mother Ruth. "It's better for my peace and me surviving here if I am in the wallpaper as much as possible. Keeping my nose down, doing a good job, and being a good nun and a good teacher are how to survive."

Regina said she had a tremendous amount of respect for Mother Ruth. "I was in awe of her accomplishments. She was a magnetic presence. She was erudite. She had a fabulous vocabulary and she used it extraordinarily well. She had a true gift for giving speeches."

Nonetheless, Sister Regina was not immune to the dysfunction in the community and Mother Ruth's treatment of some of her sisters. "I saw sisters burning out right and left. I mean literally," Regina said. "[Mother Ruth] would raise someone up, then at a drop of the hat, she would drop them. I saw that too many times.

"She was so manipulative. Emotional manipulation was what she did. I don't know how I withstood it when she was using it on me."

With Sisters Elise and Mary Christabel as Mother Ruth's military-trained lieutenants, Regina said that the convent was run by "a male power system."

Sister Mary gave this description of the hierarchy. "We all had numbers and did everything in order, everything was based on where you ranked in order of seniority—where you sat in chapel, in the refectory, in line, who went through the door first, who walked on the right or left of each other, etcetera. It was a very regimented life. I was number forty-eight and I think Mother had been SSJD 48—of course she was CHS 1." Sister Mary shared her memories with a bit of sentimentality and nostalgia.

Similarly to the military, the sisters were required to stand and salute—in the convent, however, it was stand and curtsy—when a more senior sister walked into the room. Each sister had numbers in the convent based on their entry into the community and life-profession date. Mother Ruth was number one; Sister Edith Margaret was number two; Sister Catherine was number three; and Sister Elise was four; and so on.

After ten years as a CHS sister, Sister Regina decided it was time to work for social justice in her own home. "I knew we needed a revolution and we needed it now. That's 'the 1968' popping out of me. Yes, I was a radical in the late 1970s and early 1980s.

"It was at that point I became vocal. I became visible. I became dangerous," Regina said. "I'd been working toward an evolution of the community into something healthier."

She knew the core of CHS's problems lay at the feet of the founder. Regina analyzed how Mother Ruth operated and the best ways for her to respond to it.

"I was able to recognize what she was doing. I think part of not being devastated by her emotional blackmail was to identify it as emotional blackmail. It still hurts, but at least it didn't have power over me. I think she knew those tricks, because they had been used on her. She had internalized her own oppression."

Sister Regina did not focus her radical activism on Mother Ruth, but on the community and its customs and culture. "My focus wasn't on Mother Ruth as the head of the community. My focus was on the community as my family."

She started with her own behavior and broke from customs in the community that she felt were divisive and perpetuated a pecking order and class system. "I started standing and curtsied to anyone who came into the room," Regina said. "Reinforcing seniority was not healthy. It made what was supposed to be a familial relationship more difficult than it needed to be. This was my religious family."

Unbeknownst to Regina and many of the sisters, it was Canon West, in his role as warden, who insisted on this ranking order, as documented in letters from the 1950s to Mother Ruth during CHS's formative years. It was also that way at SSJD. Sister Mary recalled a visit from one of the nuns from Canada who commented about the Community of the Holy Spirit, "this was how we [SSJD] were fifty years ago."

Sister Regina also challenged how the daily conference, Mother Ruth's review of her troops, was conducted. During the conference, sisters were addressed by Mother Ruth in order of seniority. "It was used to reinforce the hierarchy," she said. She had proposed a change in custom where the younger members were chosen to speak first. That proposal and others, including changing the black habit, were presented to the senior Sisters Elise and Mary Christabel instead of Mother Ruth.

"I thought the revolution could happen and Mother Ruth would not be hurt. I had that type of respect for her. She was a person [who] deserved all the respect given, absolutely."

As a radical nun, Sister Regina paid close attention to whether the diversity ethos of the school was being replicated in CHS. "I was so proud to be a part of that," she said about the mission of St. Hilda's & St. Hugh's School to create a diverse learning environment. "The school was wonderful. We did fabulous and amazing work. What we did was groundbreaking."

But she said it was obvious that the multicultural mission of the school wasn't being carried out in the convent. "I just assumed we would accept Black postulants. I kept being told they don't apply.

I found out they do apply, but they are shown the door. They weren't even let in the door."

Regina recalled two women who were rejected by CHS, one Black and one Filipino. "There was a Black woman with us for a few months when I was a novice, but she disappeared. Nobody said anything about why someone would disappear."

Regina recalled the woman as a St. Hilda's & St. Hugh's alumna named Elizabeth who lived briefly in the convent as a boarder. "She was Panamanian. Her father was a political person in Panama."

A short time later, "she disappeared," Regina said. Long after she left, at a Chapter Meeting, Mother Ruth told the community about Elizabeth: "She said she 'will go and serve her own people.' And that shocked me when I heard that."

When she made the "her own people" comment, Regina said she did not know Mother Ruth was "partially Black. I had been in the community for years and years before I heard that mentioned."

The Filipino woman was a maid for a family at the school. "She wanted to apply [to become a CHS sister]. I encouraged her. She was very devout and wonderful. Mother Ruth also told her she needed to go serve her people." Regina's take on Mother Ruth was similar to that of Kris Watson, who lamented that Mother Ruth really didn't want anyone from "the hood."

"There was certainly classism involved in that, too," Regina said about Mother Ruth's rejection of the Filipino maid. "I knew this type of racism couldn't be sustained in the community."

Regina said it was evident that Mother Ruth's hold on the community made it impossible to start a revolution. It became crystal clear when Mother Ruth ran for a third term as the community's superior unopposed. "The older she got, she had a tiger by the tail. And the only way she could keep things going was holding on to the tiger. Parts of that tiger were the things that would eventually destroy the community. It was tragic to watch and there was nothing I could do."

Sister Regina lived in the community for sixteen years. And unlike some of the women who left CHS, Regina did not blame Mother Ruth or the dysfunctional life in the convent for her departure.

"I burned out as a teacher first. I yelled at a kid the first day of school. I didn't yell at kids, except before the spring concert. It was out of character for me. I loved the school, but I was burnt out, that's why I left."

Another one of Sister Regina's proposed community reforms that was rejected was time off and vacation that lasted more than two weeks out of the year. "Some of us needed a whole year! I was assigned too much work. At the end of the day, I was completely exhausted. I had horrible physical and psychological symptoms that I could no longer ignore. I had a low-grade fever and arthritis. I got a life-threatening illness. I was literally burning up."

Still the radical activist nun, Sister Regina decided she was not going quietly. It was 1984, and by that time, the Reverend Mother Ruth was no longer the superior. Sister Mary Christabel became Mother Mary Christabel. She planned her departure, including the end date. "I went through the process," she said. "Part of that process included a vote by the community during a chapter meeting." She would not "just disappear" as others before her had done.

"They voted to keep me!" Regina exclaimed. She was undeterred by the vote and announced she would leave in December after the Christmas pageant. And while Mother Ruth was no longer the superior at that time, she still wielded a lot of power and still engaged in emotional blackmail. "She had no authority, but I was called into her office. She had this crucifix on her desk and she turned it toward me and said, 'tell Jesus you are going to betray him.' So I had this wonderful conversation with Jesus on the cross."

Sister Regina made sure she conveyed to Mother Ruth what she believed the crucified Jesus said back to her. "I know he understands that this is his desire for me to serve him another way."

"No, I didn't fall for the emotional blackmail," Regina said.

Mother Ruth tried to force Sister Regina to remain tight-lipped about her impending departure. "There was nothing she could do. I was able to have closure with the students. I got through the Christmas pageant and I told everyone I was leaving. I left after the pageant."

Sister Regina held the distinction in the community of being the first to demand a formal separation process and public acknowledgment of her departure so she could have closure with people.

Julian Sheffield, a St. Hilda's alumna who was enrolled as a kindergartener in 1953 during the community's and school's formative years, was notorious for being kicked out by Mother Ruth, then many years later being allowed to return.

Born Gail Sheffield (she retained her religious first name of Julian after her separation from CHS), she lived half a block from the school and was raised primarily by her father and a great-aunt. St. Hilda's & St. Hugh's School was selected because Anglican convent schooling was her family heritage.

"My family knew the nuns would take great care of me." Gail's grandparents had "convent schooling" in England at St. Mary's Wantage. It was one of the convent schools that Mother Ruth had visited during her exclaustration from SSJD in Canada.

As an eleven-year-old who was newly confirmed in the Episcopal Church, Gail said she knew who she wanted to become. Mother Ruth was her catechism teacher and prepared her for confirmation. It was an intention she shared with Mother Ruth and Sister Mary Christabel. At the school and in Mother Ruth's world, that elevated Gail to a rarified stature. During a 2020 interview on Zoom, Julian reminisced about being Mother Ruth's "golden girl."

"If you were a golden girl, nothing was too good for you and she would go out of her way for you." She recalled that Mother Ruth provided her and another favored student tickets to cultural events. "Mother Ruth gave us tickets to the Metropolitan Museum of Art for a series of talks on Egyptian art. It was what made her charismatic."

She felt privileged to see a side of Mother Ruth her fellow students and others rarely got a chance to see. "There was a lovable woman and there was this tyrant. You could have fun with this woman," she said, and recalled that she even took Mother Ruth and Sister Lucia sledding in the park. "There's a picture of it in the '65 yearbook.

"I felt I could go to her and ask for her guidance," she said. "I was a convent rat. She was very kind to me." Julian, acknowledging Mother Ruth's tyrannical reputation, abridged that statement: "Although kind can be relative with Mother Ruth. Sometimes it was the absence of horrible.

"I got to go to chapel with the Sisters and spent a lot of time with them. I hung out with the nuns." Gail also grew close to Sister Mary Christabel. "I was in fifth grade when Sister Mary Christabel was a novice. She was my fifth-grade teacher. Sister Mary Christabel became my surrogate mother. I adored her."

By ninth grade, Gail's family life had become more difficult. Gail's parents were divorced by the time she entered first grade. "My mother disappeared from my life," she recalled.

"When my great-aunt Geraldine died, my life fell apart that year." Compounding that grief, Sister Mary Christabel disappeared from ninth-grader Gail's life when the upper school was opened and the older students were moved to Charterhouse.

"Then I got a little wild," Julian said. "I was brought into Mother Ruth's office and she said to me—'you don't want to end up like your mother, never able to finish anything.' It was all shaming. That was pretty brutal. Mother Ruth made no attempt to find out what was wrong with me. She wasn't sympathetic, it was more like finger-wagging."

Although Julian conceded she was not a model student, she still felt secure in her relationship with Mother Ruth. "I was a mess because of a lot of the family things that were going on. But I always felt I could go to her."

By tenth grade, Gail said, things got better. She was the first teenager to become an associate in the Community of the Holy Spirit's Confraternity. After graduating from St. Hilda's & St. Hugh's, Gail attended Western College for Women in Oxford, Ohio. While she was a student there, Mother Ruth paid her a visit. The woman who gave her cuddles as a kindergartner and went sledding with her as a teenager spent an entire weekend visiting Gail.

"I made sure she had her four and half minute soft boiled egg," she recalled from the visit. "I had gone back to deciding that I was going to be a nun the first year I was in college."

In 1968, Gail did not return to Western College for Women. Instead, she returned to St. Hilda's convent to become a postulant and later entered the novitiate. Gail became Sister Julian.

Long before she entered the monastic enclosure of St. Hilda's convent, Sister Julian was an insider. She had spent fifteen years of her life in a close relationship with the CHS sisters as a school student and "convent rat." Subsequently, Sister Julian's entry into religious life wasn't the brutal and jarring culture shock other postulants and novices experienced. She came into the community with no delusions about the Reverend Mother Ruth. If anything, she brought intelligence that some of the other novices and even life-professed sisters were not cognizant of. During Gail's two years in college, she had become acquainted with nuns in other religious communities who knew Mother Ruth.

"I knew sisters in other communities who had known her when she was a sister in Canada, so I think I was probably more aware of her dark side earlier than anyone else. I knew she was charismatic, but she was also very dark." Her relationship with the older women who had entered CHS in the 1950s when Gail was a student—sisters Lucia, Lavinia, and Mary Christabel—also made her privy to some of the convent's secrets and gossip about Mother Ruth. (All three of those sisters have passed away.)

"Sister Lavinia, because she was a nurse, she talked often about Mother Ruth being Black. She couldn't help but know. The other person who talked about it was Sister Lucia. She would talk about Mother Ruth's hair. Even though we had these night veils, you could see [her hair]. Sister Lucia would say her hair was nappy."

Julian also indicated that members of the Younger family had made appearances at both the convent and the school. "Sister Lucia told me her brothers would come to the community and they would be drunk at times," she said. "I heard from Sister Lavinia that more than one brother showed up and they were blackmailing her. [Mother Ruth] kept a discretionary fund. [The brothers] would [threaten to] reveal that she was their sister, and therefore Black. Mother Ruth was told that she should never reveal to anyone that she was Black, because she would be unable to be effective as a head mistress to the school."

From cherished cuddles to cruel condemnation, Sister Julian over two decades experienced the highs and lows of life with Mother Ruth. And with that came well-tested strategies on how to deal with the Reverend Mother. There were two tactics that were critical to Sister Julian's initial survival in religious life with Mother Ruth. First, even when Mother Ruth was wrong about something, never correct her or even let her know she had made a mistake.

"You had to turn a mistake around into a question, to ask for her help," Julian said. This strategy allowed Mother Ruth to be the powerful, benevolent matriarch. The second strategy Sister Julian said she and many of the senior sisters employed to enact change in the community was to tacitly float and reconstrue new ideas in such a way that Mother Ruth could take credit for it, as if she had come up with the idea herself.

"It really wasn't any different from how people worked in the corporate environment," said Julian, in an astute and accurate parallel of life under the authoritarian Mother Ruth and in corporate America's top-down management culture.

Sister Julian relied on her childhood "surrogate mother," Sister Mary Christabel, also Mother Ruth's most loyal lieutenant, to "run interference." Other buffers that enabled Sister Julian to cope and get along in Mother Ruth's world were longtime relationships with other powerful figures in the New York diocese. "Madeleine 'L'Engle' Franklin and Canon West were supportive of me all the way through," said Julian, adding she had become close to the book author as a student and L'Engle writing circle member. In a 1968 letter from Mother Ruth to Madeleine, she wrote to confirm the student's attendance at "Gail Sheffield's clothing as a novice."

It appeared evident, however, that Sister Julian's protection from both outside and within had limits. Sister Julian tested Mother Ruth's rules and ultimatums and crossed the line not just once but twice. And Mother Ruth's wrath was harsh and swift. As with the 1950s board members and 1970s parents, who circumvented Mother Ruth by going directly to Bishop Donegan, Sister Julian would learn that he was Mother Ruth's most staunch defender and great protector.

First, Sister Julian was AWOL (absent without leave) from the convent for three days. Admittedly, Julian said she was emotionally distraught over a situation with another sister. "I had basically lost my mind. I was completely irrational and not thinking clearly," Julian said. "That was the thing about Mother Ruth; she couldn't see when people were floundering." However, other sisters tipped Mother Ruth off that perhaps Sister Julian needed psychological help. When Sister Julian returned, she went directly to Mother Ruth's office.

"I went to Mother Ruth; to report back, because that's what you'd do," Julian said. Mother Ruth questioned Sister Julian about whether she needed psychological help. "I had this interaction with Mother Ruth. At some point, she said to me, 'some of the sisters are saying you need psychological help, you need a psychiatrist, you need to talk to some counselor. But you don't need that. You are just being difficult, aren't you?' And of course, I said yes."

Although Julian realized she did in fact need help at that time, she had been programmed to always agree with Mother Ruth. "She told me I didn't need help and I agreed with what she said. You didn't argue with Mother Ruth."

There were consequences and punishment that Sister Julian had to pay for going AWOL. The CHS had changed its constitution in which sisters took two profession vows. Within the convent there was a middle strata, "the juniorate," that followed after novices took their first vows before election to life profession. After going AWOL, Sister Julian was "demoted" in rank. Then things went from bad to worse.

"While I was out those three days, one of the sisters went into my cell and took my journal and gave it to Mother Ruth," Julian said. The Reverend Mother refused to give the journal back to Sister Julian. "I won't give it back to you while you are here and I won't read it," she recalled Mother Ruth telling her. The confiscation further compounded Sister Julian's emotional and mental anguish. Shortly thereafter, Sister Julian was not elected to take her final vows of life profession.

"I asked to stay on [the juniorate]," Julian said. She went from golden girl to pariah during that time. She referred to her mental state as "Stockholm syndrome," because she had a fervent desire to remain in the community. As time went on during Sister Julian's "demotion," it became increasingly important to get her journal back. She sought the assistance of Canon West. The effort, in which Mother Ruth incorrectly assumed Sister Julian had gone directly to Bishop Donegan, led to a final showdown between the women. During the war of words, Mother Ruth expelled Sister Julian from CHS.

"It was unilateral. It was completely illegal. It should have been voted on by the chapter," Julian said. "Mother Ruth told me to take off my habit and get out. Of course, I didn't take off my habit because I didn't have any other clothes to wear, but I left."

THE INCOGNEGRO AND BLACK EPISCOPALIANS

New York City traffic was one of the rare instances in which the Reverend Mother lowered the barrier that separated her religious and secular worlds and exposed that she had once been an impoverished, tragedy- and adversity-plagued Younger from Harlem. The abrupt turns that careened the convent car off course, illegal U-turns, and other dangerous traffic maneuvers were common when shuttling the Reverend Mother Ruth on busy city streets. At all costs, the mother's assistant and chauffeur, Sister Mary Winifred, was ordered to avoid driving in proximity to cement mixer trucks. Mother Ruth was still haunted by the harrowing 1923 cement mixer–bus accident that resulted in horrific scalding from steam and severe burn injuries that claimed the life of her sister Loretta. The sight of a cement mixer was cause for panic by Mother Ruth, Sister Mary said.

Not only from the convent car's driver seat, but while Sister Mary Winifred cleaned Mother Ruth's cell, office, and private bathroom then ultimately became her business assistant, Sister Mary Winifred had undisputedly a close-up and intimate view of all aspects of Mother Ruth's final decade of life. "Gradually, over the years, I took on a lot more of caring for her, sometimes covering for her, keeping track of money at the convent and school," she said.

One area Mother Ruth maintained tight control over was CHS's finances. But maintaining the order's books, as she once had, became too much. Bookkeeper was added to Sister Mary Winifred's assistant duties along with chauffeur, maid, and errand nun.

"I was horrible at math. There were sisters who taught math," Sister Mary said. "Mother did not trust a lot of people, but she trusted me. I remember I called the man who was our auditor, who I really trusted. I sat in bed trying to figure out our books, because everything was done by hand. I was like, 'oh my God, I don't get it.'" The auditor gave Sister Mary Winifred a crash course in bookkeeping.

Along with the convent's finances, the bookkeeping at the school was plagued with problems. This included an accusation of misappropriation of a donation intended to provide a scholarship to a student in need. The donor was a former teacher, Olive Kelsey, whose husband passed away while her children were students at Mother Ruth's school. In 1981, the scholarship fund was established in memory of Olive's daughter Holly, who was killed in an automobile accident caused by a driver operating under the influence of alcohol. Holly, who was twenty-four years old, had graduated from Middlebury College with a degree in French literature and was on an outing with coworkers when the accident happened. Olive had lost her husband Everett thirteen years earlier and was grief-stricken by the untimely death of her oldest child. With the help of Chase Bank (Olive's employer after quitting work at the school), she donated a $10,000 fund with an agreement that the interest would be used to provide an annual scholarship to a student in need.

"I sat in Mother Ruth's office and told her exactly how I wanted that money used," Olive said. "They were not to touch the principal, only use the interest and earnings to pay out the scholarship."

Olive attended a ceremony for a student who was awarded the first scholarship. A few years later, Olive decided she wanted to live abroad and moved to China for several years into the mid-1990s. It wasn't until after her return, years after Mother Ruth's death, that she would learn that only the initial scholarship had been awarded and no others followed.

"I set up that thing so the first recipient would be in the class of '82. Shirlie Harrison [another teacher] told me no other person received a scholarship from that money. That kind of deviousness wasn't supposed to be happening in an institution of the Lord. They do that on Wall Street," Olive said. "The money may have been used up somehow and disappeared. I decided I wanted that money back." Thirteen years after Holly's death, the school's board settled the misappropriation in 1994 by issuing a check to Olive Kelsey in the amount of $15,000. Sister Mary conceded that Mother Ruth "borrowed" a lot of money. "She got people to trust her, and they gave money to help the school."

Under Mother Ruth's leadership, only one African American teacher was hired at St. Hilda's & St. Hugh's, Olive Kelsey. After Olive departed, there were no Black teachers. In 1982, with no Black faculty on staff at St. Hilda's & St. Hugh's, Mother Ruth had the opportunity to hire a man who by some measures seemed to embody the ideal teacher for the school. He was Brother Reginald-Martin Crenshaw, a newly life-professed monk with the Epsicopal Order of the Holy Cross in West Park, New York. He was a job candidate who appeared to tick all the boxes. He was Black, Canadian, a trained teacher in religion, a new resident of Harlem, and a member of the very religious order that accepted the teenaged Ruth Younger as a lay associate in its confraternity and whose founder had helped her to become a nun. Brother Reginald had been assigned to live in the Order of the Holy Cross's Absalom Jones Priory in Harlem. The prior, the Reverend Carl Sword, arranged for an interview with eighty-four-year-old Mother Ruth.

That first and only meeting was so memorable, Brother Reginald recalled every gesture, every nuanced phrase, and even the arrangement of one very specific item, a portrait, on Mother Ruth's desk in exacting detail. He likened the photograph and interview to the brown paper bag test aphorism of the blue-vein society—the denigrating relic of colorism that determined a person's "Blackness." He said Mother Ruth judged him to be "too Black."

"I had come back from Toronto for this interview," he recalled four decades later, during a phone interview. "I had to wait outside for a moment before I was brought into Mother Ruth's office. Mother Ruth was sitting at her desk, and Father Sword, who was my prior, was talking to her. They began to have this conversation about me as if I was not present, which is an old-old fashioned way superiors treated their subjects." He said even back then as a new monk, he heard that Mother Ruth had mannerisms and customs in the convent that mirrored a draconian, pre–Vatican II Roman Catholic religious order.

"I was sitting there for fifteen minutes. I was never introduced," he recalled, adding that he looked down at his feet most of that time. "As I looked up, I noticed a photograph of a light-skin Black woman. It was turned toward me in the seat I was sitting in, so I could look at it. I thought that was odd, because normally when you have a photo on your desk, it is facing you. It seemed deliberately turned around to face the chair where I would be sitting, so I could make some connection."

Eventually, Father Sword acknowledged Brother Reginald's presence in the room and excused himself so that the interview between Mother Ruth and her job applicant could commence.

"Mother Ruth and I began this conversation about our different philosophies on education. Clearly, we clashed. We clashed over that, we clashed over how one would teach religion. I wasn't trying to convince her. I was saying what was on my mind. I was very courteous, very mannerful. I was aware this was a religious superior and I was a religious subject. The whole tone of the interview was based off of those types of categories and hierarchical relationships. We talked for about forty-five minutes to an hour. She was very pleasant."

Then Mother Ruth made a silent gesture that Brother Reginald received as a non-verbal acknowledgment of a shared connection and understanding.

"She never pointed to the photograph, although she looked at it once and then she looked at me. I pretended like I didn't see that and I kept looking at her and talking. So there were these interesting little connections she was trying to make. She was letting me know she was of African American descent or some type of diasporan descent. I thought it was a very odd gesture to do that."

The photograph was verified by Sister Mary as Mother Ruth's deceased sister Loretta. Although Mother Ruth indicated that she would contact Brother Reginald directly about the position, he learned from his superior at the Absalom Jones Priory that he did not get the job. He shared with Rev. Sword, the prior, his theory about the placement of Loretta's photograph in his line of sight. In turn, Rev. Sword agreed with Brother Reginald that the portrait's placement was intended to elicit a reaction. "I sought counsel from him about it. Carl, being a psychotherapist, tried to interpret what that symbolized," Brother Reginald said.

After his official move to Harlem later in 1982, Brother Reginald sought and developed a relationship with what he called "the Black Episcopal Establishment" within the New York diocese. He was active in the diocese and nationally in Black Episcopal circles, including the Union of Black Episcopalians (UBE). It was one of the successor organizations to the nineteenth-century Conference of Church Workers Among Colored People, a group that Ruth herself had some affiliation with in the early 1900s as a sister in Toronto who authored her manifesto on the "problem with the races." Another connection Brother Reginald made was with the New York diocese's Suffragan Bishop Walter Dennis, who became New York's second African American bishop. He succeeded the diocese's first Black suffragan bishop, the Right Reverend Harold Lewis Wright, who died of a heart attack in 1978 at age forty-eight. Brother Reginald questioned these new church acquaintances about Mother Ruth. "That's how I found out that she had attended St. Philip's [in Harlem]," he said.

Dennis first came to New York to attend law school at New York University in 1952, the same year that CHS was founded. However, he changed career direction and enrolled at General Theological Seminary in Manhattan. In 1956, he was the first African American priest to serve as full-time clergy at St. John the Divine Cathedral. He was an assistant there until 1960. During that time, he developed conferences for both the New York diocese and the national church on race relations. In 1968, he was one of seventeen Black priests who met at Mother Ruth's childhood parish, St. Philip's in Harlem, and founded the Union of Black Clergy and Laity, which was later renamed the Union of Black Episcopalians.

With Bishop Dennis's long history at the cathedral and in New York, there is no doubt he crossed paths with Mother Ruth. Brother Reginald characterized the relationship between the two as "a major feud."

"What I remember hearing was around the fact that she refused to acknowledge her background. The friction between the two was around the issue of race—the refusal to acknowledge the African part of her at all and that she basically cut off the African American community in New York. So there was some tension there," he said, acknowledging that the information came from secondhand accounts from priests. "There were Black clergy—many now dead—who were aware of that feud and talked about Mother Ruth from time to time. She had nothing to do with the internal Black organizations of the Episcopal Church, UBE, nothing to do with it at all. For people that remembered her, there was anger and resentment around that; that she turned her back on us."

Admittedly, Sister Mary said she was not privy to all of Mother Ruth's relationships, but she confirmed that the bishop and Reverend Mother had diametrically opposing views on racial issues. "They respected each other, but each had their own way and own approaches that went in opposite directions." Mother Ruth opposed the idea of groups that were "Black only," even an affinity organization created by Black clergy. According to minutes from a 1960s-era chapter meeting, "the Reverend Mother here mentioned that the sisters had been invited to teach at an all-Negro school and that this had not been considered it would involve the community in segregated work. She also noted that our presence at St. George is temporary."

Despite Mother Ruth's refusal to engage with Black Episcopalians, there remained one Black Episcopalian whom she called "Sister" and appeared to make peace with—Constance, SSJD from Baltimore. Like her American compatriot did two decades earlier in 1938, Constance was forced to migrate to Canada to pursue her vocation by the racist and discriminatory practices of the Episcopal Church's religious orders. The two Americans clashed in the late 1940s during their time together in Canada's western prairie school. Sister Ruth had made Sister Constance's life difficult at the Qu'Appelle school through her defiance and disobedience, and by undermining the authority vested by the SSJD superior in Sister Constance. Despite Ruth's cutthroat separation from her Canadian order in 1949, she did return to Canada often, usually staying with friends and acquaintances. In 1979, however, she stayed in the SSJD convent in Toronto. While there, Sister Constance extended an olive branch. She wrote,

The Convent, S. S. J. D.

May 1st, 1979

Reverend and dear Mother Ruth,

For some thirty years now I have hoped the opportunity might be given me to write you a letter in peace. And now you are at the S. S. J. D. Convent and in the cell called "Peace," and in the spirit of peace.

I am seventy-five, so you must be around eighty. I would not have us be on the "home stretch" and not be reconciled, so I say, "God bless you." Much has happened in these last thirty years, many great things have been accomplished, and you have more than ever earned the "Well done." I salute you, and ask His continued blessing of you.

Lovingly in Christ,
Constance, S. S. J. D.

Apparently, Sister Constance's olive branch was accepted because during the 1980s, she returned to the United States and spent her "rest time" at St. Hilda's in New York.

"Sister Constance came to visit us at least once," Sister Mary said. "It was my impression there was a little thing between them—Mother Ruth and Sister Constance—a rivalry. They were nice to each other on the surface, of course. All of us were fascinated to meet her. Here was someone who was Mother Ruth's contemporary in SSJD." While there was Sister Edith Margaret who was also an SSJD contemporary, Sister Constance was an African American nun who was a peer. Sister Mary added that the CHS sisters' captivation with Sister Constance "didn't go over very well with Mother Ruth." Incidentally, Sister Constance wasn't as close to the "home stretch" in the 1980s as Mother Ruth. Sister Constance lived to be 109 years old and died in 2013.

21

THE BEGINNING OF THE END

While the 1980s marked a regime change in St. Hilda's convent with Mother Mary Cristabel's election as the Mother General, at the bishop's headquarters on Amsterdam Avenue, leadership change occurred a decade earlier. In 1972, Bishop Donegan handed over the bishop's crozier to his coadjutor Bishop Moore. While there were communications with the new generation of Episcopal clerics, it wasn't with the same frequency or reverence Mother Ruth extended to Donegan and West. Their retirements eroded the support system the octogenarian had relied on over the last four decades. In 1981, the one remaining priest who had empowered Mother Ruth, Canon West, retired from his position as subdean and canon sacristan of the Cathedral Church of St. John the Divine.

With her enablers no longer in power and her circle of support ever shrinking, Mother Ruth's most loyal and staunch companion, along with Sister Mary Winifred, was a pet Airedale terrier named Jonathan Hugh. The Airedale, by no small coincidence, was a breed that hailed from the Aire River valley region from Mother Ruth's beloved Yorkshire, England. He became an integral part of not only convent life but also the school. In one 1980s-era marketing booklet for the school, Jonathan's single portrait appeared on the inside cover page directly beneath the group photo of the board of trustees. Jonathan often did her bidding and biting. Evidently, he took his behavior cues from his "Mother," because the Airedale's relationship with the other CHS sisters was fraught with acrimony.

"Jonathan was a biter," Sister Mary said. Some of the sisters had caretaking responsibilities for the dog, including feeding, nightly walks, and attaching a big red bow to his collar at Christmas time. Jonathan's duties would often result in his teeth piercing a sister's skin. He even once chomped down on Mother Ruth's hand with such severity that he drew blood. The bite required an emergency room visit. Fearful that animal control officials might take her beloved Jonathan away, when the hospital's caregivers asked how she obtained the injury she offered a half-truth. "She said she stuck her hand under the table," Sister Mary said, which was true. That's where Jonathan was lying when he took a bite out of her hand. After injuring his "Mother," Jonathan Hugh was forced to participate in a weekly Chapter of Faults. In his case, the sisters offered a long list that detailed his many transgressions in the convent. After the number one fault, "Bit Mother's hand," furniture, book, and habit chewing and swallowing a habit's girdle cord were among more than two dozen faults that followed on the paper. Jonathan Hugh was viewed as a religious monastic canine since he was cloistered with the sisters. So he was often scolded for barking "at secular cats and dogs," according to his Chapter of Faults.

As for Mother Ruth's other constant companion, Sister Mary Winifred, her loyalty was rewarded with even more work and responsibilities. Even as a septuagenarian and octogenarian, Mother Ruth was a workaholic. Sister Mary wrote in an email, "She slept very little and so did I! She had to take huge amounts of aspirin because of arthritis pain."

Reverend Mother's dependence on her assistant grew exponentially as she got older. Because of her severe arthritis, when she entered her eighties, Mother Ruth was getting around mostly in a wheelchair chauffeured by Sister Mary Winifred. Despite all the intimate caretaking, there was little in the way of friendship, by secular standards, or overt expressions of affection from Mother Ruth toward her assistant. In turn, Sister Mary said she was not under any delusions that her many years of service to the Reverend Mother culminated in a friendship.

"I was the help," Sister Mary said flatly. The closest Mother Ruth came to acknowledging that the two had a special relationship that was more like a partnership was in a 1981 handwritten note part of the convent's custom of sending Easter greetings to all the CHS sisters. In

2024, along with Mother Ruth's portrait on her desk, Sister Mary still possessed the handwritten note as a cherished keepsake. Or, as she put it, "Evidence that Mother and I had a special bond and connection."

Easter 1981

To my very dear Sister,
    With loving joy and gratitude that the Lord is Risen and that He has given us the privilege and responsibility of sharing His work together.

    Ruth, CHS

"One of Mother's favorite closing prayers was by St. Augustine," Sister Mary remembered and recited it. "God, grant us to observe all these things as lovers of spiritual beauty, having our life fragrant with the sweet savor of Christ, not as slaves under law but as made free under grace."

"We did have a great spiritual connection," Sister Mary said. In spite of their "connection," the assistant's good faith efforts to engage Mother Ruth on a personal level sometimes ended in extreme rebuke. Sister Mary Winifred was one of only a few subordinates and subjects who truly revered her as inspirational on a spiritual level. However, the bond was strong insofar as Sister Mary was in total agreement with her superior.

"Once she said she didn't agree with me the conversation came to an end," she said.

One of Mother Ruth's beliefs that she conveyed to Sister Mary Winifred completely contradicted her lifelong conviction that God spoke directly to her, as she wrote in her 1935 manifesto. "I believe God has personal individual relations and God pays attention to individual people. She did not believe that," Sister Mary told me during our interview. "Mother said that was ridiculous. She believed God had a personal relationship with humanity, not individuals." Sister Mary Winifred knew she could not question the Reverend Mother on her stance. After that, "the conversation came to an end."

In the final five years of Mother Ruth's life, when she was no longer the superior, chief among all of Sister Mary Winifred's responsibilities was message courier between the Reverend Mother Foundress and Mother Superior Mary Christabel. Mother Mary Christabel's leadership efforts were routinely usurped and even sabotaged by the Reverend Mother Ruth. This dynamic was widely known and discussed among all the Episcopal religious orders.

"Even when Mother Ruth left office and Christabel succeeded her, everyone knew, or at least we gossiped, this was within the religious communities, that Christabel in fact was just a figurehead and Mother was still ruling," Brother Reginald said.

Decades of Mother Ruth's sometimes cruel, heavy-handed rule had climaxed into a tug-of-war of control between the two mothers, which led to further fissures and widespread dysfunction across CHS. The toxicity of her authoritarian leadership style and, as one sister likened the culture, a Soviet Union–era "KGB-like" atmosphere that was abetted by disgruntled, demoralized, and disenchanted sisters required years of clergy and therapist intervention that continued well into the next century.

In 1984, despite Mother Ruth's both physical and mental decline, she fought desperately hard to retain the one leadership position she still held—headmistress of the school. A multi-strategy operation commenced to push Mother Ruth out of the position, which began shortly after Brother Reginald's 1982 interview. Parents continued to lodge complaints about Mother Ruth's leadership at the school. An organized group of students staged a graffiti protest campaign and vandalized the school building with mailing labels with the words "Mother Ruth is a Drug Addict" printed on the stickers. Other complaints about Mother Ruth's competency were coming directly from inside the convent and made it to the desk of Bishop Moore.

The multi-prong approach by the school board and CHS sisters, led by Mother Mary Christabel, to push Mother Ruth into full retirement was met with resistance and failure. Even the strong arm of a diocesan bishop was unable to solve the problem of Ruth.

"I socialized with a lot of powerful people in the diocese, bishops, and priests," said Dana Catherine, goddaughter of Madeleine

L'Engle, who was in St. Hilda's inaugural first grade class in 1952. "I would be at cocktail parties, I heard priests and even bishops say they were absolutely afraid of her."

The Mother Ruth situation was elevated to the presiding bishop of the Episcopal Church, the Very Right Reverend John Maury Allin. It appeared he alone had the power to make Mother Ruth surrender.

Thirteen of the senior CHS sisters made a final effort. On July 22, 1984, led by Mother Superior Mary Christabel, the thirteen nuns signed a letter of petition to their Mother. While praising her for the two institutions she built, they beseeched her to retire. On the convent's letterhead, they wrote,

To our Mother Ruth—holy and beloved in the Lord,

We address you thus with all our hearts. You have devoted yourself with all the powers of body, mind and spirit to the Lord—guided by his Holy Spirit, you have built a Community in which we believe and to which, by his grace, we belong.

With the same strength and the same guidance, you have built a school of which we are justly proud. We believe it is a great school, and we believe in its future.

But we also believe that the time has come when you must give the running of it into other hands. We know there is no one to fill the office of head in the way or with the great care and judgment with which you have filled it. But others may have other gifts to bring.

We have been with you and watched you these last three or four years with great care and anxiety—coping with one physical handicap after the other—handicaps that don't go away at the age of 86 or 87. We have seen you suffer what must have been 2, if not 3, small strokes this last year, and we have watched your efforts to make a comeback that are nothing short of valiant.

Please believe that we say these things in reverent love to you, and in gratitude for all that God has given us in you and through your hands.

Your loving daughters

True to Mother Ruth's unyielding nature, she put up a fight. She stood her ground and doubled down. She wrote directly to Mother Mary Christabel: "I have been working on the plans for 1984–1985 and trying to find the right combination of faculty for 1984-85, the new curricula, etc. etc. . . . I am quite unwilling to leave 'my' work under GOD which He has given me to complete." She did offer the timetable of June 1985, exactly fifty years after she proclaimed to SSJD that God had appointed her to deal with the "problem of the races," as "my date for completing my work." Mother Ruth would be eighty-seven years old in June 1985.

Presiding Bishop Allin paid a visit to St. Hilda's convent and addressed the sisters, with a special message targeted at Mother Ruth. Mother Mary Christabel followed up with a handwritten letter to reinforce that message:

Dear Mother, This morning was a tremendously importance [*sic*] experience for all of us. It was wonderful to hear the Presiding Bishop ask you to do such an important and much needed task. I know that he is right in saying that this is the job you need to do especially (and moreso) for the Church as a whole. It is an urgent task and noone [*sic*]—but no one—is equipped as you to do it.

That "much needed task" Bishop Allin asked Mother Ruth to do for both her community and the entire Episcopal Church was to write her biography.

Mother Mary Christabel emphasized to Mother Ruth the magnitude of Presiding Bishop Allin's request. The directive from the Primate was not only on-par, but Mother Mary Christabel insinuated that it superseded the initial order to create the school four decades earlier from New York's diocesan Bishop Gilbert. She wrote, "When you came from Toronto you began the School because you were asked to. Now we have all heard you asked by no less a person than the Presiding Bishop to do an equally important task." Mother Mary Christabel astutely played to Mother Ruth's ego and belief that she was appointed by God. Echoing words from Mother Ruth's 1935 manifesto, she added, "What you have to say from your unique experience can truly point the way forward for God's people."

The request was answered not only with Mother Ruth's usual obstinance, she went so far as to question the authority of the presiding bishop to make such a request of her in the first place. She responded to Mother Mary Christabel: "I would not think of disparaging the Primate's most kind and generous suggestions but as I understand our Constitution, the authority and therefore the permissions are vested in the Episcopal Visitor and the Warden of the Community."

The bishop visitor during that time was the Right Reverend Frank Griswold, coadjutor bishop of the Diocese of Chicago, who later would also become the Episcopal Church's presiding bishop.

One of Mother Ruth's most powerful protectors, Bishop Donegan had retired as head of the diocese. Yet he remained in his position on the school's board of trustees. In a direct reply to Mother Mary Christabel, she invoked his name with her rebuttals. Regarding her medical conditions, she wrote that she would "have a complete physical examination to discover truly what is the condition of 'me.'" And "I will submit all of this to Bishop Donegan on his return in August and then a clear decision can be made by the suitable authorities."

Those authorities, who included Bishop Allin, did make a decision. Mother Ruth was sent to Hawaii to begin work on the book that became *In Wisdom Thou Hast Made Them*. Mother Ruth did not want to go, according to Sister Mary, but felt she had no choice.

"We have a poverty of time" was one of Mother Ruth's recurring lines. And in this instance, she probably had an inkling her time was running out.

The pair stayed in Kilauea in a newly renovated guest apartment at Christ Memorial Episcopal Church's Parish Hall. While she was in Hawaii, a new head of school moved into Mother Ruth's office at St. Hilda's & St. Hugh's and began the work to open the 1984–1985 school year.

"When Mother Ruth and I left for Hawaii, I knew she was not going to be head of school when we came back, but she hadn't gotten that message," Sister Mary said. "I did feel kind of guilty, but I couldn't do anything either to make her retire, so off we went."

A letter was sent to Mother Ruth in Hawaii notifying her that she had been removed as headmistress and that a new school leader had been installed. "Mother Mary Christabel said I was the sacrificial lamb. If Mother Ruth got really angry, it would be at me (because I was there with her in Hawaii) and not at the rest of them back in New York." But she didn't get angry. "She was very depressed," said Sister Mary. "It was scary."

Mother Ruth did very little work on the book after that. When the Reverend Mother and her assistant returned from Hawaii, the book work was taken up by four of the CHS sisters, including the ejected Sister Julian. She had been allowed to return with the help of her childhood surrogate mother and now superior, Mother Mary Christabel.

Up until the last two months of her life, Mother Ruth was active and traveling. While Sister Mary Winifred was with her, she took two major trips. One was a return to Toronto in 1984 for the 100th anniversary celebration of the founding of the Sisterhood of St. John the Divine. There she was reunited with three of the living sisters who had been in the order with her, including "rival" Sister Constance.

The other long-distance trip was to Washington, DC. It had been Mother Ruth's wish to visit President John F. Kennedy's grave at Arlington National Cemetery. Sister Mary Winifred, although still quite young in her mid-thirties, struggled to push the Reverend Mother in her wheelchair through the vast cemetery to the site of the Eternal Flame. President Kennedy was another of Mother Ruth's "White Saviors."

"She thought Kennedy had done a lot for the races," Sister Mary said, and confirmed he was Mother Ruth's Civil Rights hero. "I really never heard her talk about Martin Luther King, but she adored President Kennedy."

In what might have been a final blow that further diminished and crippled Mother Ruth's ability to wield power and authority in the convent, her one loyal remaining staff, subordinate, and lackey, Sister Mary Winifred, was removed from her role as "Mother's assistant." In 1985, Mother Superior Mary Christabel assigned the assistant to the CHS branch convent sixty miles away from St. Hilda's House in upstate Brewster. Her new assignment was to run the retreat house, St. Cuthbert. Sister Mary Winifred was in fact desperately needed to manage the retreat house, which was without sufficient staff because of the departure of another sister. Initially, Sister Mary Winifred protested the new assignment that separated her from her Mother. However, Mother Ruth told her to take it. "She's giving you a plum," she told Sister Mary.

"I absolutely loved Mother and felt like that is where I was called to be," Sister Mary said. And although she had other jobs in the admission office of the school and within the convent, it was her role as Mother's assistant that defined her life in the community. As often as she could, Sister Mary Winifred visited Mother Ruth back in New York City.

As her health deteriorated, Sister Mary Winifred tried to offer comfort. Following one of Mother Ruth's many hospitalizations during her waning months, Sister Mary Winifred erroneously thought that Mother Ruth might want to connect and reconcile with her biological family.

"Mother Ruth rarely spoke of her family, although when she did, she often mentioned Loretta and Arthur," Sister Mary said. "She was at the end of life. Before she died, I thought she might want to be in touch with her family."

She did some detective work with the goal of locating one of Mother Ruth's living siblings to provide her with contact information. She focused on Arthur, because he was the one living sibling she had talked about. Sister Mary Winifred successfully located the address and contact information for Arthur, who had moved to New Mexico. When she presented the contact information to Mother Ruth and suggested she should call him, the reaction wasn't what Sister Mary Winifred anticipated.

"She was absolutely furious with me," said Sister Mary, who indicated that despite her frail condition, Mother Ruth was able to muster up enough strength to chastise her longtime assistant. Her anger was fierce. "She said, 'no, I absolutely will not call him.' She was so mad at me."

Mother Ruth accepted visits from other lay people in her waning

days, most notably Madeleine L'Engle and her goddaughter, Dana
Catherine. Since her high school graduation, Dana had maintained
a friendship with Mother Ruth. During her adult years, she called her
"Reverend Mum." And like many of Mother Ruth's relationships,
Dana's relationship with her teacher and friend over three decades
was a roller coaster of highs and lows. Dana had returned to New
York after living in Mexico with her husband, from whom she had
separated. After her return, she attempted to get a job as a switchboard operator at St. Hilda's. Instead of showing her charity, which
Dana had experienced in the past, the Reverend Mother chastised
her. Dana, who shared an excerpt from her journal from that time,
wrote in June 1980 after a meeting with Mother Ruth,

> She told me I couldn't have the job for two reasons. 1) I couldn't
> handle it and 2) she didn't approve of what I was doing, i.e. liv-
> ing up here not being divorced—she said she'd told me to either
> go back be noble and put up with it—"be a saint" or stay up here
> and get divorced and "don't look back." It was devastating to
> say the least—I couldn't keep the tears from rolling down my
> cheeks. I felt humiliated, incompetent, let down, put out, as in
> a stray, unwanted and unloved. She also told me I couldn't hold
> my own as a translator or a teacher, which irritated me because
> I know I can and I have and she doesn't know that part of me
> and it hurt me badly.

Mother Ruth did end up giving Dana a job and she even sent her
children to St. Hilda's & St. Hugh's, paid for with some scholarship
money. In another journal entry, Dana wrote that Mother Ruth told
her, "you have been like a light to me and I am happy to be able to help
you in any way." Dana ended that entry with, "I was astounded."

On November 14, 1986, after Dana's last visit with Mother Ruth,
she wrote in her journal,

> Madeleine and I went to see Mother Ruth in the hospital today.
> Madeleine first then I. I just came to say "I love you" and "the
> boys send their love, too"

"And I love you" she said with great difficulty "tell them I
send love" Tell them
I cried.

By stark contrast, Dana characterized Madeleine's reaction to the
dying Mother Ruth as cold. The celebrated author even criticized
Dana for shedding tears. The next day, Dana wrote, "I am upset over
Madeleine's reaction to my tears yesterday. I cry so rarely in front of
people. My sense of loss was real—and I felt she tried to stop it by
telling me that this was an ok death."

In early December, Sister Mary Winifred flew home to Texas to
spend two weeks with her family. Instead of returning to Brewster
after her flight back, Sister Mary Winifred stayed in New York with
Mother Ruth. "She was so much worse than when I left," she recalled. Although she was still able to get up and go to the bathroom,
for the most part the Reverend Mother was bedridden. A hospital
bed was rented, and Mother Ruth was moved from her cell into the
much larger adjoining room that had served as her office for the last
thirty years. The final day of her life, Mother Ruth floated in and out
of sleep and consciousness. That night, about eight of the sisters,
including Mother Mary Christabel, gathered around Mother Ruth's
hospital bed for Compline, the final prayers of the Divine Office before the Great Silence. Mother Ruth was awake and alert for Compline. The sisters recited the Nunc Dimittis, the Canticle of Simeon
from the Gospel of Luke.

> Lord, now lettest thou thy servant depart in peace accord-
> ing to thy word.
> For mine eyes have seen thy salvation,
> Which thou hast prepared before the face of all people;
> To be a light to lighten the Gentiles and to be the glory of
> thy people Israel.

After the Canticle, the gathered sisters except for one, Sister
Mary Winifred, retired to their cell for the night. Sister Mary Winifred stayed alone in the room in a bedside chair with the Reverend

Mother. Through a good portion of the night, she was awake and talking. "She was very thirsty and asked for water several times."

Over the fleeting hours of the night that marched into the wee early morning dawn of December 22, 1986, Sister Mary Winifred repeatedly grabbed Mother Ruth's hand both to squeeze it to let her know she was still there and to check to see how Mother Ruth was doing. By approximately 2 a.m., Mother Ruth's hands had grown cold, although she was still breathing. Sister Mary Winifred checked her feet, which were also cold. She knew Mother Ruth was slipping away. She had promised to awaken Mother Mary Christabel if there was a change. For the first time in hours, Sister Mary left Mother Ruth's side to get the CHS superior. A couple of hours later, shortly before all the CHS sisters would arise to end the Great Silence for Morning Lauds, Mother Ruth died. The former assistant and superior were by her side. The two women removed Mother Ruth's nightgown and washed her body. Then, they dressed her in her habit. Later in the morning as news spread through the convent, other CHS sisters arrived in the room and gathered around the bed where she lay. They prayed the Divine Office's Lauds of the Dead:

> Into your hands, O merciful Savior,
>   we commend your servant Ruth.
> Acknowledge, we humbly beseech you,
>   a sheep of your own fold,
> a lamb of your own flock, a sinner of your own redeeming.
> Receive her into the arms of your mercy,
> into the blessed rest of everlasting peace,
> and into the glorious company of the saints in light. Amen.
>
> May her soul and the souls of all the departed, +
>   through the
> mercy of God, rest in peace. Amen.

It wouldn't be until around noon when the funeral home arrived to remove Mother Ruth's body. Mother Mary Christabel and Sister

Mary had to fulfill one last order that a lucid Mother Ruth demanded be carried out at the time of her death.

"She wanted us to put her dentures in her mouth before the funeral home came to take her body away," Sister Mary said.

Following Ruth (for Ruth Elaine Younger)
By Sister Mary

We weren't exactly
Elijah and Elisha-like
Tramping over Gilgal, Bethel, and Jericho,
All the way to the Jordan River,
But there were always miracles
And outrageous events;
Visions that no one else quite saw,
Almost as spectacular as fire from heaven,
And just as dangerous, too.
And there was a company of prophets,
Following, chattering questions,
Staring, finally mute and pseudo-pious,
From a great distance.
But it was our agreement,
Unwritten contract on life's balance,
That I've rather kept to since that dawning
When I watched your bed grow chariot wheels
And the sheets white and flame-like
Carried you from here to there.
I wrap your cloak around my shoulders,
Knowing and half afraid of knowing
What a double measure
Of your spirit will incur.

22

ELEGY

"There was more in him to be praised, than to be pardoned," and in the life of Mother Ruth one might add, or to be faulted or resented.[1]

The Reverend Mother Ruth's Memorial Eucharist was celebrated on the Reverend Dr. Martin Luther King Jr. federal holiday. It was the second year the holiday was celebrated after congressional and presidential enactment. The now deceased Father Leslie Lang said during his sermon that the legendary Civil Rights hero was "so greatly admired by Reverend Mother, and with special reason, for to use her own words, which are revealing, she had a 'strain' of that 'other blood,' the blood that flowed in the martyr's veins. She knew prejudice most painful."

Sister Mary mailed me the printed leaflet of that sermon in 2018, along with the University of Toronto science research medal and other boxes and padded envelopes full of mementos and historical records of Mother Ruth's life. However, I waited to read that sermon in its entirety until more than six years later, on the day that I completed this biography. The reason was that when I began my research on Mother Ruth's life in earnest, I decided I wanted to conduct it in as close to chronological order as I could, beginning with Ancestry .com. I also settled on this approach because I wanted, in a manner

---

1. Borrowed from Ben Jonson's quote about William Shakespeare by the Reverend Dr. Leslie John Alden Lang for his sermon at the Memorial Eucharist for the Reverend Mother Ruth Monday, January 19, 1987.

of speaking, to grow up with Ruth Elaine Younger. And along the way, I did.

As I got to know Mother Ruth, I grew to love her. She became family to me. I communicated to Sister Mary in an email that I too, now loved Mother Ruth. She wrote back. "Mother Ruth was difficult, but I loved her and am thrilled to find that someone else cares about her too." Along the way I found many others who cared about her. Author of the book *Mama's Girls*, Janette McCarthy Louard wrote in her acknowledgments that "Reverend Mother Ruth saw the potential in me and refused to accept anything other than my best effort."[2] Now known as Janette McCarthy Wallace, she is the general counsel for the NAACP. In school alumna Karen Watson's first email in reply to my interview request, she wrote, "I am so excited that you have reached out to me and would be delighted to talk with you. Mtr. Ruth was a very significant influence in my life and made a major impact on who I am today."

Mother Ruth was and is an iconic archetype of a strong Black woman, who I realized wasn't just familiar to me, but to many. This archetype was embodied in my great-grandmother Clara Anderson Allen. She was a woman I never met but was a force to be reckoned with, I learned through family stories. And while this may be presumptuous of me to conjecture, this fierce Black woman archetype was also known to the former First Lady Michelle Obama. While I was deeply immersed in my early interviews with people who knew Mother Ruth—prioritizing people in their seventies, eighties, and nineties—a friend gifted me Mrs. Obama's biography *Becoming*. More than anything in that book, I was completely enraptured by the former First Lady's aunt Robbie, whom she called "a terror" in her life. As the first Aunt Robbie story unfolded in Mrs. Obama's biography, the resonance to Mother Ruth's personality was instantaneous. I am embarrassed to admit I never finished reading *Becoming*. My last memory of the biography was Mrs. Obama referencing the death of Aunt Robbie, which was probably why I never completed reading the book.

---

2. Janette McCarthy Louard, *Mama's Girls* (Sepia BET Books, 2002).

Another book I intentionally sought out was Walter Isaacson's biography of Steve Jobs, another visionary who was also loathed for his nasty streak. It was uncanny the number of identical personality traits—especially his leadership style, ambition, and tenacity—that the iconic technology mogul shared with this monastic mogul that was Mother Ruth. Humanity, all of us, are easily drawn to and are in awe of people, especially American leaders, with great character flaws. It makes heroes more human. Even fictionalized popular culture has produced these nasty, beloved, flawed lead characters such as in *The Godfather*, the Fox TV show *Empire*, HBO's Tony Soprano, and the leader of the pack Jax Teller of *Sons of Anarchy*. Hollywood comedy even produced a wildly amusing, lovable sliver of a likeness to Mother Ruth. She existed in the character of the pious, Bible thumping, and pocketbook slinging Aunt Esther, the comic foil and nemesis of Redd Fox's Fred Sanford in the 1970s hit sitcom *Sanford & Son*.

As Alice Parker, the White woman who said Mother Ruth was identical to her mother, demonstrated, the soul of Mother Ruth is everywhere: women you both feared and respected. And as Kris Watson, who never doubted Mother Ruth's racial background, pointed out, many of those traits were in her own mother, whom she feared more than Mother Ruth.

The Order of the Holy Cross monk Brother Reginald-Martin Crenshaw offered a surprisingly objective opinion on Mother Ruth's personality and lasting legacy. In spite of being roundly rejected by her, his hindsight view decades later, coupled with being a church insider and person of African descent, was sympathetic while blunt and critical. He didn't mince words. He made it clear he vehemently despised her and chose not to attend her funeral. Still, he echoed others, especially a few African American people who knew Mother Ruth, in viewing her caustic personality as internalized trauma and internalized oppression.

With a ministry focused on anti-racism training; and diversity, inclusion, and equity work, Brother Reginald's views were compassionate and academic. Decades after Mother Ruth's death, he was invited to return to St. Hilda's House to develop an anti-racism workshop for the CHS sisters. While the CHS sisters opted not to participate in Brother Reginald's sessions, during the initial dialogue, Mother Ruth's backstory was revealed to him.

"She was threatened," he said. "In terms of founding the school, if she didn't do what they wanted, she would be exposed for passing for White, her career and her community would go down the tubes, and basically they would destroy her in some ways.

"I was surprised to learn all that. I had a slight change of heart about her, very slight, about who she was and what she wanted to do," he said. "Her treatment of the sisters probably had a lot to do with the anger she felt in terms of the boxes she was in. One of those boxes she created, the other was created by the society she lived in at that time. She had very little room, and within that room she was absolutely abusive. Here were White men telling her what to do and how to do it. And what was under her were White women who did what she told them to do. I don't think there is a disconnect on some level around internalized oppression and White supremacy." He said Mother Ruth's trauma from internalized oppression had an impact on the relationships among the women within that community that lasted into the present day.

An example of Mother Ruth's impact on the community played out in 2009, and one person who ended up getting hurt by it was Sister Mary. "My relationship with CHS is complicated too, maybe because I was close to Mother Ruth," she said. "Before the Sisters moved to the new convent in the city, they invited sisters who had left CHS to a celebration, but I wasn't included. I heard about it, after the event, from another sister who had left before I did."

The fractures and lingering dysfunction were apparent to me also. When I arrived at Melrose, the sisters were divided into two camps. The five city sisters lived in the new convent in Harlem, and the three farm sisters lived in Brewster. They rarely saw each other in person, only in online meetings. In December of 2019, the New York City real estate firm Denham Wolf sold the four-story, 10,600-square-foot building for $7.4 million. At that time, only two sisters were living in it. One sister moved to Melrose, and the other two (now deceased), Sister Mary Elizabth and Sister Elise, lived out their remaining years in the nursing home close to Melrose in Danbury, Connecticut. The two "city sisters," as they were often called, today live in an opulent, three-bedroom luxury penthouse apartment in Morningside Heights near the cathedral.

During my time in Brewster, I became disillusioned by the community. In 2019, it became apparent that the majority of the sisters were in retirement mode. Launching the farm ministry at their age and with a small community for women of color coming out of incarceration was far-fetched. I ended up returning to my former profession, public relations and communications, landing a part-time job at the Upper West Side Manhattan Episcopal parish, St. Michael's Church. In addition, I became a regular volunteer for the charity operating out of the old Melrose School, Second Chance Foods. The secular organization dedicated to reducing food waste and providing meals to those suffering with food insecurity was the closest I came to the desired ministry and vocation I had spent a decade searching for. My work with Second Chance Foods, volunteering in food preparation and as an unofficial assistant to its cofounder, Martha Elder, jolted me into the realization that in order to live the gospel, I needed to find a life outside of the Episcopal Church.

I continued to live at Melrose for another year, helping the sisters with the upkeep of the farm and St. Cuthbert's House and caring for the sisters themselves. I even took one of the sisters to the hospital and stayed with her after she became ill. I decided it was time to move on after the CHS sisters said that I, along with the others who had come to Brewster to start this new ministry, needed to pay them rent to live in St. Cuthbert House. The three farm apprentices from Ghana left immediately after receiving the email and departed a month later. All of us who were invited to live at Melrose were resigned to the fact that the sisters were not in the position to, nor did they have the ability to, start a new ministry or charity.

About a month before the pandemic lockdown, I moved in with another Episcopal order of nuns, the Community of St. John the Baptist (CSJB). I was accepted into their Alongsider Program. For the first time, I lived inside the monastic enclosure. My room for six months was a twelve-by-ten-foot "cell" in the century-old Tudor Revival convent listed on the National Register of Historic Places in Mendham,

New Jersey. I lived among all White women; all but two were in their seventies and eighties. The youngest had become the superior, Sister Monica Claire of viral TikTok video and commercial fame. My time there confirmed a second self-discovery: that this enclosed life with all White women living under a restrictive and regimented life in a cell was no place for a middle-aged African American woman with my personality. Living in that cell (a word I pondered a lot over my six months with CSJB) and my efforts to follow their lifestyle were demoralizing and repressive. There was little room for individuality and creativity in the way I needed to express myself. The pandemic lockdown, the murder of George Floyd, the deaths of my brother Richard Lloyd Allen, who succumbed to his cancer back in my hometown of Dayton, Ohio, and another relative, all exacerbated that experience, for sure.

I interviewed Regina while at CSJB when she told me the story of that Black Panamanian woman, Elizabeth, who was rejected during her novitiate. I had to wonder if Mother Ruth did her a favor by turning her away from CHS "to serve her own people."

I threw myself into my research work, interviewing sources, and writing Mother Ruth's biography. Living within that monastic enclosure of CSJB was the period Mother Ruth morphed into a hero for me, someone I was growing to admire, because I had this vantage point that Brother Reginald talked about of "living in a box." I, too, like Mother Ruth, felt trapped inside some boxes. And honestly, in my case, many of those boxes were also of my own making. I also came to realize through my work that Mother Ruth was being birthed again for a third time by and through me. She was an Ancestor who became a very human Matron Saint to me. In the quiet of the Great Silence in the CSJB convent, I heard Mother Ruth's voice in my head.

Collectively, I have spent nearly three years living in all-White religious communities for women. In addition to my two years with the CHS sisters and the six months with the St. John the Baptist sisters, I had short stints living in convents. I spent nearly six months in the guest wing of the convent of the Community of the Transfiguration in Cincinnati, and a three-week long retreat in Maidenhead, England, at the eleventh-century Burnham Abbey with the Sisters of the Precious Blood, and a weekend with Community of the Sisters of the Love of God in Oxford, England. I am indebted to all of these communities and remain highly appreciative and honored to have been welcomed into their world as a retreatant, temporary resident, and guest. Many of these sisters ministered to me at times in my life when I was in crisis. They prayed for me, they helped me, and they loved me. However, I never felt like I was a part of those communities, even as an associate of Transfiguration, nor did I belong in their communities. And much of that sentiment stemmed partly from my identity as an African American woman. I was truly never 100 percent comfortable, nor did I ever truly feel like I fit in.

To a lesser degree, that was now my overall feeling about the Episcopal Church. Like the awakening of the nation in 2020 in the post-Obama presidency, the election of the Very Right Reverend Michael Curry as presiding bishop of the Episcopal Church did not mark a new post-racial era in the denomination.

After working for two years for the diverse congregation, St. Michael's parish on Manhattan's Upper West Side, a place that I adored but did not give me a livable wage, I became the director of communications at the very affluent, Upper East Side Episcopal parish, St. James' Church on Madison Avenue. I often described the socio-economic profile of the parishioners as ladies who lunched, or as Truman Capote might have called them, swans who lunched and carried purses that were worth more than my car. There, instead of the church potlucks I grew up with and was accustomed to at other parishes that I attended and worked at, St. James' gatherings with food were catered with fifty-dollars-per-plate fare from Butterfield's Market, which advertised itself as an "upscale" grocery and catering company on Lexington Avenue. Two Hispanic women, St. James' housekeeping staff, often stood at the ready by a beverage table pouring coffee and tea during these events. Even Garrison Keillor, a parishioner at St. Michael's whom I became pandemic pen pals with, bemoaned my departure from the Upper West Side church and emailed me: "Wow. St. James'. We'll need to buy you some silk stockings and white gloves."

The first day I walked into St. James' for work in 2020—my interviews were over Zoom because of the pandemic—I immediately knew I didn't fit in that predominantly White world either. My biggest comfort while working at St. James' was knowing it was the very parish where Bishop Donegan served before becoming a diocesan bishop. We held meetings in Donegan Hall, and I would often position myself directly across from his large portrait. I had conversations with him in my head about Mother Ruth and, on occasion, I'd ask him what I was doing there. I was very unhappy; I found the clergy, staff, and parishioners less welcoming than at St. Michael's. And I admit my performance wasn't up to par and I wasn't meeting the huge demands of the job during the pandemic.

After two years working there, I had a very painful separation in which the rector, a White woman, asked me not to return to the parish and didn't allow me a proper good-bye with my colleagues I had worked with for nearly two years. The man in charge of human resources reiterated that in an email, asking me not to show up for the weekly free lunch that was open to the public, where I had hoped to say good-bye to the staff. As Olive Kelsey decried when the memorial fund she set up for her deceased daughter was misappropriated, "that kind of deviousness wasn't supposed to be happening in an institution of the Lord." Dr. King said it best, that "sin is separation."

Back in Brewster, Melrose was up for sale. Throughout this book, I referred to the site as Melrose, the original name that Mother Ruth gave the property. The farm sisters had renamed the property Bluestone Farm and Living Arts Center. The Aaron Copland Society purchased the entire site for three million dollars, which included twenty-four acres of woodlands, all the buildings, St. Cuthbert's Pre-Revolutionary War manor, and the former Episcopal grade school and three other buildings.

Two of the Brewster sisters ended up in a nursing home in Ridgefield, Connecticut. Two others are living in separate apartments in Woodstock, New York. And two sisters remained in the city in the penthouse apartment in Manhattan's Morningside Heights near the cathedral. Netting ten million dollars in real estate deals, and no longer having any ties to the St. Hilda's & St. Hugh's School, the six CHS sisters were far from living a life of poverty.

I visited Melrose one last time in May 2023, after the first offer was made by the Aaron Copland Fund for Music, which ultimately acquired the Brewster estate. In preparation for the realtor's showings, the cluttered and dilapidated school building had been painted, cleaned, and decorated for showing. For the first time, Mother Ruth's large photo, along with the three other founding sisters, was hung prominently on the wall near the entry doors.

On April 27, 2024, the ashes of Mother Ruth and thirteen deceased CHS sisters removed from the Melrose columbarium, along with the ashes of three other deceased sisters, were entombed in niches at the Cathedral Church of St. John the Divine, the very place where Mother Ruth was enshrined in 1952 as the Reverend Mother and the Community of the Holy Spirit was officially received into the Episcopal Church through the Diocese of New York.

During my last walk through the Melrose School and as I drove past the St. Hilda's & St. Hugh's School again in Manhattan, I recalled Father Lang's 1987 eulogy of the Reverend Mother Ruth that culminated with these words:

> Because she was the way she was, she created something unique in the annals of academic history. There was in her the essence of refinement, most beautiful manners, a shy sweetness, not always apparent (she was not always self-assured as she seemed to be). She was a lady! She was an abbess! She knew she was called and wanted to be, a Saint. And, maybe, it is the wanting that becomes in the end the making of it. She will go on from strength to strength.

ACKNOWLEDGMENTS

All the initial work and the crucial letters that provided missing links were the efforts of one woman, Sister Mary (a.k.a. Sister Mary Winifred née Emily Shepherd). She remains the one and only living person who was closest to the Reverend Mother. Over six years, Sister Mary and I exchanged countless emails and talked for hours on the phone. I visited her for three days on the Eastern Shore of Maryland for face-to-face interviews. This book would have been so much more difficult to research and write if it hadn't been for Sister Mary. Also, a special thanks to the Younger family, Peter, Art, and Jacyln.

I am appreciative beyond measure to my book editor, Sulay Hernandez of Unveiled Ink. Sulay was more than an editor; she was an answered prayer. Working with Sulay was copy editor Susan Afanuh—my former CDC colleague and a dear friend; together they were a creative and editorial dream team.

My research travels and technical support were made possible through grants from the Historical Society of the Episcopal Church and the Episcopal Women's History Project. Other significant financial support and retreat writing space were provided by the Community of the Transfiguration, Glendale, Ohio.

For residencies, retreats, and other places to write, eat, sleep, and commune with nature: Community of St. John Baptist, Mendham, New Jersey, and Order of the Holy Cross, West Park, New York. For use of the artist apartment, the Presbyterian Church's Stony Point Center in Stony Point, New York, and during my 2020 bereavement the Society of St. Margaret's Duxbury, Massachusetts. Mrs. Evelyn New, York, Maine, and during the most lonely periods of the pandemic, Shut up and Write! Dayton (OH) Metro Library; the Nyack (NY) Library; and my office at Wholly Grounds Tearoom and Coffeehouse in Dayton and the life-giving tea blends created by owner Amy Williams.

Crucial support was provided by Rick Hamlin, Joan Marans Dim, Vanessa Parks, James Amorello, Beth Castrodale, Sophfronia Scott, fellow Buckeye the Rev. Sister Constance Joanna Gefvert, SSJD, Wayne Kempton, Sister Victoria Michelle, CSJB, CHS sisters Heléna Marie, Catherine Grace, Emmanuel, Faith Margaret, Claire Joy, and Elise (deceased), the Reverend Sister Promise Marie, SSM, the Rev. Stacy Salles, the Rev. Charles Graves IV, Patty Mitchell, Martha Elder, Samuel Harps, and Garrison Keillor.

Invaluable access to archival records: the Community of the Holy Spirit; the Episcopal Diocese of New York; Sisterhood of St. John the Divine, Toronto; the Putnam County Historian, Brewster, New York; and the National Archives of the Episcopal Church.

My agents at Folio Literary Management, Sonali Chanchani & Claudia Cross, and my supportive editor, Andrew Knapp. Artie Isaac, for getting me unstuck.

And faraway, round-the-clock, and never-ending support of family and dear friends. My beloved brothers, William Lawrence "Larry" and James Edward; sister-in-love Vivian; nephews Maurice Emmanuel and Daniel James; my god-family, Julian, Miles, Maya, and Sara; cousins Cece and Joe; my Ghanian roomies, Duke, Judith, and Abraham "AB." So many dear friends, especially Anissa, Olive, Wanda, Jan, Christol, Suzette, Angela P., Erica P., Theresa W-T, and Doris.

PHOTOS

Pinkie Ruth Younger |
Photo courtesy Peter A. Younger

William Younger | Photo courtesy Peter A. Younger

STATE OF NEW YORK
Department of Health of The City of New York
BUREAU OF RECORDS
STANDARD CERTIFICATE OF DEATH

1 PLACE OF DEATH
BOROUGH OF **Manhattan**
No. **676 St. Nicholas Ave.**
Character of premises, whether tenement, private, hotel, hospital or other place, etc. **Tenement**
Registered No. **21811**

3 FULL NAME **Ruth Younger**

4 SEX **Female**   5 COLOR OR RACE **Colored**   6 SINGLE, MARRIED, WIDOWED, OR DIVORCED (Write the word) **Widowed**

15 DATE OF DEATH **September 2 1925** (Month) (Day) (Year)

6 DATE OF BIRTH ______ , 1 (Month) (Day) (Year)

7 AGE **51** yrs. ___ mos. ___ ds.   If LESS than 1 day ... hrs. or ... min.?

8 OCCUPATION (a) Trade, profession, or particular kind of work **Domestic**
(b) General nature of industry, business or establishment in which employed (or employer)

9 BIRTHPLACE (State or country) **Washington, D.C.**
(A) How long in U. S. (if of foreign birth) **Entire Life**   (B) How long resident in City of New York **50 years**

PARENTS OF DECEASED
10 NAME OF FATHER
11 BIRTHPLACE OF FATHER (State or country) **Virginia**
12 MAIDEN NAME OF MOTHER **Ruth Houston**
13 BIRTHPLACE OF MOTHER (State or country) **Virginia**

14 Special INFORMATION required for deaths in hospitals and institutions and in deaths of non-residents and recent residents. (Former or usual Residence)

16 I hereby certify that the foregoing particulars (Nos. 1 to 14 inclusive) are correct as near as the same can be ascertained, and I further certify that I attended the deceased from **Feb. 20, 1925** to **September 2, 1925** that I last saw her alive on the **2nd** day of **September 1925**, that death occurred on the date stated above at **1 P.M.**, and that the cause of death was as follows:

Cardiac Disease (Chronic Endocarditis)   duration **1** yrs. ___ mos. ___ ds.

Contributory (Secondary) **Chronic myocarditis**   duration **1** yrs. ___ mos. ___ ds.

Witness my hand this **3rd** day of **Sep.** 1925.

Signature **Percy M. Rubinstein** M. D.
Address **2337 Grand Concourse**

FILED 1925 SEP

17 PLACE OF BURIAL **Cypress Hill Cemetery**   DATE OF BURIAL **September 6th 1925**
18 UNDERTAKER **Est. of J. Wesley Lane, Inc.**   ADDRESS **112 West 133rd St.**

James R. McLeod 5730

Death certificate of Pinkie Ruth Younger

Sister Ruth

The Rev. Charles Cuthbert Canterbury Corbin Jr. in a group photograph; Corbin is ninth from the left, indicated with an arrow above his head

Sister Ruth and several sisters, including Sister Edith Margaret and Sister Constance, in Toronto for the 100th anniversary of SSJD in 1984

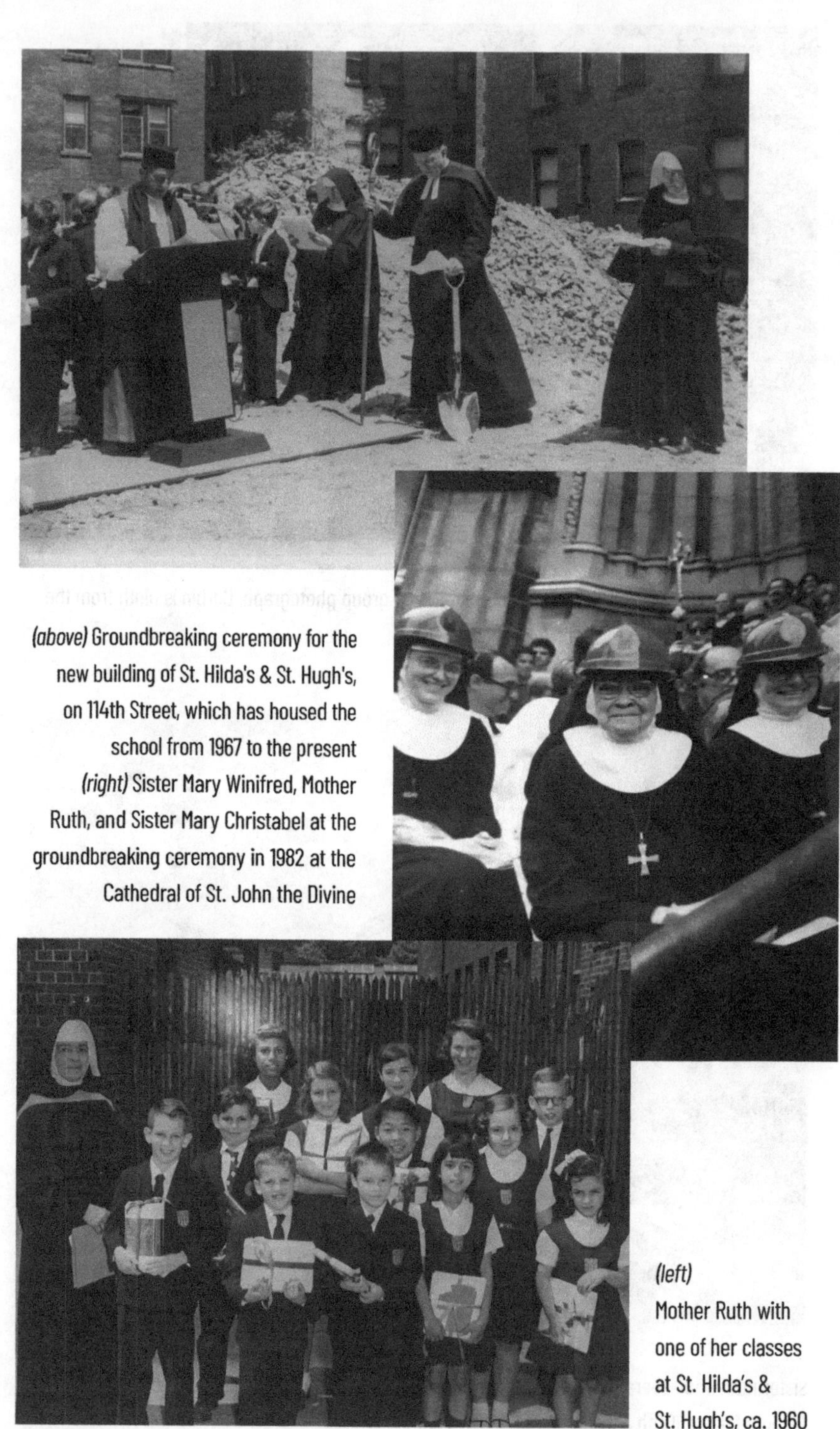

(*above*) Groundbreaking ceremony for the new building of St. Hilda's & St. Hugh's, on 114th Street, which has housed the school from 1967 to the present
(*right*) Sister Mary Winifred, Mother Ruth, and Sister Mary Christabel at the groundbreaking ceremony in 1982 at the Cathedral of St. John the Divine

(*left*)
Mother Ruth with one of her classes at St. Hilda's & St. Hugh's, ca. 1960

Photograph of Mother Ruth, discovered in the basement of the Community of the Holy Spirit in 2023 | Courtesy Community of the Holy Spirit

Mother Ruth on the basketball court

Students at St. Hilda's & St. Hugh's in procession

(top) Mother Ruth playing a game with students
(middle) Mother Ruth feeding pigeons in Riverside Park
(bottom) Mother Ruth at her desk

Mother Ruth with students at the Metropolitan Museum

Mother Ruth holding a young child

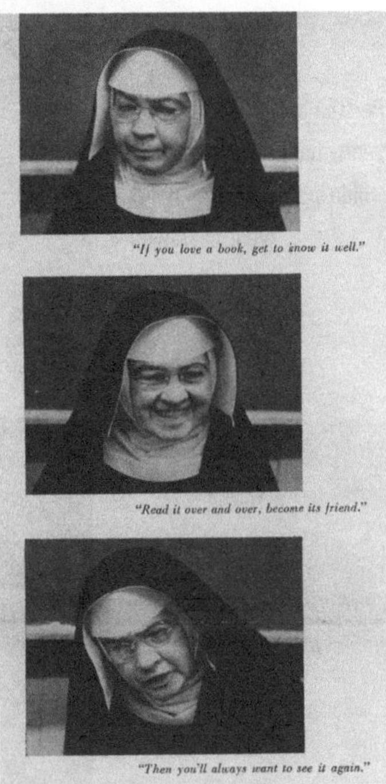

Three photos of Mother Ruth

Mother Ruth's dog, Jonathan Hugh

Portrait of Mother Ruth that currently hangs in the foyer of St. Hilda's & St. Hugh's School (year unknown)